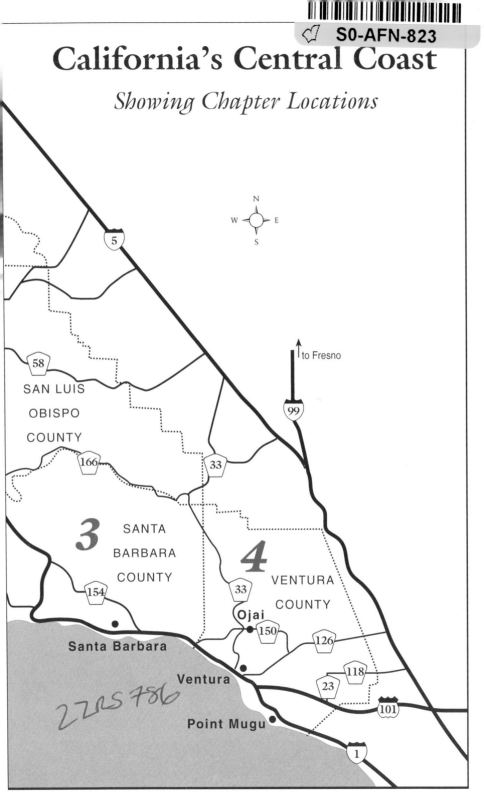

From the foothills to the Pacific Ocean

Mountain Biking California's Central Coast
Best 100 Trails

Big Sur to Point Mugu

By Delaine Fragnoli

Contributions by Don Douglass, Jamie Griffis,
Mark Langton, Mickey McTigue, and Kevin Woten

MountainBikingPress.com

AN IMPRINT OF
FINE EDGE PRODUCTIONS

IMPORTANT LEGAL NOTICE AND DISCLAIMER

Mountain biking is a potentially dangerous sport, and the rider or user of this book accepts a number of unavoidable risks. Trails by nature have numerous natural and man-made hazards; they are generally not signed or patrolled, and they change with time and conditions.

While substantial effort has been made to provide accurate information, this guide-book may inadvertently contain errors and omissions. Any maps in this book are for locator reference only. They are not to be used for navigation and are intended to complement large-scale topo maps. Your mileages will vary from those given in this book. Contact land managers before attempting routes to check for suitability and trail conditions.

The editors, authors, contributors, publishers, and distributors accept no liability for any errors or omissions in this book or for any injuries or losses incurred from using this book.

Credits:
book design: Melanie Haage
copy editing: Cindy Kamler
diagrams: Faith Rumm
cover photos: © Jason Houston
all other photos by the authors, except as noted

Library of Congress Cataloging-in-Publication Data

Fragnoli, Delaine, 1962–
        Mountain biking California's Central Coast best 100 trails, Big Sur to Point
Mugu / by Delaine Fragnoli ; with chapters by Don Douglass . . . [et al.].
                p.   cm.
        Includes bibliographical references (p.   ) and index.
        ISBN 0-938665-59-6 (pbk.)
        1. All terrain cycling—California—Pacific Coast—Guidebooks.
    2. Bicycle trails—California—Pacific Coast—Guidebooks.
    3. Pacific Coast (Calif.)—Guidebooks.   I. Title.   II. Title: Mountain
    biking California's Central Coast best 100 trails, Big Sur to Point Mugu.
    GV1045.5.C22P334   1999   98-46441
    917.94--dc21   CIP

Address requests for permission to:
Mountain Biking Press™
FineEdge.Com (Fine Edge Productions)
140 North Valley View Road, Swall Meadow, CA 93514

TABLE OF CONTENTS

Chapter 1: Big Sur
By Delaine Fragnoli
Andrew Molera State Park

Chapter 2: San Luis Obispo County
By Delaine Fragnoli
Morro Bay State Park/Cabrillo Peaks

Chapter 4: Ventura County
By Mickey McTigue, Kevin Woten, Jamie Griffis,
Mark Langton and Delaine Fragnoli

Appendix

Acknowledgments

I wish to thank Don Douglass and Mickey McTigue for the many routes that they pioneered in the Ventura and Santa Barbara backcountry. Chapters three and four are based largely on their books, *Mountain Biking the Coast Range— Ventura and the Sespe, Guide 4,* and *Mountain Biking the Coast Range— Santa Barbara County, Guide 5.* Jamie Griffis and Kevin Woten have provided invaluable in-the-field research and updates for those chapters. Thanks also to Mark Langton for contributing the rides in the Santa Monica Mountains.

Special appreciation goes to Jan Arnold for traipsing through the San Luis Obispo outback with me during wretched El Niño and post-El Niño conditions. As always, my thanks go to Jim MacIntyre, whose love and support make all my projects possible.

Delaine Fragnoli

Safety Precautions

One of the joys of mountain biking on dirt is the freedom to experience nature. However, mountain biking in the backcountry involves unavoidable hazards and risks that each cyclist accepts when leaving the pavement behind. You can increase your safety by being aware of potential dangers, preparing ahead, and respecting and remaining alert to the environment in all its variety and changes. Just because a trail is described in this book does not mean it will be safe or suitable for you.

Trails in this book cover an unusually wide range of terrain, elevation, and weather patterns that require different levels of skill and conditioning. A route that is safe for one rider may not be safe for another. It is important that you know and heed your own limitations, that you condition properly both physically and mentally, and that you give thought to your equipment as well as to trail and weather conditions.

En route, take appropriate action, including turning back at any time your judgment and common sense dictate. This book is not a substitute for detailed mountain survival or for cycling texts or courses. We recommend that you consult appropriate resources or take courses before you attempt the more strenuous or remote routes. When you have a question about route suitability or safety, consult local bike shops and land management offices.

Jason Houston

Trail Daze, trail maintenance on the Cold Springs Trail

WELCOME TO MOUNTAIN BIKING CALIFORNIA'S CENTRAL COAST

Central California offers mountain bikers year-round opportunities and challenges found nowhere else . . . from urban, palm-lined beaches to remote desert canyons and gorges, from gently rolling oak-covered hills for the family to twisting gnarly singletrack for the technical expert, from dramatic ridgetop rides to bluffside trails with shoreline vistas of the Pacific Ocean.

We assembled the who's who of mountain biking authors in Central California and asked them for their favorite rides. This book is a result of their collective efforts. You will benefit from their years of experience and know-how as they share with you areas and rides—from the well known to the not-yet-discovered—that have helped make mountain biking America's fastest-growing sport.

The authors—experts in their own areas—include the founders and directors of a number of successful regional mountain biking clubs, members of federal, state, and local trail advisory groups, and two editors of mountain biking magazines. Their collective experience is a history of the activity to which they are dedicated.

HOW TO USE THIS BOOK

With so many great trails to choose from, selecting the best was difficult. Obviously "best" means different things to different people. Some rides were included for their outstanding scenic value, others for their historical significance, others simply for their "fun factor." A few were included because they were quintessentially Californian in some way. The chosen rides represent a variety of terrain and levels of difficulty.

We have organized all this information in an easy-to-use way. Each chapter is dedicated to a particular area. The chapters are organized from north to south, starting in Big Sur and traveling down the coast to Ventura. Within each chapter we have grouped together rides that are in the same vicinity.

At the beginning of each ride you will find capsule information to let you decide quickly if a ride is for you or not. Ride **distance** is included as is a rating of **difficulty**. Mileages shown are approximate and may vary among riders and odometers. We rated the rides for strenuousness (from easy to very strenuous) and for technical difficulty (not technical to extremely technical). The ratings are a subjective assessment of what the route would be for an average fit rider (acclimatized to elevation). If you are a racer, you may consider some of our difficult rides to be moderate. If you are new to the sport, you may find our mildly technical rides challenging. Know your limits and be honest in evaluating your skill level. Check with local bike shops and land managers for their evaluation of your fitness for a particular ride. We do not know your skill level and consequently cannot be responsible for any losses you may incur using this information. (Please see the important legal notice and disclaimer.)

Elevation information pertinent to a particular ride is included. Rides with lots of elevation gain and loss are noted as are rides at high elevations. **Ride type**

Jason Houston

Chris King, organizer and sponsor of "Trail Daze," Cold Springs Trail

lets you know if the ride is a loop, an out-and-back trip, a multiple-day tour or if it requires a car shuttle. It also tells you the trail surface; for example, fire road loop with singletrack return. **Maps** refer to USGS 7.5-minute topos unless otherwise noted. The best **season** for riding each route is also noted. Last, we let you know if **water** is available and where to find it. If after reading the capsule information you are not sure if a ride is for you, the text of each ride description should give you additional information with which to make a decision.

Please note that the routes described in this book are not patrolled and contain natural hazards. Trail conditions and surfaces are constantly changing. Check with local land managers for latest trail and access conditions. Pertinent phone numbers are included in the Appendix (*Agencies, Mountain Bike Clubs, and Visitors Centers*).

We have tried to be consistent in presentation while retaining some of the character and tone of each individual author. Mountain biking is a very individualistic sport, and we think that should be reflected in any writing about the sport.

We hope you will find that this book is like a group of friends getting together to tell you about their favorite bicycling spots and that our authors' enthusiasm is contagious.

KNOW BEFORE YOU GO:
SPECIAL CONSIDERATIONS

To enhance your pleasure and safety we ask that you observe the following Special Considerations:

1. **Courtesy.** Extend courtesy to all other trail users and follow the golden rule. Observe the IMBA Rules of the Trail. The trails and roads in Central California are popular with many user groups: hikers, equestrians, fishermen, ranchers, 4-wheel drive enthusiasts, hunters, loggers, and miners. Mountain bikers are the newest user group, so set a good example of courtesy and respect.

2. **Preparations.** Plan your trip carefully; develop and use a check list. Know your abilities and your equipment. Prepare to be self-sufficient.

3. **Mountain Conditions.** Be sensitive at all times to the natural environment: the land, beautiful and enjoyable, can also be frightening and unforgiving. The areas covered by this book often provide extremes in elevation, climate and terrain. If you break down, it may take you longer to walk out than it took you to ride in! Check with your local Red Cross, Sierra Club, or mountaineering textbooks for detailed mountain survival information. Know how to deal with dehydration, hypothermia, altitude sickness, sunburn and heatstroke. Always be prepared for:

Intense Sun: Protect your skin against the sun's harmful rays by wearing light-colored long-sleeved shirts or jerseys and hats with wide brims. Use sunscreen with a sufficient rating. Wear sunglasses with adequate protection. Guard against heatstroke by riding in early morning or late afternoon when the sun's rays are less intense.

Low Humidity: East-facing slopes and high elevations usually have low humidity. To avoid headaches or cramps, start each trip with a minimum of two or more large water bottles. (Gallons of water may not be sufficient for really hot weather or hard rides.) Force yourself to drink *before* you feel thirsty. Carry water from a known source; treat any water gathered from springs, streams or lakes. Untreated drinking water may cause Giardiasis or other diseases.

Variations in Temperature and Weather Conditions: Carry extra clothing—windbreaker, gloves, stocking cap—and use the multi-layer system so you can quickly adapt to different weather conditions. Afternoon thundershowers can occur in the high country, so keep an eye on changing cloud and wind conditions and prepare accordingly.

Fatigue: Sluggish or cramping muscles and fatigue indicate the need for calories and liquids. Carry high-energy snack foods such as granola bars, dried fruits and nuts to maintain strength and warmth. To conserve energy, add layers of clothing as the temperature drops or the wind increases.

Fire Closures: Many mountain and foothill areas are closed to the public during times of high fire danger. Please check ahead of time with local authorities and observe such fire closures. Always be extremely careful with fire.

Smog Alerts: Although most of the rides in this book are outside the Los Angeles Basin, if you cycle within the Basin during the summer we recommend that you listen to the smog forecasts over local radio stations. If you know the zip code for your riding area, you can get a smog report by dialing 800/242-4022. Heavy exercise is unwise at midday or during smog alerts.

4. **Maps and Navigation.** The maps in this book are not intended for navigation and should be used with the forest or USGS topographic maps that we recommend you carry and use. In case you lose your way (it's easy to do!), have a plan ready in advance with your cycling group. En route, record your position on the trip map(s), noting the times you arrive at known places. Be sure to look back frequently in the direction from which you came in case you need to retrace your path. Do not be afraid to turn back when conditions change, or if the going is tougher than you expected. Before you leave on a ride, tell someone where you're going, when you expect to return, and what to do in case you don't return on time. Ask that person to call the proper officials if you are more than six hours overdue and give them full details about your vehicle and your trip plans.

5. **Horses and Pack Animals.** Some of the trails in Central California are used by recreational horse riders as well as cyclists and hikers. Horses can be spooked easily, so make them aware of your presence *well in advance of an encounter.* A startled horse can cause serious injuries both to a rider and to itself. If you come upon horses moving toward you, yield the right-of-way, even when it seems inconvenient. Carry your bike to the downhill side and stand quietly, well off the trail in a spot where the animals can see you clearly. If you come upon horses *moving ahead of you in the same direction,* stop well behind them. Do not attempt to pass until you have alerted the riders and asked for permission. Then, pass on the downhill side of the trail, talking to the horse and rider as you do so. It is your responsibility to ensure that such encounters are safe for everyone. Do not disturb grazing sheep or cattle.

6. **Respect the Environment.** Minimize your impact on the natural environment. *Remember: Mountain bikes are not allowed in Wilderness Areas and in certain other restricted areas.* You are a visitor, so ask when in doubt. Leave plants and animals alone, historic and cultural sites untouched. Stay on established roads and trails and do not enter private property. Follow posted instructions and use good common sense. If you plan to camp, you may need a permit. Contact the nearest land management agency for information.

7. **Control and Safety.** Crashes usually don't cause serious injury, but occasionally they can and do. Stay under control and slow for the unexpected. Wear protective gear—helmet, gloves, and glasses to protect yourself from scrapes and impacts with rocks, dirt, and brush. Guard against excessive speed. Avoid overheated rims and brakes on long or steep downhill rides. Lower your center of gravity by lowering your seat on downhills. Lower your tire pressure on rough or sandy stretches. In late summer and fall, avoid opening weekend of hunting season, and inquire at local sporting goods stores as to which areas are open to hunting. Carry first aid supplies and bike tools for emergencies. *Avoid solo travel in remote areas.*

Good friends always snap a photo of your crash <u>before</u> helping you up.

8. Trailside Bike Repair. Minimum equipment: pump, spare tube, patches and 2 tubes of patch glue or glueless patches, 6" adjustable wrench, Allen wrenches, chain tool and spoke wrench. Tools may be shared with others in your group. Correct inflation, wide tires, and avoiding rocks will prevent most flats. Grease, oil, and proper adjustment prevent most mechanical failures. Frequent stream crossings wash away chain grease; carry extra.

9. **First Aid.** Carry first aid for your body as well as your bike. If you have allergies, be sure to bring your medicine, whether it's for pollen or bee stings. Sunscreen saves your skin, and insect repellent increases your comfort in many seasons. Bring bandages and ointment for cuts and scrapes, and aspirin for aches that won't go away. Additional first-aid items you might want to carry in your kit are antiseptic swabs, moleskin, a single-edged razor blade, a needle, an elastic bandage, and waterproof matches. For expedition trips, consult mountaineering texts on survival for additional suggestions.

RULES OF THE TRAIL
International Mountain Bicycling Association © 1998

Thousand of miles of dirt trails have been closed to mountain bicycling because of the irresponsible riding habits of a few riders. Do your part to maintain trail access by observing the following rules of the trail:

1. RIDE ON OPEN TRAILS ONLY. Respect trail and road closures (ask if not sure), avoid possible trespass on private land, obtain permits and authorization as may be required. Federal and State wilderness areas are closed to cycling. Additional trails may be closed because of sensitive environmental concerns or conflicts with other users. Your riding example will determine what is closed to all cyclists!

2. LEAVE NO TRACE. Be sensitive to the dirt beneath you. Even on open trails, you should not ride under conditions where you will leave evidence of your passing, such as on certain soils shortly after a rain. Observe the different types of soils and trail construction; practice low-impact cycling. This also means staying on the trail and not creating any new ones. Be sure to pack out at least as much as you pack in.

3. CONTROL YOUR BICYCLE! Inattention for even a second can cause disaster. Excessive speed maims and threatens people; there is no excuse for it!

4. ALWAYS YIELD TRAIL. Make known your approach well in advance. A friendly greeting (or bell) is considerate and works well; startling someone may cause loss of trail access. Show your respect when passing others by slowing or even stopping. Anticipate that other trail users may be around corners or in blind spots.

5. NEVER SPOOK ANIMALS. All animals are startled by an unannounced approach, a sudden movement, or a loud noise. This can be dangerous for you, others, and the animals. Give animals extra room and time to adjust to you. In passing, use special care and follow the directions of horseback riders (ask if uncertain). Running cattle and disturbing wild animals is a serious offense. Leave gates as you found them, or as marked.

6. PLAN AHEAD. Know your equipment, your ability, and the area in which you are riding, and prepare accordingly. Be self-sufficient at all times, keep your machine in good repair, and carry necessary supplies for changes in weather or other conditions. A well-executed trip is a satisfaction to you and not a burden or offense to others. Keep trails open by setting an example of responsible cycling for all mountain cyclists.

Dedicated to the appreciation of and access to recreational lands, non-profit IMBA welcomes your support. IMBA, P.O. Box 7578, Boulder, CO 80306-7578
Phone: (303) 545-9011 • Fax: (303) 545-9026
E-mail: imba@aol.com • Website: www.imba.com

FOREST ADVENTURE PASS

As of June 1997, the four Southern California National Forests (Angeles, Cleveland, Los Padres, San Bernardino) have instituted a demonstration user-fee project, a Forest Adventure Pass, that amounts to a parking fee. Any vehicle parked within one of the above forests must display the Forest Adventure Pass. If you drive into a U.S. Forest to park and ride your bike, your vehicle must display one of these passes. If, on the other hand, you park outside the U.S. Forest and ride your bike in, you do not have to have a pass. Note that all or part of the book chapters describe rides located in the Los Padres National Forest.

You can purchase a $5/one-day pass or a $30/annual pass at Forest Headquarters or at local sporting goods or outdoor supply stores. If you buy an annual pass, it's valid for all four areas. If you have already paid a facility fee (e.g., paid for camping at a Forest Service campground), you do not have to buy a Forest Adventure Pass as well. Residents and those using an educational or organizational camp or facility are also exempt.

When and how vigorously the program will be enforced is unclear. What citations and fines may be issued also remain to be seen. Note that the project is a "demonstration" project, meaning it may or may not become permanent.

The fees were initiated as part of a larger program to raise revenues for budget-crunched federal land management agencies. Other federal agencies (National Park Service, Fish and Wildlife Service, Bureau of Land Management) are also developing recreation user-fee programs and selecting test sites, so you may find yourself paying fees elsewhere as well. Supposedly, 80% or more of the Forest Adventure Pass fees raised will go directly back into maintaining and building recreational facilities in the area where the fees were collected.

Reaction to the programs from the outdoor community has been mixed. For more details on the pros and cons of the issue, contact IMBA. For more information on user-fees in your area, call the appropriate land management agency. (See *Agencies, Mountain Bike Clubs and Visitor Centers* in the Appendix.)

Backcountry Ethics

All cultural resources on Public Lands are protected for the enjoyment and scientific analysis of present and future generations by federal laws, including the Antiquities Act of 1906 and the Archeological Resources Protection Act of 1979. Please take only pictures and memories, leaving our historic heritage for others to enjoy.

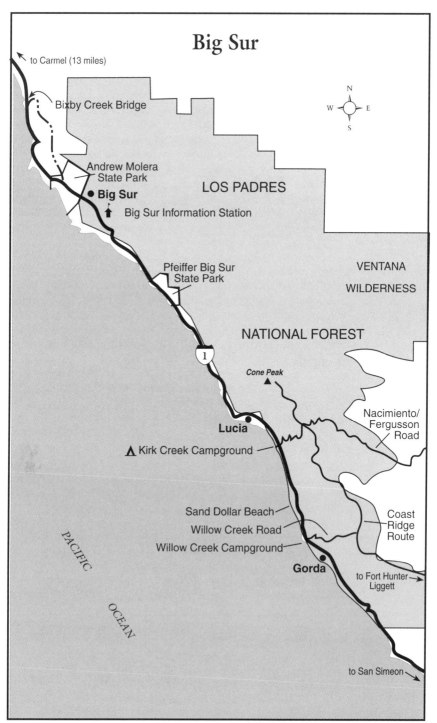

Big Sur

to Carmel (13 miles)

Bixby Creek Bridge

Andrew Molera
State Park

● **Big Sur**

LOS PADRES

Big Sur Information Station

Pfeiffer Big Sur
State Park

VENTANA

WILDERNESS

NATIONAL FOREST

Cone Peak ▲

Nacimiento/
Fergusson
Road

Lucia ●

Λ Kirk Creek Campground

Sand Dollar Beach

Willow Creek Road

Willow Creek Campground

Coast
Ridge
Route

Gorda ●

to Fort Hunter
Liggett

PACIFIC

OCEAN

to San Simeon →

©1999 Fine Edge Productions

CHAPTER 1

Big Sur

By Delaine Fragnoli

Henry Miller called California's Big Sur coast "the face of the earth as the Creator intended it to be." It's hard to disagree once you've visited this storied landscape of plunging rock and splashing foam. Rugged doesn't begin to describe the deep ravines and knife-edge ridges of the Santa Lucia Mountains as they drop precipitously into the Pacific Ocean. Large portions of the area are inaccessible or barely accessible. When El Niño rains forced evacuation of Big Sur during the winter of 1997–98, residents had to be airlifted by helicopter.

Big Sur coastline

Unfortunately, what sheer ruggedness hasn't made inaccessible, legislation and the military have: the huge Ventana Wilderness and Fort Hunter-Liggett leave only a few patchy sections of Los Padres National Forest open to mountain bikes. The paltry legal routes are dirt roads and 4WD doubletracks. Apparently the Creator did not intend for mountain bicyclists to ride singletrack.

However, He or She did intend to give anyone who hikes or bikes in the region poison oak. When most people think of the area's flora, they visualize towering redwoods. The trees certainly rank in the jaw-dropping category, but the poison oak—impressive not just for its proportions but for its virulence—leaves a lasting impression. My husband believes it is "the poison oak that *other* poison oak runs from." My theory is that it does not lie helplessly alongside the road or trail waiting patiently for you to brush against it; rather, it spits at you as you pass by from what you think is a safe distance.

The beauty of the region—waterfalls, redwoods, huge ferns dripping with water, banana slugs inching along—makes up for these deficits. There is no more gorgeous place to explore, and a mountain bike is the perfect vehicle for traversing the ridge routes which are legal to ride. You can find legal singletrack at Andrew Molera State Park and inland at Lake San Antonio

While there are all kinds of charming, rustic accommodations in the town of Big Sur, my recommendation is to camp at Pfeiffer Big Sur State Park. All the rides in this chapter are easily accessible from there. Most services are available in Big Sur, but for a bike shop you'll have to go north to Carmel or Monterey. Access is by Highway 1, the Pacific Coast Highway (PCH). The only paved through-route from the coast to Highway 101 is Nacimiento-Fergusson Road through Fort Hunter-Liggett.

Andrew Molera State Park

Bisected by Highway 1, Andrew Molera State Park occupies a narrow strip of land between the Big Sur River and the Big Sur coast on its west side. Most of the park's 4,800 acres sit across the Pacific Coast Highway (PCH). Largely undeveloped, these lands contain several trails, open to mountain bikes, which looked largely unrideable to me. The Old Coast Road (see Ride 3) takes off from this part of the park. Most of the park's trails and all of its facilities (port-a-potties, primitive walk-in camping and a small picnic area) are on the beach side.

Ridgeline and cliffside beach trails afford stunning coastal views, while other trails circle meadows and meander along the river. Giant coastal redwoods, madrone, coast live oak and ponderosa pine all grace the park. In January, the park is a popular spot for viewing the gray whale migrations. Other animals you may see include deer, boar, sea otters, seals, sea lions and a variety of shore birds. Banana slugs, too! Add to that the heavily forested banks of the Big Sur River and you've got a spectacular slice of landscape.

Note: The park trail map is not particularly accurate, nor is the information about which trails are open to bikes very clear. The following trails are legal to ride: River Trail north of the Beach Trail, Beach Trail, Ridge Trail, Bluffs Trail for 1.2 miles between the Ridge Trail and Spring Trail, the Trail Camp Trail, and East Molera Trail.

1 Creamery Meadow Loop with Ridge Option and Bluffs Option

Distance: 10 miles.
Difficulty: Easy, mildly technical; ridge climb is strenuous and more technical.
Elevation: Minimal; the Ridge Trail climbs 1,200'.
Ride Type: Loop on dirt roads and trails with two out-and-back spur options.
Season: Year-round. Spring brings great wildflowers. Seasonal footbridges for crossing the Big Sur River go up in early spring. In the fall and winter, expect a cold, wet portage. Be careful—water levels can change considerably.
Map: Trail map and pamphlet available at the park or any of the nearby Big Sur parks.
Water: Spigot near port-a-potties.
Comments: The park charges a day-use fee. If you've stopped at any of the other Big Sur State Parks, you can enter for free.

Overview: Although Andrew Molera State Park (AMSP) is small and offers limited riding, the scenery more than makes up for these deficits. An easy loop around Creamery Meadow via the Beach and River trails makes a good choice for beginners; they may want to venture along the Bluffs Trail as well. More advanced riders can add a vigorous climb up the Ridge Trail. You have views of the beach, cliffs and the spectacular Big Sur coastline from the Ridge Trail and the Bluffs Trail. Ferns, redwoods and oaks add to the Ridge Trail's scenic appeal.

Getting There: AMSP is 22 miles south of Carmel on Highway 1. It's a short 10-minute drive north from Pfeiffer Big Sur State Park, an excellent choice for camping. The parking lot is on the west side of the highway, or you can park at one of the walk-in gates along PCH north of the main park entrance.

Route: From the main parking area, backtrack past the ranger kiosk and go right under the *Molera Horseback Tours* sign. Follow this level dirt road for 0.1 mile to a gate with a Fire Road sign on your right. Take the path around the gate and drop down to the Big Sur River.

Bluffs Trail, Andrew Molera State Park

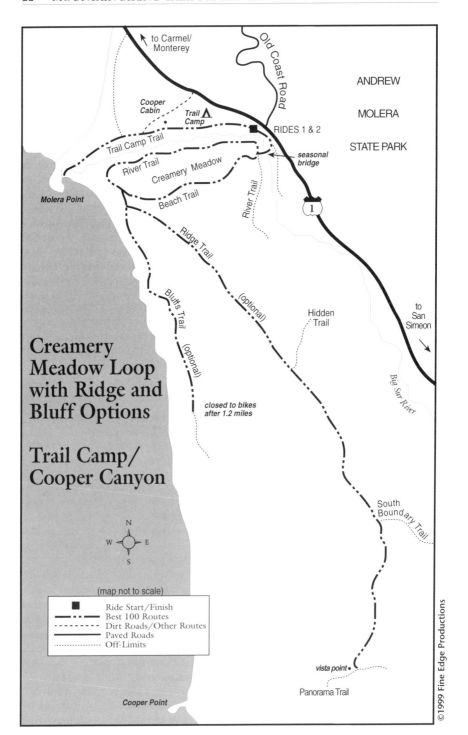

Creamery
Meadow Loop
with Ridge and
Bluff Options

Trail Camp/
Cooper Canyon

(map not to scale)

■ Ride Start/Finish
━·━· Best 100 Routes
------ Dirt Roads/Other Routes
━━━ Paved Roads
············ Off-Limits

©1999 Fine Edge Productions

Big Sur River, Andrew Molera State Park

turnoff to Ridge and Bluffs trails on your left. Intimidating in its steepness, this pitch is rideable. If you want to explore either or both of these trails, ride and push up the 0.1-mile climb. At the top, the Bluffs Trail takes off to the right and the Ridge Trail climbs at an even steeper grade off to the left.

Ridge Option: If you're up to the challenge, go for the Ridge Trail. If you're not, skip ahead to the description of the Bluffs Trail. This first pitch is the worst. Honest. You make your way up the ridge in five or six anaerobic bursts like this one. Surrounded by grasslands, you are rewarded with great views toward the ocean. At least that's what I'm told by people who have been here on a clear day. The March day I was here it was too misty to see anything.

At 1.9 miles total, you reach an intersection with Hidden Trail (closed to bikes). This intersection is at the bottom of a downhill and is obvious from some distance. Don't bother to slow down for it! Keep your momentum up for the next climb.

About a mile later, 2.8 miles total, you come to another intersection (South Boundary Trail), also closed to bikes. The worst climbing is definitely over at this point, although you continue to gain elevation.

The vegetation gets thicker and denser along here and soon you enter a world of big trees and ferns. An incredible forest of coast live oaks arch overhead. Madrone, ponderosa

In the fall and winter you have to portage across the river, but in summer simply cross on the plank bridge. I had to walk up the sandy embankment on the other side.

Just as the sand becomes rideable, there's an intersection and a trail sign. The sign indicates you are on Beach Trail (legal), while the trail to your left is the River Trail (closed to bikes). Immediately past here, a singletrack on the right is signed Parking Lot. This singletrack is also the River Trail and is open to bikes. At the end of the loop you will return to this intersection via this legal portion of the River Trail.

For now, continue on the Beach Trail toward the signed Creamery Meadow. At 0.8 mile, you reach the

Ridge Trail, Andrew Molera State Park

noticed them on the way up, and they have "endo" written all over them on the descent. Practice that front-wheel lift!

At 6.2 miles, you're back at the intersection of the Ridge Trail and the Bluffs Trail. You can either fork left to do the Bluffs Trail or drop back down to the Beach Trail.

Bluffs Option: From the Ridge/Bluffs intersection, fork right. Very shortly you come to a Y intersection. Go left. (The right fork, although not signed as closed to bikes on this end, soon drops to the beach where it *is* signed as closed to bikes. Uh huh.)

Stay on the main trail as it parallels the bluffs with views of the beach and ocean. There are a few mildly technical ups and downs, but in general the trail rolls along for 1.2 miles. At that point, 7.4 miles total including the Ridge option, a sign declares that bikes are not allowed beyond here. Retrace your tire tracks. Yes, it seems silly to backtrack, but the point here is to take in the dramatic Big Sur coastline.

Back at the Ridge/Bluffs intersection, (8.6 miles if you did both options), turn left and drop back down 0.1 mile to the Beach Trail (the trail you began on). Go left. Just 0.1 mile later (8.8 miles total), take a sharp, unmarked right turn. [**Side trip:** You could continue straight about 0.2 mile to the beach if you're ready for a break. I would recommend carrying your bike when the trail starts to get real sandy. Wet sand isn't exact-

pine and coast redwoods poke through thickets of Douglas iris, thimbleberry, blackberry, redwood sorrel, wake-robin, ferns and, of course, poison oak. Ample reward for your climbing efforts. You have a little bit more climbing to do, but by now you won't care.

You reach a vista point at 3.6 miles (total). I couldn't see anything but fog; however, I've heard from others that the point does indeed provide quite a vista. Here the Ridge Trail turns into Panorama Trail which is closed to bikes. You have no choice but to return the way you came.

The trip down is a lot faster and a lot more fun. But watch out for the drainage ditches! You probably

ly a great lubricant for bearings.]

Back to that unsigned right-hand turn. This trail takes you through Creamery Meadow, the site of a habitat restoration program. Past agricultural use has left the meadow open to colonization by non-native plants. The Park Service, aided by volunteers, is trying to rehabilitate the area and plant the meadow with native grasses.

At 9.5 miles, the trail ends at a T. Go right. At 9.7 miles at the Y, go right. There's a short rocky section, but the trail soon smoothes out. Here you pass a trail sign and map indicating that you are on the River Trail and are heading toward the Beach Trail.

At 9.8 miles you reach a T-intersection. Go left onto the Beach Trail. (This is the trail you started on.) Cross the plank bridge over the river. Go around the gate and left onto the dirt road. You're back at your car at 10 miles.

2 Trail Camp/Cooper Canyon

Distance: 2.2 miles.
Difficulty: Easy and not technical except for one short pitch.
Elevation: Negligible.
Ride Type: Out-and-back on singletrack and dirt road.
Season: Year-round.
Map: Trail map and pamphlet available at the park or any of the nearby Big Sur parks.
Water: Spigot near port-a-potties.
Comments: The park charges a day-use fee. If you've stopped at any of the other Big Sur State Parks, you can enter for free.

Cooper Cabin, Andrew Molera State Park

Overview: An easy jaunt for beginners, or a nice addition to the previous ride, this route takes you past the historic Cooper Cabin on your way to a beach. The trail to the beach is both smooth and scenic, a good introduction to those who've never ridden singletrack.

Getting There: See the previous ride for directions.

Route: Head toward the far end of the parking lot away from the ranger kiosk. Follow the Trail Camp signs. The trail climbs steeply at first, then drops even more steeply around a tight switchback. Signs here ask cyclists to walk their bikes—a prudent suggestion.

Just beyond, you can resume riding the singletrack which soon runs into a fire road. (A right turn here would take you up to PCH.) Continue straight through Trail Camp. This is flat and easy cycling. You pass Cooper Cabin on your right where another spur climbs up to PCH. Cooper Cabin belonged to sea captain John Cooper who acquired this land in 1840. His descendants sold the land to the Nature Conservancy in 1968, and it became a State Park in 1972.

At 1.0 mile, go right. (The very short left fork goes to the water and stops.) You pass Headlands Trail (closed to bikes but worth the hike) on your right. Here you are on singletrack, curving through criss-crossing trees. Just as you're thinking, "this is cool," the trail ends at the beach, 1.1. miles.

Retrace your route for a 2.2-mile trip.

Coast Ridge Road

Before Highway 1 was completed along the Big Sur coast, several dirt roads pitched up and down inland ridges, tracing the spine of the Santa Lucia Mountains. Often these were the only routes through and to certain areas. Until the Bixby Bridge was built, one such dirt road, the Old Coast Highway, ran from present-day Andrew Molera State Park in the south into and out of several drainages before emerging at the north end of present-day Bixby Bridge.

Another stretch of road, called the Coast Ridge Road, sections of which are often referred to on maps as the North, Central or South Coast Ridge Roads, used to wind from what is now the Ventana Inn in Big Sur south all the way to the San Luis Obispo County line.

I can only imagine what it would have been like to bikepack the length of it—a possibility that no longer exists thanks to the Ventana Wilderness area (closed to bikes) and the machinations of privacy-loving landowners in the area. But chunks of these routes can still be ridden.

The Old Coast Highway remains open to vehicles—be sure to stay on the road as virtually all of the surrounding land is private. The 25-mile northern section of the Coast Ridge Road from the Ventana Inn to the Ventana Wilderness (where it turns into a trail) is, however, at the center of an access controversy. This is a Forest Service-maintained road, meaning our tax dollars go to maintain it. But local landowners have pressured the Forest Service to close the road, and its gate is currently plastered with No Trespassing signs. I agree with Andrew

Rice who, in his book *Adventure Guide to Northern California*, says: "Frankly, the Forest Service maintains this road with your tax dollars, and it is historically a public easement. You should be allowed to ride here. The whole thing smells like yesterday's fish to me. Call the Forest Service (408/385-5434) and tell them what you think. Write them a letter. I'm not advocating trespassing, but I rode it anyway and no one said a word."

If you choose to practice a bit of civil disobedience yourself, be sure to stay on the road—this is *not* trespassing—and avoid all spurs, most of which are driveways. Riding these would be trespassing. Also, do not park in the Inn's lot or its restaurant lot. There's a pullout on Highway 1 where you can park, or park at Big Sur Station and ride to the Inn to begin.

The central and southern sections of the Coast Ridge Road are more accessible, but they, too, have their limitations. The northernmost access route is the paved Nacimiento-Fergusson Road, while the southernmost access route is the dirt Willow Creek Road. Partway between these two east-west roads is another former access road, Plaskett Ridge Road. Here a single landowner has succeeded in cutting off all through access. As of 1996, this person had constructed a locked gate at his property line beyond which vehicles could not pass. And from the looks of things, he seems prepared to vigorously enforce his No

Chris Hatounian

Bixby Bridge, Pacific Coast Highway

Trespassing signs. Once again, this is a maintained Forest Service road. Also be warned that, as of winter 1997, at its west (beach) end, the road has no signs indicating that it is not a through road, nor is it shown as closed on the USFS map. It is, however, signed as closed at the east (ridge) end.

What this means is that you have just two access points many miles apart. (USFS maps show Mill Creek, Prewitt Ridge and Willow Creek trails as through routes, arousing desire for a singletrack descent from the ridge. These routes are a mapmaker's fantasy. Yes, *parts* of the trails exist, but most of these parts are completely unrideable. As through routes, they are cruel jokes. I know. I tried.) Thus, fashion-

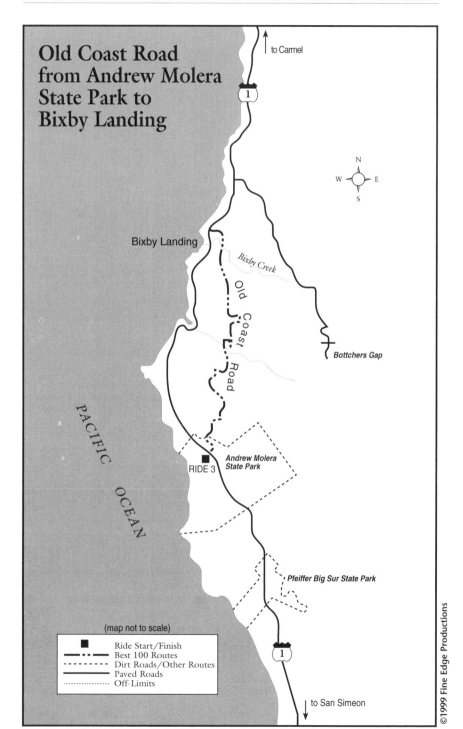

Old Coast Road from Andrew Molera State Park to Bixby Landing

to Carmel

Bixby Landing

Bixby Creek

Old Coast Road

Bottchers Gap

RIDE 3

Andrew Molera State Park

PACIFIC OCEAN

Pfeiffer Big Sur State Park

(map not to scale)

■	Ride Start/Finish
—■—■—	Best 100 Routes
- - - -	Dirt Roads/Other Routes
————	Paved Roads
··········	Off-Limits

to San Simeon

©1999 Fine Edge Productions

ing any kind of loop is out of the question, unless you want to do some loaded touring or can arrange for a 4WD sag vehicle. Even a shuttle would make for a long and difficult day ride. The easiest access, by car or bike, is Nacimiento-Fergusson Road, which is still exceptionally steep (3000' gain in 7 miles). If you do want to do a multi-day loop, I would recommend going up Nacimiento Road, traversing the ridge from north to south, and descending Willow Creek Road.

Otherwise, it's best to do the Coast Ridge Road in sections: out and back from Nacimiento Summit north to Cone Peak; one way from Nacimiento Summit to Willow Creek Road (although you can do this section as an out-and-back from either access road); out and back from Willow Creek Road south to road's end at Lottie Potrero. All of these options are described in more detail in the following section.

Now, you may be wondering, why go to all this trouble? Good question.

In one word: views. As the road winds from the west side of the ridge to the east, views alternate from ocean vistas to wilderness expanses. At some points you can see both the Big Sur coast and the peaks of the Ventana Wilderness at the same time. Add in that the area is remote and seldom visited (especially the southernmost end) and you have as close to a Wilderness (and certainly a wilderness) experience as possible on a bike.

Three more *cautions*: The riding here is rugged, remote and (with the exception of Cone Peak) difficult. Be self-sufficient. Second, from Plaskett Ridge Road south to the road's end at Lottie Potrero, the ridge road follows the boundary of Fort Hunter-Liggett—*no public access!* Do *not* descend east (inland) from the ridge. Third, the whole ridge road is open to motor vehicle traffic, although you won't see too many cars. The section to Cone Peak is the most heavily trafficked as hikers use it to access Wilderness trailheads.

3 Old Coast Road from Andrew Molera State Park to Bixby Landing

Distance: 10.5 miles one way; 18.5 miles as a loop; 21 miles out and back.
Difficulty: One way or as a loop, it is strenuous and mildly technical; as an out-and-back venture, very strenuous and mildly technical.
Elevation: Over 1,800' one way or as a loop; more than 3,700' out and back.
Ride Type: One-way shuttle on dirt road; loop on dirt road and pavement; out-and-back on dirt road.
Season: Year-round. Spring, with wildflowers and without lots of tourists, is best.
Map: AAA Monterey Bay Region.
Water: At Andrew Molera State Park.
Comments: Nearest facilities are at the road's southern end in Andrew Molera State Park. The road is open to vehicle traffic. After the first mile, be sure to stay on the road as all land beyond that point is private (and emphatically signed as such).

Overview: Before the Bixby Bridge was completed in 1932, the Old Coast Road was the main route from

Big Sur into Carmel. Today the graceful bridge is not only a lovely concrete structure, but it lets cars

Old Coast Road, Bixby Bridge and the Pacific Ocean

zoom through on Highway 1, leaving the Old Coast Road to you and me and our two-wheeled friends.

The old road can be ridden from Andrew Molera State Park in the south to Bixby Bridge in the north or vice versa. I prefer to start at AMSP. The parking situation at AMSP is better, there are facilities available in nearby Big Sur, the view as you descend to Bixby Bridge is spectacular, and on your return route down Highway 1, the ocean is on your right and the wind is usually at your back.

Either way you do plenty of steep climbing as you make your way up and through the ranch land of the Big Sur Valley, into and out of the old-growth redwoods of the Little Sur drainage, and into and out of the Bixby drainage on your way to the ocean at Bixby Landing.

I prefer the loop option, but you can arrange to have a friend pick you up at Bixby Landing if the vehicle traffic on Highway 1 makes you nervous. As an out-and-back, the Old Coast Road is a burly undertaking—although I know people who have done it.

Getting There: Start at Andrew Molera State Park. (See directions for Ride 1.)

Route: From the parking lot, climb 0.1 mile back out to and across Highway 1. The Old Coast Road takes off from the dirt pull-out directly across the highway. You can't miss it. There's a street sign which reads *Coast Highway/Cabrillo Highway* and several yellow signs declaring *Entering State Park Property* and *Impassable When Wet.*

The road climbs immediately. About 0.1 mile up, a trail takes off to the right. It's signed as being open to bikes, but a quick hike up it convinced me it's not particularly rideable—at least uphill. At 0.3 mile you begin to get views of the coast. A turnout at 0.6 mile offers a nice vista of the beach and ocean. The hard-packed gravel road turns inland just beyond here.

At 0.8 mile, you cross a cattle-guard and gate with signs indicating private property on both sides of the road for the next 6 miles. In other words: stay on the road. Route-finding for the rest of the ride is easy as there are no other roads or trails you can take.

At 1.5 miles the grade lessens a bit before pitching upward again. One more mile and you top out and begin a 2-mile downhill. It's over at 4.5 miles as you begin the ride's toughest climb. You grunt through several steep, tight switchbacks with loose gravel and rocks. You will loathe these. To add to the misery factor, this portion of the climb lacks any shade.

Fortunately, the agony lasts "only" 2 miles. When you top out at 6.5 miles, you are greeted by an awesome 3-mile descent through a cool, old-growth redwood forest. These are the best trees on the ride. Although the coastal views are long gone, this is my favorite part of the route. This is the main reason, in my mind, for doing the ride.

At 9.5 miles you have one final climb. Thankfully, it is shorter than the earlier ones. At just under 10 miles, you can see Bixby Bridge and the ocean—a great photo op.

At 10.1 miles, start your descent to Highway 1. A left turn onto the highway and an 8-mile spin back to your car completes the loop. Or, if you've arranged a shuttle pick-up, your ride ends here.

4 Central Coast Ridge Road from Nacimiento Summit to Cone Peak

Distance: 13 miles.
Difficulty: Moderately easy; not technical.
Elevation: 1,100' gain/loss.
Ride Type: Out-and-back on dirt road.
Season: Year-round.
Maps: Cone Peak; or Los Padres National Forest: Monterey and Santa Lucia Ranger Districts; or AAA Monterey Bay Region.
Water: None.
Comments: A half-mile past Nacimiento Summit on Nacimiento-Fergusson Road is Nacimiento Station, a fire station where you *may* be able to get emergency help. Note that the Ridge Road is open to motor vehicles.

Overview: By far the easiest, and the easiest to arrange, of all the Coast Ridge Road rides, this out-and-back venture travels a corridor into the Ventana Wilderness. Other than the road itself, all else around you is wilderness. That means you need to stay on the road. Fabulous views inland (road stays on the northeast side of the ridge for most of the route) and a few ocean vistas mark this highly scenic jaunt. To reach the summit of Cone Peak itself, you have to stash your bike and hike the 2 miles (it felt longer) to the lookout. The 100-mile views from the top are worth the effort. Try to do this ride early in the morning before fog and mist roll in and obscure the views. The area is also home to the rare Santa Lucia fir.

Getting There: Nacimiento-Fergusson Road is off of Highway 1, one

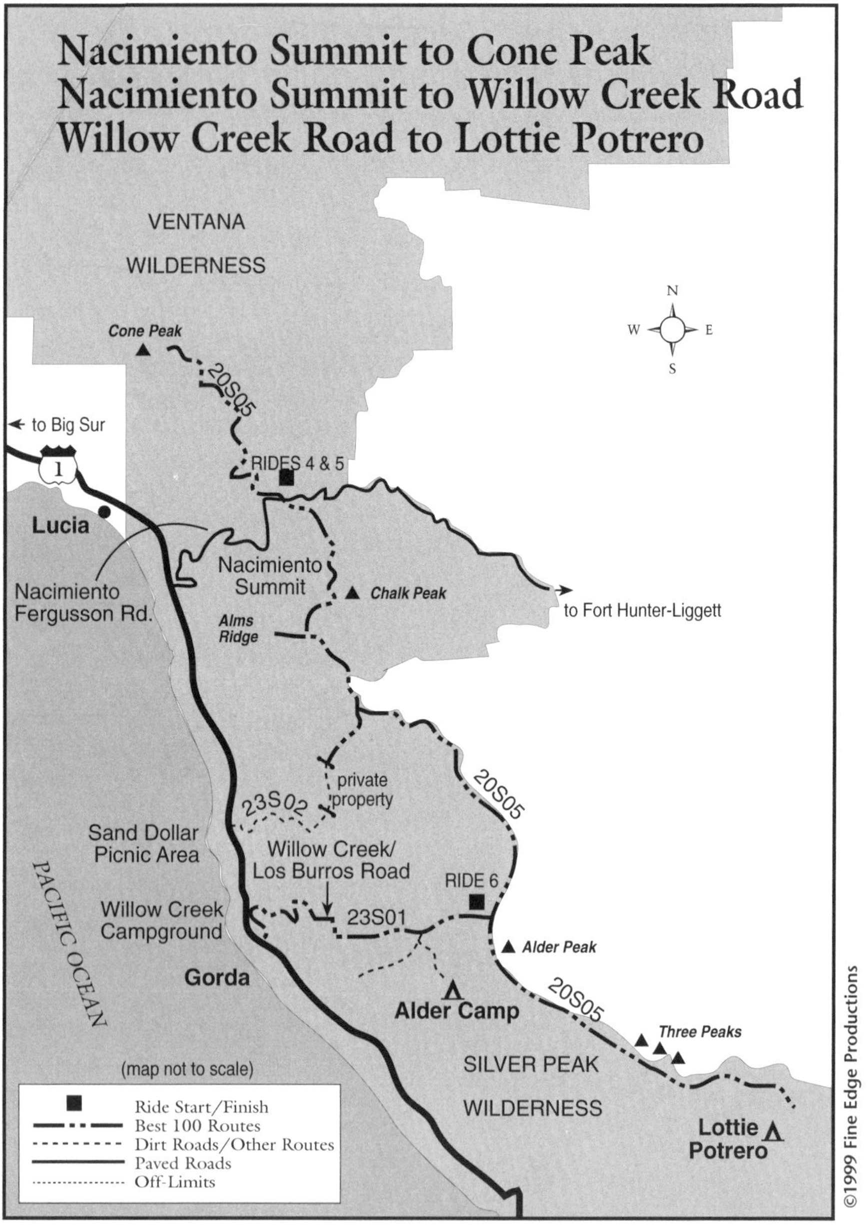

Nacimiento Summit to Cone Peak
Nacimiento Summit to Willow Creek Road
Willow Creek Road to Lottie Potrero

VENTANA

WILDERNESS

▲ Cone Peak

20S05

← to Big Sur

(1)

Lucia ●

Nacimiento
Fergusson Rd.

RIDES 4 & 5 ■

Nacimiento
Summit

▲ *Chalk Peak*

to Fort Hunter-Liggett

*Alms
Ridge*

private
property

23S02

Willow Creek/
Los Burros Road

Sand Dollar
Picnic Area

Willow Creek
Campground

Gorda

23S01

20S05

RIDE 6 ■

▲ *Alder Peak*

Alder Camp △

20S05

▲ *Three Peaks*
▲▲

SILVER PEAK

WILDERNESS

Lottie △
Potrero

N
W ✦ E
S

(map not to scale)

PACIFIC OCEAN

©1999 Fine Edge Productions

■	Ride Start/Finish
	Best 100 Routes
	Dirt Roads/Other Routes
	Paved Roads
	Off-Limits

mile south of Kirk Creek Campground. There's a cattleguard and a
sign indicates: *Jolon, 22 miles; Fort
Hunter-Liggett, 18 miles.* Head up
this steep, paved road for 7.2 miles

(there are mile markers on the side of
the road) to Nacimiento Summit,
where the dirt Coast Ridge Road
crosses. A sign on the left reads:
Central Coast Ridge Road; Vincente

View toward the Pacific Ocean from Coast Ridge Road

Trail, 4 miles; San Antonio Trail, 5 miles; Cone Peak Trail, 6 miles, North Coast Ridge Trail, 6 miles. A sign on the right reads: *South Coast Ridge Road 20S05; Prewitt Ridge Road, 5 miles; Plaskett Ridge Road, 7 miles.* Park here, being careful not to block the road.

Route: You take the road to the north signed as Central Coast Ridge Road (20S05) to Cone Peak. The route begins with a gentle downhill before turning upward, then repeating the pattern as the road grows a bit rockier. At 2.5 miles you get some very good views to the northeast as you make your way around the ridge's north side. Here you are surrounded by moss, ferns and manzanita trees.

Just under 4.0 miles, the road gets steeper and you pass a trail sign on your right for San Antonio Trail (5E04). Stay on the road; the trail drops into the wilderness area. The going along here is steeper as you

pedal past some white rocks. A turnout a little beyond offers views of the ocean to the west. The grade abates a bit but the road surface remains rocky. A little bit of a downhill brings you to a small saddle with a pullout at 4.9 miles. Again you have an ocean view—photo op.

Gawk all you want and then proceed another 0.4 mile (5.3 total) to the Cone Peak trailhead. [**Side trip:** A sign indicates the peak is 2 miles away. I highly recommend bagging the summit. Hide your bike or lock it up (although if you're up here in the middle of the week such precautions are probably unnecessary). The going gets tougher the closer you get to the 5,155-foot summit, where the 1923 structure still serves as a fire lookout. It was unmanned when I was there. An ancient volcano, the peak is just 3 or 4 miles from the beach, making its western slope one of the steepest escarpments in the state.]

Once back to your bike, you can

head back to your car from here. [**Side trip:** You can follow the road another 1.2 miles to its end at the Ventana Wilderness where it turns into North Coast Ridge Trail (3E10), bringing ride mileage to 13 miles round trip. It's pretty easy going with more fabulous views inland, but there are no grand vistas or anything like that at road's end.]

5 South Coast Ridge Road from Nacimiento Summit to Willow Creek Road

Distance: 24.5 miles.
Difficulty: Strenuous; somewhat technical.
Elevation: Endless ups and downs; most are short but can be *very* steep.
Ride Type: One-way; can be done as an out-and-back of whatever length you desire; a loop or shuttle can also be arranged.
Season: Year-round.
Map: Los Padres National Forest: Monterey and Santa Lucia Ranger Districts. *Note:* On some maps Willow Creek Road is referred to as Los Burros Road.
Water: Some available en route but not dependable; any that you do find should be treated.
Comments: Nearest services are along Highway 1. Emergency help could be sought at Nacimiento Station just past Nacimiento Summit on Nacimiento-Fergusson Road or, perhaps, at residences along Willow Creek Road.

Overview: This is classic ridge riding with innumerable ups and downs as you wind from the west (ocean) side to the east (inland) side of the ridge. As you ride past oak and bay forest surrounded by coastal canyons and enveloped in fog, you feel like you're truly riding on top of the world. Such a feeling is hard won as this ride is a workout.

You can explore this section of road by riding out and back from the top of either Nacimiento Road or Willow Creek Road. Nacimiento is the easier drive as dirt Willow Creek is steep, rutted and washboarded. No matter which way you do it, the riding is tough.

For a loop, the easiest route would be up Nacimiento Road, along the Coast Ridge Route, down Willow Creek Road and along Highway 1 to your starting point. This would be around 45 miles. Or you could arrange a shuttle, dropping off at Nacimiento Summit and picking up at the bottom of Willow Creek Road. (After all your hard work, you might as well enjoy the descent of Willow Creek Road!) This would be about 25 miles and is the option described below.

The town of Gorda, one mile to the south of Willow Creek Road on Highway 1, or Willow Creek picnic area, 0.5 mile north on Highway 1, would make good pick-up points for a shuttle, or parking points if you decide to loop it.

Getting There: Follow directions for Ride 4. Park in the same place or, if doing a shuttle, drop off here.

Route: Head down South Coast Ridge Road (20S05) away from Cone Peak. You have views toward the ocean as you make your way up and

View from South Coast Ridge Road

down. In general, the rollies are steeper and the going is tougher than on the Cone Peak ride. At 3.0 miles you hit a brief section of pavement followed by a steep downhill—the first extended downhill stretch on the ride. Less than 0.5 mile later you are back on dirt. Just under 4.0 miles you pass a nice campsite on your left with a picnic table, awesome tree and small pond (in November at least).

At 4.5 miles you reach a junction. The right is signed: *Prewitt Ridge Camp, Alm's Ridge.* The left is signed: *South Coast Ridge Road, Chalk Peak 3/4 mile, Nacimiento-Fergusson 5 miles, Plaskett Ridge Road, Highway 1.* [**Side trip:** Head right toward Alm's Ridge. Bypass spurs to campsites as you make your way up and down several steep rollers. This area burned recently and you can see the effects of the fire. However, there are some beautiful oaks still standing. At 5.3 miles, you reach a view point. The vista point is on a bluff to your left, while the road continues down to the right. A sign here indicates that it is a rough road with a dead end. Go left

to the view point. From here you can see the ocean, Nacimiento-Fergusson Road, Mill Creek drainage and the ridge road you've just ridden. This is a popular spot for hang gliders to take off from, and you'll probably see a few up here when you visit. When you're done looking around, head back to the junction of Alm's Ridge and South Coast Ridge Road, reached at 6.1 miles.]

From the junction, continue south on South Coast Ridge Road through a burned area. (The following mileages assume you took the side trip.) At 7.4 miles you pass a road on the left: *McKern Road, Dead End 3 miles, 4WD Recommended.* You continue straight on Ridge Road. A mile later (8.4 miles total), you pass Plaskett Ridge Road (20S02) on the right. A sign indicates the road is closed ahead (this is the road that has been closed by a private property owner that I mentioned in the introduction to this section). You continue on the left fork uphill, signed South Coast Ridge Road (20S05).

About 0.5 mile later (8.9 miles

total), pass a 4WD spur on the right. I explored this spur, hoping it went through to Highway 1—no such luck. Continue on the ridge. In the next few miles, you have good views as you pass through more burned area. You bypass a campsite on the left before encountering some truly steep ups and downs. Indeed, the hardest riding seems to come in the last few miles— or maybe I was just tired.

Around 13 miles, you hit some granny gear pitches, and at 13.5 miles you stay right. Here you have great views to the southeast. On clear days you can make out San Antonio Reservoir and Nacimiento Reservoir.

A mile later, a road on the left leads to Fort Hunter-Liggett. *Do not enter.* I understand that unauthorized entry to a military facility is a federal crime. Any of the 4WD roads dropping east of the ridge should be avoided. You continue straight on the Ridge Road.

At 16.7 miles, you reach a Y intersection. The South Coast Ridge Road continues to the left. Willow Creek Road/Los Burros goes right. Decision time. You can head back the way you came (yikes). You can continue on the Ridge Road (see Ride 6). Or you can descend Willow Creek Road to Highway 1.

To descend to Highway 1, go right on Willow Creek Road/Los Burros Road. At 18.2 miles, you pass private residences on the right, then on the left. Stay on the main road and watch for dogs. At 18.5 miles, you

reach a junction. Los Burros/Willow Creek Road goes right. A sign indicates Highway 1 is 5 miles away, San Martin Top is 2 miles straight ahead, and Alder Creek Camp is 2 miles to the left. If you're doing the Coast Ridge Road as a multi-day trip, you could spend the night at Alder Camp. Reportedly, drinking water is available, but I did not confirm this.

Continue on Willow Creek Road to the right. Once past several more "residences" (I use the term loosely), the real descent begins. Be forewarned: it's not *all* downhill, but most of it is—and very welcome. Enjoy. At 24.5 miles you're at Highway 1. Whew.

Nacimiento / Fergusson Road

6 South Coast Ridge Road from Willow Creek Road to Lottie Potrero

Distance: 16 miles.
Difficulty: Strenuous; somewhat technical.
Elevation: Lots of short, steep ups and downs with one extended climb.
Ride Type: Out-and-back on dirt road.
Season: Year-round.
Map: Los Padres National Forest: Monterey and Santa Lucia Ranger Districts.
Water: Stream water at Lottie Potrero should be treated.
Comments: All services are available along Highway 1. You might be able to find emergency help at residences along Willow Creek Road.

Overview: This is my favorite section of the Coast Ridge Route. The views strike me as particularly stunning. It is probably the least-visited portion and feels the most remote and wild.

You can explore it as part of a multi-day venture along the Coast Ridge Route or as a day ride. No matter which you choose, it is an out-and-back venture since there is no southern outlet. The easiest way to do it is to drive up dirt Willow Creek Road to the junction of the Ridge Route. Some passenger cars may have trouble, particularly in wet weather. An-

other option is to ride up Willow Creek Road, which would add a very steep 8-mile climb to the ride's start, but a fun 8-mile descent at the end. A final option is to get dropped off at the top of Willow Creek Road and then picked up along Highway 1. As with the previous ride, the town of Gorda or Willow Creek Campground would make a good rendezvous point.

Getting There: Willow Creek Road (also called Los Burros Road), heads east off of Highway 1 about 1 mile north of the town of Gorda and a

Ocean view from South Coast Ridge Route

half-mile south of Willow Creek Campground. Drive up Willow Creek Road 7.8 miles to its signed junction with South Coast Ridge Road. Do not block the road when you park.

Route: Head south on South Coast Ridge Road. The beginning section is mostly a gradual downhill on a smooth, twisty dirt road. When I was there in November, shrubs crowded the road's edges and I saw a bobcat.

Soon the road turns upward and grows rockier. At 1.2 miles there's a lookout point/campsite on the right. The road continues left. This is followed by a steeper downhill section interrupted by a couple of steep rollies.

At 2.5 miles the road winds away from the ocean and you lose the grand ocean views, only to have them replaced by awesome views to the north and east. As you roll and dip along a smooth ridge top you can see all of the Ventana Wilderness and Fort Hunter-Liggett. At points you regain the ocean view as well.

At 4.3 miles you reach a signed junction. Sign reads: *South Coast Ridge Road 20S05, Salmon Creek Trail 1/4 mile, Dutra Trail 2 1/2 miles, Lottie Potrero 4 miles.* It also indicates that Lion Den Camp is 1 mile to the right, but the road has been roughed up and has a Road Closed sign. Continue on the Coast Ridge Road.

The going soon gets tougher. At 4.5 miles, you pass the signed Salmon Creek Trail on the right. Immediately there begins a *very* steep, loose, rutted uphill. If you can clean this, more power to you. At 4.8 miles, a rusted white sign on the left marks a road into Fort Hunter-Liggett. Avoid all roads dropping inland toward the military base.

You begin to get views of some nicely craggy peaks ahead, including the Three Peaks. At 6.6 miles the road forks. There's a sign: *Pack it in, pack it out.* Left goes to Hunter-Liggett; you continue on the South Coast Ridge Road. From here you begin a consistent, steep downhill. If you're feeling tired, you may want to turn around here as the only way out is back up this descent.

At 8.0 miles, you cross a stream and the road ends at a campsite. This is Lottie Potrero. A picnic table sits amid oaks and sycamores, the stream running beside it. This would make a most pleasant campsite if you're doing the Ridge Road as a bike packing venture. Treat all water!

Rest and munch some food. When you're ready, it's a pull back up to the ridgeline. Backtrack the way you came to the junction with Willow Creek Road. If you got someone to drop you off, you can now enjoy the 8-mile descent to Highway 1. If you parked here, your adventure is over—at least for the day.

Highway 1

Outside the rugged ridges and canyons of the Los Padres National Forest, there is not much legal riding in the Big Sur area. There's almost no riding immediately adjacent to Highway 1. This is unfortunate for the less-experienced rider. There is, however, one nice spot for families and beginning riders to try. It is a bluff-side trail extending from near Plaskett Creek campground in the south to Pacific Valley in the north. The coast along here is part of a state game refuge, and on one visit I watched a sea otter frolic just offshore. So pack a lunch and some binoculars when you explore this area.

7 Bluff Trail

Distance: 3 miles.
Difficulty: Easy; mildly technical.
Elevation: Negligible gain/loss.
Ride Type: Out-and-back on trail.
Season: Year-round.
Map: Cape San Martin.
Water: Available at Sand Dollar campground/picnic area.

Overview: This easy trail traces the bluffs along the edge of Pacific Valley. The ride makes for a nice leg-stretcher if you're driving the coast; a good family lunch stop with optional ride.

Getting There: Start at Sand Dollar Campground/Picnic Area, about 4 miles north of Gorda on the west side of Highway 1.

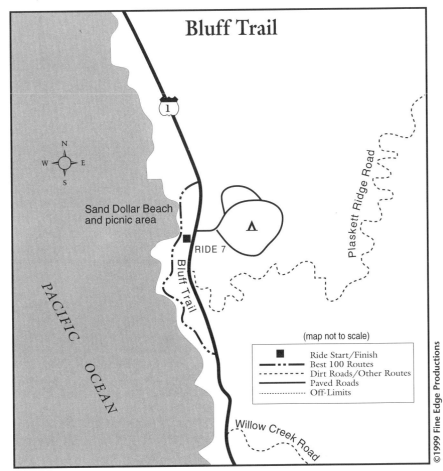

©1999 Fine Edge Productions

Route: Access the trail in the northwest corner of the picnic area. It goes for about one mile to the north. Several trails drop down the bluffs to ocean vista points. If you venture down one of these, be forewarned that it's a steep climb back up. In general, you want to stay high. You really can't get lost, sandwiched as you are on a narrow strip of land between Highway 1 to the east and the ocean to the west. The trail does drop into and climb out of several drainages. These sections are the only "technical" parts of the ride and the only spots that may give families or beginning riders pause. They are, however, short enough to walk. When you're done exploring to the north, you can return to the picnic area. (If you want, you can travel about half a mile to the south, then retrace your path back to your car.)

Lake San Antonio

The Monterey County Parks Department has done an excellent job of developing and signing mountain biking trails in the oak and chaparral landscape along the south shore of Lake San Antonio. Just north of Paso Robles, the lake is the county's premier freshwater recreation area. Fishing, swimming and boating opportunities abound. In May the 3,000-acre park hosts the famous Wildflower Triathlon. One of the largest bald eagle winter habitats in central California, the park runs Eagle Watch boat tours Friday through Sunday in January and February.

The trail system here is a land access success story for mountain bicyclists. Trail development started 20 years ago when rangers realized that many of the park's fire breaks would make great hiking trails. Too much motorized recreation during the 1970s led to trail damage and the park began roughing up the fire breaks so that they were impossible to ride. During the 1980s, the Wildflower Triathlon brought more hikers, runners and bicyclists to the area, and a local mountain bike club began using the park as a race course. Although the trail system was temporarily closed to mountain biking because of concerns over liability and resource preservation, those issues have been resolved. Now the Parks Department is committed to building, rating and signing trails for all levels of riders.

8 Long Valley Loop

Distance: 7.1 miles.
Difficulty: Moderate; mildly technical.
Elevation: Lots of ups and downs, but no major climbs.
Ride Type: Loop on dirt roads, fire breaks and singletrack.
Season: Year-round; can be extremely hot in summer.
Map: Monterey County Parks Department produces a very good map, available at park entrance.
Water: Water and bathrooms at Visitor's Center.
Comments: This is a pretty contained area so hazards are few.

Overview: This loop takes you through oak and chaparral along the Harris Creek arm of the lake, away from the boat launches and more developed shoreline of the main reservoir. In addition to 26 miles of hiking and mountain bike trails, the south shore of the lake has a full-service

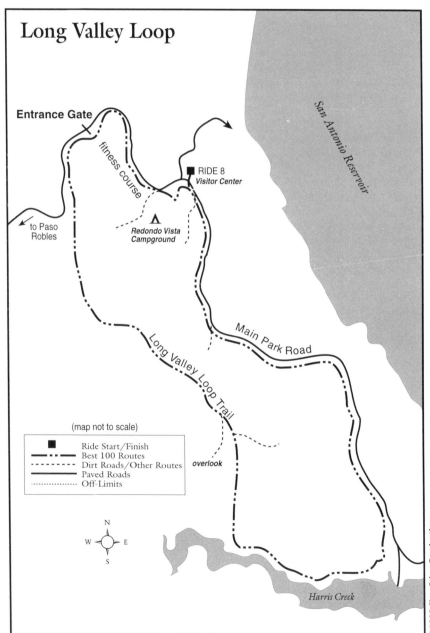

Long Valley Loop

Entrance Gate

fitness course

to Paso Robles

RIDE 8
Visitor Center

Redondo Vista Campground

San Antonio Reservoir

Main Park Road

Long Valley Loop Trail

(map not to scale)

■ Ride Start/Finish
–··– Best 100 Routes
----- Dirt Roads/Other Routes
——— Paved Roads
········· Off-Limits

overlook

N
W   E
S

Harris Creek

©1999 Fine Edge Productions

Long Valley Loop

resort with grocery store, restaurant, gas station, marina and cabin rentals.

Getting There: From Paso Robles, take G-14 north/northwest. (In town, G-14 is 24th Street. Outside of town it is signed Nacimiento Lake Dr. As you exit Highway 101 or 46 in Paso Robles, signs direct you to G-14.) Follow the signs for Lake Nacimiento and Lake San Antonio. At 8.5 miles, G-14 makes a right. At 16.3 miles, it curves right and crosses a dam (Lake Nacimiento). At 17.9 miles, go left on G-14/Interlake Road just past the sign indicating North Shore (straight) and South Shore (left). At 24.8 miles, cross the Monterey County line. At 25.7 miles, go right on San Antonio Road (signed South Shore) to the park entrance. There is a $6 day-use fee. Take the main entrance road and follow signs to the visitor's center. Park here.

Route: Backtrack to the entrance road. Immediately on your right is a bunch of big white boulders. Ride between them and you can see the backside of a trail sign. Pick up the Long Valley Trail here. Go right to begin the loop. We did the loop in a counterclockwise direction, but it could just as easily be done in the opposite direction. Neither way appears much harder or easier than the other. In both cases you have a few short, steep climbs.

At 0.1 mile, cross a paved road. The trail continues on the other side. It is clearly marked here and throughout the loop. Continue following signs for the Long Valley Loop, alongside the fitness course. You parallel the entrance road here. Although the surroundings are not pristine wilderness, we did see deer here.

At 0.4 mile, start the first of two short hills. At 1.0 mile, you come to a fence. Be sure to close the gate behind you as there are cattle in the area. Just under 2.0 miles, the doubletrack you're on swings left and begins a short pain-in-the-butt climb. It tops out at 2.1 miles and immediately passes through another fence. You can walk through the gate on the side, albeit awkwardly. Watch the barbed wire.

Go down a steep, loose section and keep left at the fork at 2.3 miles. Not the least bit tempting, the right fork is a very steep uphill doubletrack. This junction, like the others, is clearly signed. On the left fork, you begin a fun singletrack section along a creek.

At 2.5 miles, merge with a fire road and continue straight. (Once again, well-signed.) Just beyond, you fork right and roll up and down for awhile. Be on the watch for a single-track on your left at 2.9 miles. If you're not paying attention you can blast right past it. Going straight takes you 0.2 mile up a steep rocky climb to Harris Valley Overlook. We rode up to it and concurred that it was not worth the trouble. So head left down the singletrack through braking bumps and a short rocky section.

At 3 9 miles, go straight; Badger Trail branches left. A half-mile later, the singletrack begins skirting the Harris Creek arm of the lake. This is the prettiest part of the ride. You are away from campgrounds and the entrance road, surrounded by oak-graced hills, the cool blue waters of the lake, and possibly a few fishermen. Adding a spooky, surreal touch, dead tree limbs poke out of the water, marking trees that were drowned when the reservoir was created.

Follow the fun singletrack as it rolls beside and above the lake for a mile. At 4.5 miles, go straight up the steep, rocky climb. You may have to dismount and push up this short sec-tion. At 4.6 miles, go straight where a doubletrack merges from the right.

Begin a rolling dirt road climb—steep and loose in spots. It can be hot and exposed here, but when we did it we were blessed with a breeze. Soon enough, 5.6 miles, you begin a rolling downhill. At 5.8 miles, cross another dirt road (Oak Hill Loop) and continue straight. Things get more park-like and less like wilderness as you once again closely parallel the main park road.

At 6.2 miles, veer right, cross the paved road and catch the trail to the right on the other side of the road (clearly signed). After this you cross a variety of other dirt trails and roads. Stay on the clearly-signed Long Valley Loop parallel to the main paved park road.

You're back at the boulders at 7.1 miles—at least that's what my computer said. The park map says this loop is 8.1 miles. Go figure. From the boulders, take a right and head back to the Visitor's Center (water and bathrooms available).

Harris Creek at Lake San Antonio

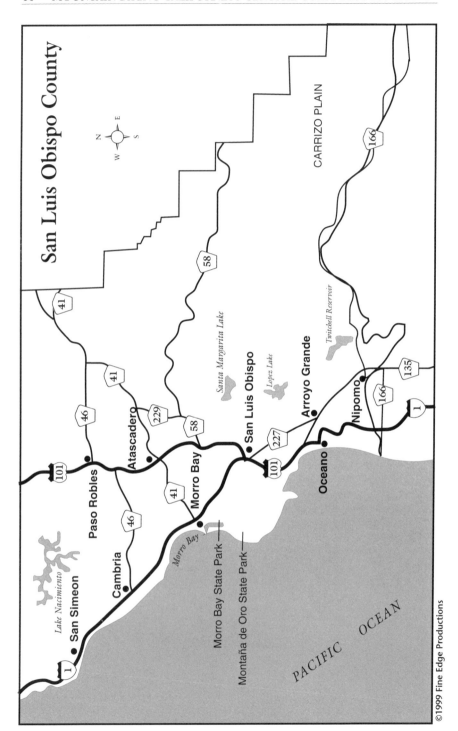

CHAPTER 2

San Luis Obispo County

By Delaine Fragnoli

Tucked between Santa Barbara County and the Los Padres National Forest to the south and Monterey County and the Santa Lucia Mountains to the north, San Luis Obispo County offers excellent road and mountain biking opportunities. Best known for its lovely beaches, San Luis Obispo County boasts 80 miles of coastline, including Pismo Beach and Morro Bay, the latter punctuated by the striking Morro Rock. Morro Rock is one of the Seven Sisters or Nine Morros, a series of ancient volcanic plugs which dominate the landscape. Farther north is San Simeon and Hearst Castle, the fantasy estate of newspaper magnate William Randolph Hearst.

Predictably, the best riding here is at the beach. A State Park, Montaña de Oro, contains perhaps the most scenic coastal mountain biking in all of the state. Just inland, Los Padres National Forest continues into San Luis Obispo County from Santa Barbara County, while another chunk of the forest stretches from San Simeon almost to Carmel. Unfortunately, much of it is designated wilderness and is thus closed to bikes. The areas that are open for mountain biking provide very steep climbing as the Santa Lucia mountain range rises from sea level to over 5,000 feet in a mere few miles.

There are several other pockets of rideable terrain scattered throughout the county, such as those near Cal Poly San Luis Obispo and in the remote Carrizo Plain, and around Lopez and Santa Margarita lakes. Since the area averages sunny days 78% of the year, you can ride here year round.

The hub of the county, the city of San Luis Obispo has several bike shops and a variety of accommodations. Camping is available at the beach, in the Los Padres National Forest, at Lopez and Santa Margarita Lakes, and at Montaña de Oro and Morro Bay State Parks.

Morro Bay State Park/Cabrillo Peaks

The network of trails at Cabrillo Peaks is part of Morro Bay State Park. It offers lots of different trail surfaces, terrain and vegetation in a small area, not to mention cool rock outcroppings. There are lots of ups and downs but no really extended climbs, and the trails are good for honing singletrack skills. I couldn't help thinking the area would make a nice, fast race course. The trails are well signed, at least the major trails are, although some junctions are not. Innumerable loops are possible, making the park a good choice for a quick workout or after-work ride.

9 Portolo Point Singletrack Loop

Distance: 6 miles.
Difficulty: Moderate; somewhat technical in spots.
Elevation: 1000' gain/loss.
Ride Type: Loop on singletrack.
Season: Year-round.
Maps: Morro Bay South; or SLO Adventures' Mountain Biking San Luis Obispo & Coastal Areas.
Water: Bring all you will need.
Comments: Not recommended in wet weather.

Overview: The loop described here takes in most of the park's trails and includes a good view of Morro Bay and Morro Rock from Portolo Point. Don't let my suggestions constrain you. This is a good place to explore willy-nilly. As long as you stay on the south/southwest sides of Cerro Cabrillo and Hollister Peak, and keep oriented to South Bay Boulevard, you shouldn't get lost.

View of two of the Cabrillo Peaks

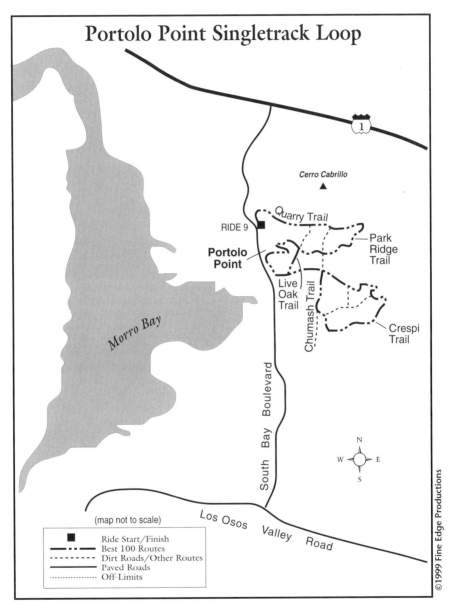

Portolo Point Singletrack Loop

Cerro Cabrillo

RIDE 9

Quarry Trail

Portolo Point

Park Ridge Trail

Live Oak Trail

Chumash Trail

Crespi Trail

Morro Bay

South Bay Boulevard

N
W · E
S

©1999 Fine Edge Productions

(map not to scale)

Los Osos Valley Road

■ Ride Start/Finish
–·–·– Best 100 Routes
– – – – Dirt Roads/Other Routes
——— Paved Roads
··········· Off-Limits

Getting There: From Highway 1, exit at South Bay Boulevard. The off-ramp is signed with a brown Morro Bay State Park sign. Take South Bay Boulevard about 1.5 miles to a parking area on the left. There's another smaller parking area just down the road, but the first one is better.

From Highway 101, exit at Los Osos Valley Road and head west. Go right on South Bay Boulevard and park in the second parking area on the right.

Route: Start at the information

One of the Cabrillo Peaks in Morro Bay State Park

the ocean. I flailed around some here, and my computer read just over 2 miles at the top of Portolo Point. Enjoy the view.)

Backtrack down the switchbacks—much more fun in this direction—to the 4-way Live Oak Trail intersection. Go right and down a handful of waterbars. (A left would take you back to Quarry Trail if you've had enough.) You soon encounter several Y intersections. Bearing right will take you down toward South Bay Boulevard. To continue the loop, keep bearing left until you T into Park Ridge Trail, actually a doubletrack at this point. Go left and up Park Ridge about 0.1 mile to Crespi Trail.

Stay on Crespi Trail (well-signed, although some of the signs have weathered so that the name reads "respi" in places) when it crosses Chumash Trail and when several spurs jut off. Crespi is my favorite trail here. It winds up and down, and its prettiest section includes a couple of switchbacking corners through a grove of beautiful oaks hung with Spanish moss. Very cool. This little drainage feels "remote" from nearby, and busy, South Bay Boulevard.

At about 4.8 miles (once again, my mileage was not totally accurate), Crespi Ts into Chumash Trail. Go right. When Chumash crosses Crespi again you can go straight on Chumash or veer left onto Crespi. You should recognize this intersection from when you began the Crespi loop. Both options will deposit you on Park Ridge Trail. Go left (down-

board. Take the singletrack Quarry Trail uphill. Initially a steep climb, it soon mellows. Enjoy the cool rock formations on the flanks of Cerro Cabrillo on your left. Bypass Live Oak Trail on your right and Park Ridge Trail, also on your right. Just under a mile, take the second Park Ridge Trail uphill.

After some ups and downs, Park Ridge Trail crosses Chumash Trail. Go straight to a small saddle. Continue straight, then bear right at a series of trail junctions. It's a bit confusing through here, but you drop into a gully before climbing across Live Oak Trail (a distinct 4-way intersection) and up several switchbacks to Portolo Point. (You're basically heading due west toward South Bay Boulevard and

hill) on Park Ridge Trail. This is a quick doubletrack.

You bypass Live Oak Trail (the section you took down from Portolo Point) on your way toward South Bay Boulevard. Just before the gate, you can catch another section of Live Oak Trail that parallels the road and take it back to your starting point. Or, if you're lazy like I was (hey, cut me some slack, it was my second ride of the day), you can descend to the pavement and go right on the road back to your car for a more-or-less 6-mile ride.

Montaña De Oro State Park

West of San Luis Obispo and just south of Morro Bay (you can see Morro Rock from spots in the park), Montaña de Oro has eight trails, mostly singletrack, open to bikes. The rides in this section take you on all but one of those trails. Please note that the trails described in Rides 10–14 can be combined in numerous ways. These are just a few suggestions.

The Park gets its name not for the precious metal, but for the brilliant gold color the landscape assumes in spring when it is covered by California poppies and other wildflowers. At over 8,000 acres and with half a million visitors each year, this is one of California's largest and most popular State Parks—and for good reason. Seven miles of shoreline offer spectacular views and cooling sea breezes. Tide pools and miles of sandy beaches add to the dramatic meeting of land and sea. Facilities include a visitor center, picnic areas and campgrounds.

10 Islay Creek/East Boundary Trail/Barranca Trail Loop

Distance: 9.5 miles.
Difficulty: Moderate with some strenuous sections, some technical sections.
Elevation: 1,000' gain/loss.
Ride Type: Loop on dirt road and singletrack.
Season: Year-round.
Map: Montaña De Oro State Park map, available at visitor center.
Water: Can be purchased at visitor center, or available at campground.

Overview: This ride combines a gradual climb up a pretty canyon with some steep and challenging singletrack. Beginners can ride up the fire road and turn around, eliminating the technical singletrack. Experienced riders will want to tackle the technical climb up East Boundary Trail and the equally technical descent of Barranca Trail.

Getting There: The park is about 12 miles west of San Luis Obispo and 7 miles south of Los Osos. From Highway 101 in San Luis Obispo, take the Los Osos/Bayward Park exit and go northwest on Los Osos Valley Road. After 12 miles it turns into Pecho Valley Road and leads into the park.

From Highway 1 near Morro Bay, take the Los Osos/Bayward Park exit. Go right on South Bay Boule-

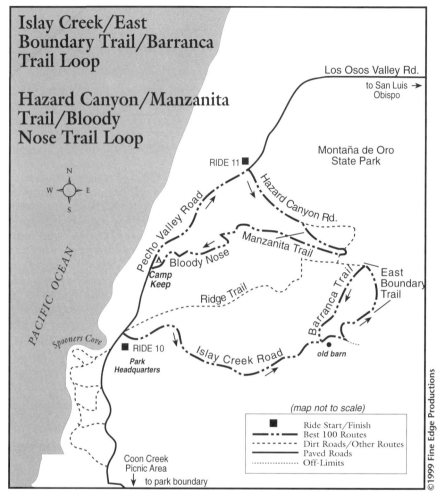

Islay Creek/East Boundary Trail/Barranca Trail Loop

Hazard Canyon/Manzanita Trail/Bloody Nose Trail Loop

vard. At 5 miles you come to a T at Los Osos Valley Road. Go right and follow Los Osos Valley Road into Pecho Valley Road and the park.

Park headquarters are 2.5 miles past the park entrance sign. Park there or at a trailhead 0.1 mile farther on Pecho Valley Road in a dirt turnout on the right. There is a pay phone and restrooms at headquarters.

Route: From the headquarters, backtrack to Pecho Valley Road and go right 0.3 mile to the gated and signed Islay Creek Road on your

right. This dirt road rolls along, gaining elevation at an easy grade as it heads inland. As you spin along you have views into lush Islay Creek with its willow, sage, purple nightshade, blackberry—and poison oak.

At 2.4 miles, you pass a trail on your right (closed to bikes). A half-mile later you pass another single-track, this one on your left. This is the Barranca Trail, your return route which drops from the East Boundary Trail. Continue climbing on the road past an old barn on the right.

At 3.3 miles, East Boundary Trail (signed) branches to the left. Ahead of you on the road you can see a closed gate which marks the park boundary. (Beginners should turn around here.) Go left onto East Boundary Trail. It starts climbing almost immediately—and gets steeper with each pedal stroke. If the incline and the rocky, loose trail weren't bad enough, you soon have to maneuver around and over waterbars as well. The longer you go, the worse it gets. I mashed, bashed, moaned, groaned and swore with a vengeance and I still couldn't clean it. Thankfully this misery ends when you top out at 4.0 miles.

From here, the trail rolls rather than pitches upward. At 4.2 miles you pass a trail marker with trail tools, donated by the Central Coast Concerned Mountain Bikers. A sign encourages you to pick up a tool and spend a few minutes on trail work. Good work to the CCCMB.

Temporarily level and then descending, the trail crosses a wooden bridge at 4.4 miles. An equestrian trail joins East Boundary here. This creek crossing is followed by a short switchbacked climb across an open slope—much easier than the earlier climb.

The trail then levels and you have great views of the steep ridges and canyons of the coastal mountains. Don't take your eyes off the trail for too long as you soon hit a technical downhill section. Curvy, with loose soil, this bit of trail was filled with braking bumps when I rode it.

At 4.9 miles, you come to a short hike-a-bike pitch (at least it was for me) past a lovely oak tree on your left. Follow the trail along the fence line marking the park boundary (thus, the trail's

name). At 5.2 miles, there's an unsigned singletrack on your left.

You have a decision to make here. This is the Barranca Trail. You can take it back down to Islay Creek Road for a lollipop-shaped 9.5-mile loop or you can continue 0.2 mile farther to the Ridge Trail (see Ride 12).

For the Barranca Trail loop, you climb 0.3 mile more, including a couple of switchbacks, to a T intersection. The left branch goes to a picnic table with an ocean view (makes a nice rest stop even if you decide to take the Ridge Trail). Take the right branch as it drops steeply through a series of sometimes tight (but rideable) switchbacks and over some rocky pitches (real butt-off-the-saddle stuff) before depositing you at Islay Creek Road. I thought the trail was a blast, but its technicality might not be to everyone's liking. At Islay Creek Road, a right takes you back to Pecho Valley Road.

East Boundary Trail, Montaña de Oro State Park

11 Hazard Canyon/Manzanita Trail/Bloody Nose Trail Loop

Distance: 6.0 miles.
Difficulty: Moderately strenuous; very technical in spots.
Elevation: 650' gain/loss.
Ride Type: Loop on dirt road, singletrack and pavement.
Season: Year-round.
Map: Montaña De Oro State Park map, available at visitor center.
Water: Buy at visitor center.
Comments: Watch for poison oak and stinging nettles!

Overview: Like the previous ride, this one includes a scenic trip up a canyon, ocean views, fun singletrack and a gnarly descent. Conditions on the Manzanita and Bloody Nose singletracks have gotten decidedly more difficult since El Niño. Beginners should turn around before heading down Bloody Nose. Advanced riders may want to connect these trails with the previous ride for a longer loop. The easiest way to access Ridge and Barranca trails would be via Hazard Canyon and Manzanita Trail, described here.

Getting There: Hazard Canyon Road takes off to the left (east) from Pecho Valley Road just inside (about 0.1 mile) the State Park boundary. A small brown post here reads *Group Horse Camp*. Park in the dirt turnout just beyond and across the road.

Route: Head down dirt Hazard Canyon Road past the horse camp. Beyond here the road rises and falls, generally gaining altitude. Continue past a second gate. Soon the road curves to the right, and at 0.8 mile you come to a junction with the Manzanita Trail off to the right. Go right and climb this singletrack out of the canyon.

View of Hazard Canyon from Manzanita Trail, Montaña de Oro State Park

Manzanita Trail rises from the wet, wooded (willow and eucalyptus) creek bed to manzanita and sage. This ascent constitutes the ride's major elevation gain. Although steep, it is rideable with a good line around most of the waterbars. Indeed, it is much easier than the previous ride's climb up East Boundary Trail.

At 1.4 miles, you come to a T intersection. Go right. Almost immediately there's another trail joining on the left. You continue straight for this loop. (Going left would take you to the Ridge Trail or, a bit farther, the Barranca Trail. See the previous ride description for details.) There's a picnic table here with a view down Hazard Canyon and to the ocean. Photo op!

Continue along the now more level Manzanita Trail. At 1.9 miles you pass a closed trail climbing steeply on the left. Continue straight. You have more views toward the ocean and into steep-walled Hazard Canyon. Your ride continues to the left. (Just beyond here there's a Y intersection. You can take the right fork that climbs steeply for 0.1 mile to a small ridgetop and viewpoint where it dead ends.)

Now you begin what can only be described as a very gnarly and bizarre piece of trail. (Beginners attempting this ride should turn around at this point unless you don't mind walking.) You are basically riding in a giant rut filled with deep sand; stands of the trail's namesake manzanita bushes line the lip of the crevice. Black plastic erosion netting here seems to serve no purpose but to knock you off your bike.

I found it quite frustrating to be pedaling so hard through the bottomless sand to go *downhill*. But it's not all sand. You get rock, hard-packed soil with ruts, waterbars, drop-offs—a wide variety of hazards and obstacles. I believe I said a swear word or two along here.

At 3.1 miles, go left at the Y. At this point you are on Bloody Nose Trail, although it is not signed as such. You go in and out of two streams, steeply of course. One waterbar-choked ascent will be a hike-a-bike for most riders. Throw in some ragged, jagged shale as well as more railroad ties and you've got yourself a challenge. Hmm, wonder how the trail got that name.

At 3.7 miles, you reach a picnic spot. Stop if you like or continue on the trail into Camp Keep. Bear right past the campsites and park residences. You are soon on pavement as you head out to Pecho Valley Road. Once there, go right for 1.5 miles to finish the loop. It's down, then up, then rolling back to your car.

12 Ridge Trail

Distance: 3 miles.
Difficulty: Moderately strenuous; somewhat technical.
Elevation: Net loss of 650'.
Ride Type: One-way on singletrack.
Season: Year-round.
Map: Montaña de Oro State Park map, available at visitor center.
Water: May be purchased at visitor center.

Ridge Trail
Bluff Trail

to Los Osos
Valley Road,
San Luis Obispo

**Montaña De Oro
State Park**

PACIFIC OCEAN

Valley Road

Pecho

Camp
Keep

Ridge Trail

Barranca Trail

East
Boundary
Trail

Spooners Cove

RIDES 12 & 13
park
headquarters

Islay Creek Road

old barn

Bluff
Trail

Coon Creek
Picnic Area

to park boundary

(map not to scale)

■	Ride Start/Finish
—·—·—	Best 100 Routes
- - - -	Dirt Roads/Other Routes
———	Paved Roads
··········	Off-Limits

©1999 Fine Edge Productions

Overview: This trail is an alternate return route for either of the two preceding rides. Instead of returning via Barranca Trail (Ride 10) or via Manzanita and Bloody Nose trails (Ride 11), you can finish either ride by descending the Ridge Trail. First it climbs Hazard Peak before beginning a spectacular drop toward the ocean. Great views!

Getting There: You can park and begin riding at park headquarters (same spot as Ride 10) or just inside the park boundary (as in Ride 11). Even if you decide to add the Ridge Trail to Ride 11, I recommend that you park at headquarters. By starting there, you get the pavement portion of the ride over with first.

Route: Follow the directions for Ride 10 up to the intersection of Barranca Trail and East Boundary Trail at 5.2 miles. Continue straight on East Boundary Trail for 0.2 mile to the Ridge Trail intersection on the left.

[*For an easier option,* follow the

directions for Ride 11 up to the T intersection of Manzanita Trail and East Boundary Trail at 1.4 miles. Go right. Almost immediately there's another trail joining on the left. Go left. Then make an immediate right onto the Ridge Trail.]

The Ridge Trail rolls west along the ridgeline above Hazard Canyon (to your right) with a few short, steep uphills. (I had to do some walking and pushing.) About 0.5 mile along the trail, there's a T intersection. Go left for another 0.5 mile before beginning the final steep ascent to Hazard Peak, at 1,076 feet, where you have fantastic ocean and shoreline views.

From here it's a sometimes steep, sometimes rutted, sometimes rocky, sometimes sandy descent toward the beach. At 2.4 miles, you cross a former fence line. Keep heading toward the ocean. At the bottom, 3.0 miles, a left turn on Pecho Valley takes you 0.4 mile back to park headquarters.

[If you started at Hazard Canyon, go right on Pecho Valley Road for 2.5 miles back to your car. If you don't want to ride the pavement, a more hard-core option would be to go left on Pecho Valley Road to Islay Creek Road. Take Islay up to the East Boundary Trail and follow East Boundary around to Upper Hazard Canyon. This would make for an 11.5-mile double loop.]

13 Bluff Trail

Distance: 3.5-mile loop; 4.4 miles out and back.
Difficulty: Easy; not technical.
Elevation: 60-100'.
Ride Type: Out-and-back on dirt road; or loop on dirt road and pavement.
Season: Year-round.
Map: Montaña De Oro State Park map, available at visitor center.
Water: Can be purchased at the visitor center, or available in campground.

Overview: This ride may have the best scenery for the least amount of effort of any ride in California. As the name implies, it follows bluffs (actually uplifted marine terraces). For drama, it's hard to beat the sight of ocean waves crashing over these jutting rock formations. Beach access and views of wave-formed sea arches add to the scene. In April and May abundant California poppies, lavender and mustard improve on the already eye-gasmic picture. Pack a lunch or snack—you'll want to dawdle on this ride.

Getting There: Park at park head-quarters or at the trailhead just beyond. (See Ride 10 for driving instructions.)

Route: Begin by dropping to cross over a wooden foot bridge. After the bridge you pass several trail junctions. Keep forking to the right, heading toward the ocean. It's pretty obvious which is the main trail. As you continue along the bluffs, there are several spurs to your right which go to coastline vista points. You may want to bypass the first few as the ones closest to the trailhead tend to be more crowded.

At 0.5 mile, a spur leads to a lookout and a trail to the beach (don't ride it). Walk to the beach, if you want to go there. Just beyond this spur, at 0.6 mile, you intersect a second wooden bridge that spans a creek. Go right, crossing the bridge. (If you go straight you end up back at Pecho Valley Road.) At 1.0 mile, overlooking Quarry Cove, there are restrooms and picnic tables—a nice rest stop.

At 1.3 miles, fork right to stay on Bluff Trail (signed). About 0.2 mile later you have views of a large freestanding rock near the shore. At 1.7 miles turn left up the singletrack leading to Pecho Valley Road. [**Side trip:** You could go straight here; doing so would lead you to a turnaround at a fence marking the park boundary. Near this junction you have great views of Grotto Rock, its arches formed by the eroding power of wind and water.]

Heading left up the singletrack, you encounter the only technical part of the ride as the trail drops into and climbs steeply out of a small ravine. This portion of trail climbs gradually toward Pecho Valley Road and can be rutted.

After 2.2 miles of pedaling, you reach a parking area and Coon Creek trailhead (closed to bikes). There are restrooms and picnic tables here. You can return to your car, 1.1 miles away, via paved Pecho Valley Road, or you can go back the way you came. I personally don't know why anyone would choose the road when you can ride along the bluffs. Riding the trail in the opposite direction gives you a new perspective and you will probably notice things you missed on the way out.

14 Singletrack Figure 8

Distance: 7.7 miles.
Difficulty: Moderately strenuous; technical.
Elevation: 900' gain/loss.
Ride Type: Figure 8 on singletrack and dirt road.
Season: Year-round.
Map: Montaña de Oro State Park, available at visitor center.
Water: Purchase at visitor center

Overview: Here's yet another way to loop most of the best singletracks in Montaña de Oro.

Getting There: Begin at Hazard Canyon Road. (See directions for Ride 11.)

Route: This ride begins the same way as Ride 11. Follow those directions (Hazard Canyon Road to Manzanita Trail) until the T intersection at 1.4 miles. At this intersection, go right. Almost immediately, there's another trail joining on the left. Take it. Bypass the Ridge Trail on your right and continue beyond it for 0.2 mile to the unsigned Barranca Trail, also on your right.

Climb the Barranca Trail up a couple of switchbacks for 0.3 mile until you come to an intersection.

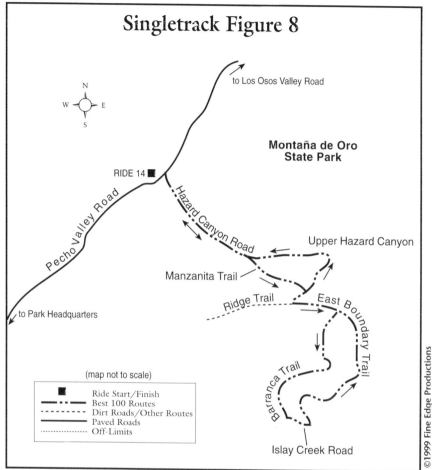

Singletrack Figure 8

to Los Osos Valley Road

Montaña de Oro State Park

RIDE 14

Pecho Valley Road

Hazard Canyon Road

Upper Hazard Canyon

Manzanita Trail

to Park Headquarters

Ridge Trail

East Boundary Trail

Barranca Trail

Islay Creek Road

(map not to scale)

■ Ride Start/Finish
—·—· Best 100 Routes
- - - - Dirt Roads/Other Routes
——— Paved Roads
·········· Off-Limits

©1999 Fine Edge Productions

The left fork goes to a picnic table with ocean views (nice rest stop) while the right fork begins a technical, switchbacked descent. At 3.2 miles the singletrack drops you onto Islay Creek Road. Go left and climb gently for 0.4 mile to East Boundary Trail on your left.

Climb and descend East Boundary Trail for almost two miles, about 5.5 miles total, back to the top of Barranca Trail. Continue straight on East Boundary Trail 0.2 mile. In quick succession you hit three inter-sections; veer right at each to stay on East Boundary Trail. [*Option:* You could choose to take Manzanita Trail and then Bloody Nose Trail (see Ride 11) down to Pecho Valley Road.]

The trail follows the park boundary fence as it drops down a series of railroad tie waterbars. Kerplunk. Kerplunk. Kerplunk. Soon you cross a stream and, at 6.5 miles, the trail turns into doubletrack. As you head down Hazard Canyon you pass Manzanita Trail on your left at 6.9 miles. At 7.7 miles you're back at your car.

Cuesta Ridge

Just north of San Luis Obispo, Highway 101 begins a steep climb to Cuesta Pass (1,521 feet), a notch which splits Cuesta Ridge into a western and an eastern section, both part of the Los Padres National Forest.

A wildfire in August 1994 denuded the western section of Cuesta Ridge, wiping out the "lush vegetation" described in earlier guidebooks. Even the Cuesta Ridge Botanical Area, formed in 1969 largely to protect the rare Sargent cypress (it reputedly grows only two other places on earth), looks scraggly. Although fire-hardy shrubs like manzanita are coming back, much of the area appears bare and exposes relics from the area's past as a shooting range (shooting is now prohibited). Broken glass and spent shell casings give an overall "trashy" appearance.

So why ride here? Put simply, the views. From the ridge you have ocean views and can see the famous Seven Sisters to the south and west. To the north and east are the Atascadero Hills and the Santa Lucia Wilderness.

A paved road, West Cuesta Ridge Road (also known as TV Tower Road, for obvious reasons, and by its Forest Service number 29S11) climbs from Cuesta Pass for 7.5 miles and turns to dirt just past Tassajera Peak before connecting with trails originating from Cerro Alto campground off of Highway 41. Riding the whole length is quite an undertaking with lots of ups and downs, although last time I was up here some ambitious roadies (!) were tackling it. Fortunately there are other options. Doubletracks and trails branching off from the ridge can be used to fashion loops. (Some riders do a shuttle by climbing the ridge and descending the trails to Cerro Alto Campground where they have left a second vehicle.)

The eastern section of the ridge, unaffected by the fire, offers an all-dirt out-and-back option with equally splendid views, especially of the Santa Lucia Wilderness and upper Lopez Canyon.

The Cerro Alto trails are worth exploring on their own. Steep and technical, they are challenging. The tough climb to Cerro Alto itself rewards with 360-degree views. The stream-side, oak-shaded campground makes a lovely base camp.

15 Stagecoach Road

Distance: 5.4 miles.
Difficulty: Moderate; not technical.
Elevation: 880' gain/loss.
Ride Type: Out-and-back on dirt road.
Season: Year-round.
Maps: San Luis Obispo, Lopez Mountain; or SLO Adventures' Mountain Biking San Luis Obispo & Coastal Areas.
Water: None.
Comments: Stay on the road as surrounding land is all private property.

Overview: This well-maintained dirt road parallels Highway 101 and was once the major route from Santa Margarita to San Luis Obispo. It was also popular with stagecoach bandits.

Today it is a relatively easy ride for beginning cyclists, or an alternate way to get from SLO to Cuesta Ridge for more advanced riders. It's a very shady ride, thanks not just to its his-

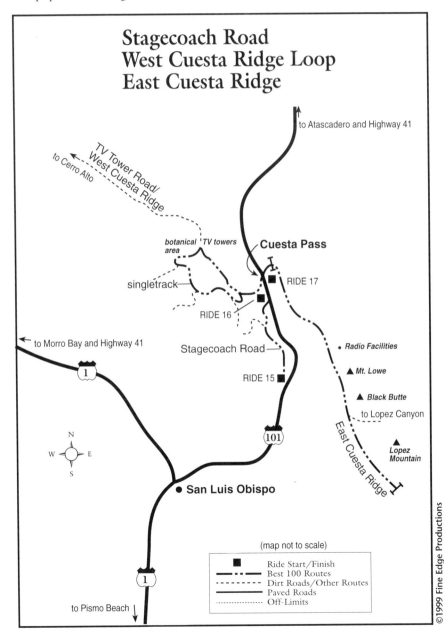

Stagecoach Road
West Cuesta Ridge Loop
East Cuesta Ridge

to Atascadero and Highway 41

to Cerro Alto

TV Tower Road/
West Cuesta Ridge

botanical   TV towers
area

Cuesta Pass

singletrack

RIDE 17

RIDE 16

to Morro Bay and Highway 41

Stagecoach Road

• Radio Facilities

▲ Mt. Lowe

RIDE 15

▲ Black Butte

to Lopez Canyon

East Cuesta Ridge

▲ Lopez Mountain

N
W — E
S

• **San Luis Obispo**

(map not to scale)

■	Ride Start/Finish
—·—·—	Best 100 Routes
- - - - -	Dirt Roads/Other Routes
———	Paved Roads
········	Off-Limits

to Pismo Beach

©1999 Fine Edge Productions

tory but to the plentiful sycamore and oak trees. Stagecoach Road is a good choice in hot weather.

Getting There: From San Luis Obispo, take Highway 101 north. Just past the Monterey Street exit and before the ascent of Cuesta Grade, turn left onto Stagecoach Road. Park off to the side of the road where your car won't block traffic.

From southbound Highway 101, Stagecoach Road is about 3 miles down from Cuesta Pass.

To start at Cerro Alto campground, follow the directions for Ride 18.

Route: For the first quarter-mile, the road is paved. After that it is well-graded, sometimes washboarded dirt. The road rises gradually for the first mile. You cross a cattleguard at 0.5 mile. At 1.0 mile you begin passing houses. From here the climb gets a bit steeper but is still quite manageable.

Just under 2.0 miles, you pass a private road. Stay on the main road. Immediately after that you cross another cattleguard. As with all good climbs, this one continues to get steeper as you make your way toward Cuesta Pass. Don't despair: from the second cattleguard you have less than a mile to go. You reach TV Tower Road (West Cuesta Ridge Road) at 2.7 miles.

Here there is a parking area, information board and pay phone. It's basically a large pull-out from Highway 101. It's a bit of a shock to go from the relative quiet of the canyon to the noise and traffic of the highway.

From this point, you can return the way you came or continue up West Cuesta Ridge on TV Tower Road (see the following ride). The descent is fast and fun, but watch for vehicles!

16 West Cuesta Ridge Loop

Distance: 8.0 miles.
Difficulty: Moderately strenuous; technical.
Elevation: 1500' gain/loss.
Ride Type: Lollipop-shaped loop on pavement, dirt road and singletrack.
Season: Year-round.
Maps: Atascadero, Morro Bay North, Morro Bay South, San Luis Obispo; or SLO Adventures' Mountain Biking San Luis Obispo & Coastal Areas; or Los Padres National Forest: Monterey and Santa Lucia Ranger Districts. *Note:* The singletrack is not shown on any of these maps.
Water: None.
Comments: The road is open to motor vehicles. Parking area is not Forest Service land so you do not need a Forest Adventure Pass.

Overview: While steep in spots, the climb of West Cuesta Ridge affords excellent coastal views. Riders are further rewarded with fun, technical singletrack—although you have to pay for it with a tough climb toward the end of the ride. Thanks to the '94 fire, the area boasts great spring wildflowers. The route can be extended by riding up Stagecoach Road (see previous ride) or by continuing toward Cerro Alto Campground.

Getting There: From San Luis Obispo, take Highway 101 north to just below the top of Cuesta Grade.

View of 3 of the Seven Sisters from West Cuesta Ridge

Use the left-hand turn lane here to turn into the pull-out on the west side of the highway. Be careful. This can be a harrowing turn as south-bound drivers hurtle down Cuesta Grade. You can choose to ride to this point via Stagecoach Road (see Ride 15).

Route: The ride begins with a steep, switchbacked climb on rough pavement up to the ridge. Once you have gained the ridge, the grade abates and the views begin. You can see the volcanic cones of Morro Rock, Cerro Cabrillo, Hollister Peak, Cerro Romualdo, Chumash Peak, Bishop Peak and Cerro San Luis Obispo. You pass several old, closed 4WD routes. Ignore them and stay on the pavement.

At 1.0 mile, you pass a gated doubletrack on your left. You will be coming up this to finish your ride. Right now, stay on the pavement and continue rolling up and down along the ridge. There is one *very* steep pitch as you make your way up to the TV Towers at 2.6 miles.

Bypass the road to the towers on your right and continue on the now more level ridge road. At 2.9 miles, you reach the Cuesta Ridge Botanical Area, marked by a bullet-riddled Forest Service sign. Stop here and look behind you to your left. There is a gated 4WD route.

Head downhill on this rough, very rocky track. Bounce along and, at 3.5 miles, start looking for a singletrack on your left. Make the abrupt left turn and get ready for even more technical challenges, namely more rocks and a narrow trail. Half a mile later, fork left.

In the spring, this area is full of flowers. What a delight, singletracking through the blooms! At 4.2 miles, the trail dips sharply into and out of a creek bottom (usually dry). Beyond it begins a series of steep uphill switchbacks (I had to push through a couple of them) and then a group of fun downhill switchbacks, just tight enough to be a bit of a challenge but rideable by the skilled mountain biker. Always there are rocks.

The trail deposits you onto a doubletrack at 5.2 miles. Although a right here promises more downhill fun, you need to go left and up. (*Please note*: Many tempting downhill tracks and trails lacing through the area provide no legal outlet. There is no public right-of-way across the Southern Pacific railroad tracks which run through the area.)

So head left and up, beginning a steep climb made technical by the rocky trail surface. Shadeless, the route can get very hot in summer months. You pass two gates, 0.5 mile apart. Just under 6.5 miles, you come to a Y-intersection. Once again go left and up. (A right would take you for a rolling 2.5 miles to the railroad tracks with no option but to return the way you came. But if you just want to add miles . . .)

From here you have another 0.5 mile of climbing, but the going is easier thanks to less of a grade and a smoother trail surface. You go around another gate and rejoin

Entrance to Cuesta Ridge Botanical Area

TV Tower Road at 6.9 miles. Go right for a fast and furious 1.1-mile descent to your car. Watch out for vehicles!

17 East Cuesta Ridge

Distance: 14 miles.
Difficulty: Moderately difficult; mildly technical.
Elevation: 1700' gain/loss.
Ride Type: Out-and-back on dirt road.
Season: Year-round; rocky trail surface makes it a good choice in rainy weather.
Maps: Lopez Mountain, San Luis Obispo; or SLO Adventures' Mountain Biking San Luis Obispo & Coastal Areas; or Los Padres National Forest: Monterey and Santa Lucia Ranger Districts.
Water: None.
Comments: Stay on the ridge as all land to the northeast is Santa Lucia Wilderness and closed to bikes. The parking area is not Forest Service land so you do not need a Forest Adventure Pass.

Overview: Like West Cuesta Ridge, this route has its share of TV towers and other electronic paraphernalia, but it feels more remote, probably because it is an all-dirt route, closed to motor vehicles (except those servicing the towers) and follows the southern boundary of the Santa Lucia Wilderness. Like the west ridge, its primary appeal is in the views. Conveniently, the climbing gets steeper as you go, so you can turn around whenever you've had enough.

Getting There: From San Luis Obispo, take Highway 101 north up Cuesta Grade to the summit. Immediately past the summit, turn right and up a switchback into a dirt parking area. There is a pay phone here. Parking is limited. Be sure not to block the gate.

Route: To begin you have to lift your bike up, over, under or around the gate—not an easy task. The road (30S10) starts climbing immediately past some impressive oak trees. It levels off before you've even gone a mile. You cross a cattleguard at 1.1 miles. Half a mile later, 1.6 miles, you pass another metal cattle grate.

From here the road climbs and rolls and you can shift into your middle ring. You have views to the west of Morro Bay and as far south as Pismo Beach. At 3.6 miles, continue straight when a road comes in from the left. It leads to some radio towers.

Soon, 3.7 miles, you pass a second road on the left leading to the Mt. Lowe microwave facilities. Go right and up. About a mile later, 4.6 miles, you pass the Upper Lopez Canyon Trail on your left. It leads into the Wilderness Area where bikes are prohibited. You can, however, enjoy the views into the wilderness, including Black Butte and Lopez Mountain.

Continue uphill to the right to a Y-intersection. Go left here. The climbing gets harder past this point. If you've had enough you might want to turn around here. The rollies get steeper and the road surface is much rockier. It's like doing a series of intervals.

At 7.0 miles, you reach a gate. Beyond is private property. This is your somewhat anti-climactic turn-around point. Enjoy the return trip. Once you make it past the rollies, it's a fun, fast descent. Watch out for the squared-off water culverts on the way down.

View along East Cuesta Ridge

18 Cerro Alto Loop

Distance: 5.5 miles.
Difficulty: Very strenuous; technical.
Elevation: 1,620' gain/loss.
Ride Type: Loop on singletrack and dirt road.
Season: Year-round.
Maps: Atascadero, Morro Bay North; or SLO Adventures' Mountain Biking San Luis Obispo & Coastal Areas; or Los Padres National Forest: Monterey and Santa Lucia Ranger Districts (not all trails shown on this map).
Water: At Cerro Alto Campground.
Comments: A good choice in rainy weather, although the streambed at the end can be muddy. Forest Adventure Pass required.

Overview: The climb to Cerro Alto ("High Peak") is extremely steep, but you are rewarded with 360-degree views and a fun, mostly singletrack descent. Don't let the short mileage fool you. This ride will kick your butt and then some.

Bottom of Cerro Alto Back Trail

Getting There: From San Luis Obispo, take Highway 101 north to Highway 41 and head west (two left turns). It's 8.1 miles to Cerro Alto Campground, on the left. You can park just off the highway or continue 0.9 mile up a narrow, paved road to the campground. The advantage of parking below is that you get a bit of a warmup before you begin the very steep climb of the bridge singletrack. If you begin at the campground, be sure to park in one of the day-use spots. Toilets and water are available at the campground.

From Highway 1, you can take Highway 41 east (Atascadero exit) for about 8 miles to the campground.

Route: Mileage is from the campground. If you start from the highway, add 0.9 mile.

The ride starts on Cerro Alto Trail (12E01) between campsites 16 and 17. It is a well-used trail and drops to a bridge over Morro Creek. After this initial drop, the trail pitches upward at a brutal grade. I was in immediate anaerobic

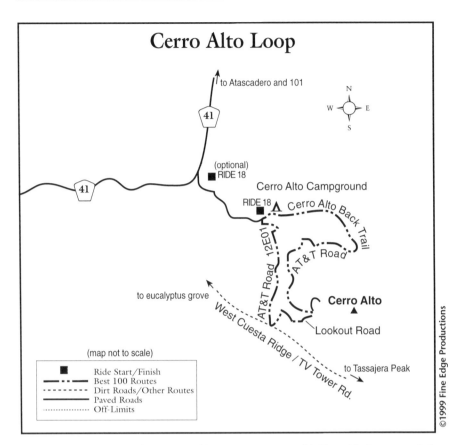

Cerro Alto Loop

to Atascadero and 101

41

(optional)
■ RIDE 18

Cerro Alto Campground

RIDE 18 ▲ Cerro Alto Back Trail

41

AT&T Road 12E01

AT&T Road

Cerro Alto
▲

to eucalyptus grove

Lookout Road

West Cuesta Ridge / TV Tower Rd.

to Tassajera Peak

(map not to scale)

■ Ride Start/Finish
—■—■— Best 100 Routes
------- Dirt Roads/Other Routes
——— Paved Roads
··········· Off-Limits

©1999 Fine Edge Productions

hell. The bad news is that it stays like this for most of the way as it climbs from the shady stream to the exposed canyonside high above the creek. The good news is it lasts less than a mile—although it was one of the longest miles of my life.

At 0.9 mile, the trail Ts into an AT&T service road. Go right. You get a very brief downhill, then more steep climbing around a corner. This is no easier than the singletrack. The road then levels a bit before a gate at 1.3 miles. Go around the gate and continue to the T-intersection with TV Tower Road/West Cuesta Ridge. (A right turn onto 11E01 would take you through a eucalyptus grove and either to Highway 41 or back to the campground.) For this loop, go left and continue climbing. The grade is not quite as steep, but still plenty stiff.

At 1.5 miles, you reach a Y-intersection with Cerro Alto Lookout Road. Go left past the very steep dirt berm and around a gate. The road turns to singletrack and then back to doubletrack, always climbing with some sections more rideable than others.

You pass a singletrack on the left at 2.3 miles. You will catch this trail on the way back. For now, continue on the lookout road. The trail surface grows rockier as it circles the peak. At 2.5 miles, you reach the bare, rocky top of Cerro Alto at 2,620 feet. Enjoy the panoramic vistas of most of San

AT&T road to TV Tower Road, Cerro Alto Loop

row with some rocky sections that definitely require your attention. A steep, rocky corner leads into a T-intersection with another singletrack. (A left would take you back to the lookout road.) To continue the singletrack fun, go right.

This singletrack is smoother and easier but still steep in spots, and there's a water crossing. At 3.7 miles, it Ts into the AT&T road. Go right. Enjoy. This is the first downhill where you can really get up some speed. It turns into a singletrack and then back into a doubletrack. Don't get going too fast because, less than a mile later (about 4.5 miles total), there's a cairn marking a singletrack on the left. It's easy to miss.

This is the Cerro Alto Back Trail. Shady, fun and not too technical. Take it as it drops into a canyon and follows Morro Creek back to the campground. Along the way there are several stream crossings to negotiate, which can be quite wet in winter, and plenty of poison oak. After a mile, 5.5 miles total, it deposits you in the campground opposite the bathrooms and the campground host's cabin.

Luis Obispo County. The name "lookout road" is a bit deceiving as there is no lookout on the peak.

When you've recovered, head back the way you came to the singletrack you saw on the way up, now on your right at 2.7 miles. This is a fun trail and it's quite a relief to be headed downhill after all the climbing. The trail is nar-

San Luis Obispo

There are only a few spots right in town where you can ride, such as the small trail network around California Polytechnic University. The following ride on the west side of town offers the most reward for the least amount of effort.

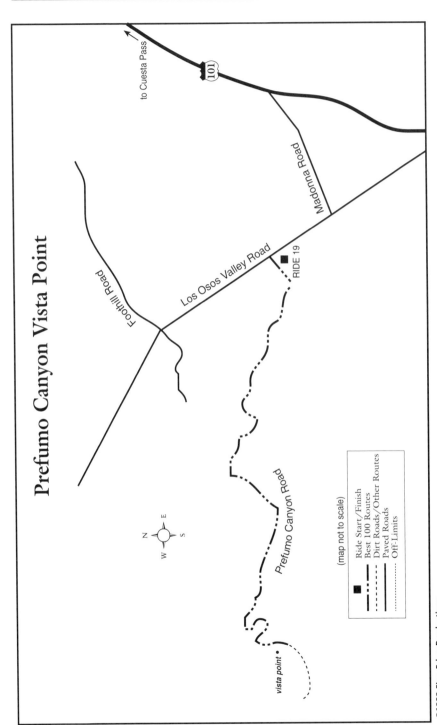

Prefumo Canyon Vista Point

to Cuesta Pass

101

Madonna Road

Los Osos Valley Road

Foothill Road

RIDE 19

Prefumo Canyon Road

vista point

N
W E
S

(map not to scale)

■ Ride Start/Finish
▬ Best 100 Routes
▬ ▬ Dirt Roads/Other Routes
▬▬ Paved Roads
⋯⋯ Off-Limits

19 Prefumo Canyon Vista Point

Distance: 9 miles.
Difficulty: Moderate; not technical.
Elevation: 800' gain/loss.
Ride Type: Out-and-back on dirt road.
Season: Year-round.
Maps: Morro Bay South, San Luis Obispo; or SLO Adventures' Mountain Biking San Luis Obispo & Coastal Areas.
Water: Not available.
Comments: Route is open to vehicle traffic.

Overview: Beginning riders will appreciate the relatively easy grade through oak-shaded Prefumo Canyon. A vista point 4.5 miles up canyon affords an outstanding view of six of the Seven Sisters.

Getting There: From Highway 101 you can exit at either Madonna Road or Los Osos Valley Road. If you exit at Madonna, go right where it Ts into

Bluffs at Montaña de Oro State Park

Los Osos Valley Road. Turn left onto Prefumo Canyon Road. It's easy to miss. It's near the junior high school. (If you hit Foothill Boulevard, you've gone too far.) Proceed 0.5 mile up Prefumo Canyon Road to a dirt turnout on the left.

Route: Head up Prefumo Canyon Road, nice and wide with a bike lane at its start. It soon narrows and the bike lane disappears. Continue climbing alongside the creek. At 2.5 miles, the road crosses a cattleguard and turns to dirt. It feels like you're out in the countryside, not anywhere near San Luis Obispo. The last time I was here I saw a doe and a fawn on this section.

About 0.5 mile later, the grade gets steeper but you should be warmed up by now. As you keep climbing, you leave the shady streamside environment behind and start crossing open hillsides. It can sometimes get windy through here, and the road is washboarded in spots.

One mile later, the road surface turns back to pavement and keeps climbing.

Go around the steep left-hand switch-back and back onto dirt. Here on your right, at 4.5 miles, is a short, very steep 4WD track. Leave your bike and hike up to the rock formation for a panoramic view of San Luis Obispo, the Sisters and the coastline. You might want to bring a windbreaker as it can get windy up here. Turn around at this point for a ride total of 9 miles.

If you want to add more mileage, the road continues for another 3 miles, climbing for 1 mile and descending for 2 miles, where it ends at a cattleguard. The rock outcropping is the scenic highlight of the ride and where I turn around. Enjoy the quick descent, but remember the road is open to motor vehicles.

Lopez Lake

This oak-shaded lake in south San Luis Obispo County is popular for water sports and with equestrians and bird watchers. Bald eagles are regularly spotted here, as are golden eagles, merlins (of both the feathered and titanium varieties), northern pygmy owls and spotted owls. Several trails are open to mountain bikers, including Upper Lopez Canyon and High Ridge Trails. Although some sources indicate that other trails are OK for bikes, the official park map shows only Upper Lopez Canyon and High Ridge Trails as bike trails. In recent years, several mountain bike races have been held here, including an off-road triathlon. You can find plenty of developed campsites at the lake as well.

20 Lopez Lake and Canyon

Distance: 17 miles.
Difficulty: Moderate; stream crossings can be technical.
Elevation: 1,100' gain/loss.
Ride Type: Out-and-back on dirt roads and pavement.
Season: Year-round; can be very wet and muddy in winter, hot and dry in summer.
Maps: Lopez Mountain, Tar Springs Ridge, Santa Margarita Lake; or SLO Adventures' Mountain Biking Eastern San Luis Obispo County; or Los Padres National Forest: Monterey and Santa Lucia Ranger Districts.
Water: At park entrance/registration building, Squirrel Campground, Quail Campground.
Comments: There is a day-use fee.

Overview: Although dry, dusty conditions in late summer and muddy, wet conditions in winter can make the going tough, this is generally an easy route. Once you get past the hustle and bustle of the park entrance/campground area, you find yourself in a steep, high-walled canyon with multiple stream crossings and two waterfalls. Since this is an out-and-back you can turn around at any time for an easier trip.

Getting There: From Highway 101, take the Lopez Lake turnoff. At the junction of Highway 227 and Lopez

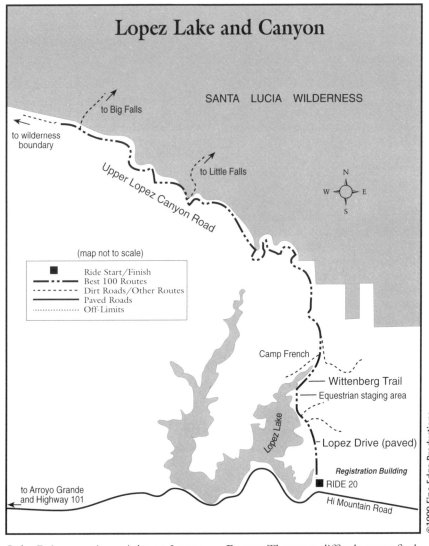

Lake Drive, continue right on Lopez Lake Drive for 8.5 miles to the junction with Hi Mountain Road. Continue on Lopez Lake Drive for almost a mile, following signs to the Recreation Area. Park on the left past the park entrance or on the right behind the registration building. For a shorter ride, continue another mile to the equestrian staging area and park there.

Route: The most difficult route-finding is making your way through the campgrounds and such to the dirt Upper Lopez Canyon Road. Once you're in the canyon, there really isn't anywhere else to go.

From the parking area, continue on paved Lopez Drive past several trailheads, Squirrel Campground, Quail Campground, Vista Lago Swim Area, a water slide, and finally the equestrian staging area. Go around the gate (locked) at 1.5 miles. A sign here reads: *Tuouski Trail/High Ridge Trail*. You are now on the dirt Wittenberg Trail.

Next you have to maneuver through Camp French. At the fork at just over 2 miles, go left, following the signs toward Tuouski Trail. Within 0.5 mile, you cross a stream and arrive at Camp French. Go right through the gate, then make a quick left onto Upper Lopez Canyon Road.

Continue uphill on the paved road. Except for a short descent, most of the rest of the route is uphill— though not as steep as this first part. You come to a Y-intersection at 5 miles. Head right to continue on the pavement. Soon you pass some buildings, then a sign: *Welcome to the Los Padres National Forest*, and finally the road turns to dirt.

Here is where the ride really starts to get interesting. You cross several streams in rapid succession as you parallel the southern boundary of the Santa Lucia Wilderness Area.

Note: Any trail to your right enters the Wilderness and is closed to bikes.

At 6.5 miles, you come to the trailhead for the Little Falls Trail. Over the next 2 miles you climb and descend until you reach, at 8.5 miles, the Big Falls trailhead. Stash your bike and make the trek to the falls— they're worth the effort. Once you've eaten, relaxed and cooled off, your best option is to turn around and return the way you came.

(The road, if it can be called that, continues for about another 2 miles to the Wilderness boundary—at least it shows that way on maps. I forded on ahead but soon found myself riding uphill *in* the streambed. For me it was too much work for too little payback.)

Pozo/La Panza

This area of the Los Padres National Forest constitutes the backcountry of San Luis Obispo. It is accessible from Pozo Road off Highway 58 east of the town of Santa Margarita. The only other town, more of a "hamlet," is Pozo, and its services are limited to a sometimes open saloon (serves food on weekends) and a USFS ranger station. You need to be self-sufficient when you travel here.

Riding centers on two areas: Hi Mountain (3,180') to the south of Pozo Road, sandwiched between the Santa Lucia Wilderness and the Garcia Wilderness, and the La Panza mountain range to the northeast. The La Panza area offers several OHV routes and is popular with the motorized crowd. It also contains two of the area's high points—Black Mountain (3,622') and Pine Mountain (3,550'). These mountains are the result of movements of the San Andreas Fault. Some geologic theories hold that the rocks here may have originated as far away as the southern Sierra or even Palm Springs!

The area's rugged slopes are home to black bear, wild boar and wild turkeys, the latter quite common around the aptly named Turkey Flat. From Pine Mountain Ridge you have views of Castle Crags and Machesna Mountain Wilderness, a reintroduction area for the endangered California condor. Flora includes live oaks, pine, manzanita, madrone and sage. Spring wildflowers can be great.

The area enjoys a colorful gold mining history (you can visit the old La Panza townsite, though there's not much to see), and reputedly was once the home of Jesse James.

Drive-in campsites include Hi Mountain Campground and, in La Panza, Friis, Navajo, La Panza and Queen Bee campgrounds. None of these have drinking water. Bring plenty, especially in summer months.

21 Hi Mountain Lookout from Pozo

Distance: 12.6 miles (out-and-back); 12.5 miles (one-way); 20 miles (loop).
Difficulty: Strenuous; mildly technical to technical depending on options.
Elevation: 2,000' gain/loss.
Ride Type: Out-and-back on dirt road; one-way on dirt road and singletrack; loop on dirt road, singletrack and pavement.
Season: Year-round; can be hot in summer.
Maps: Santa Margarita Lake; or SLO Adventures' Mountain Biking Eastern San Luis Obispo County; or Los Padres National Forest: Monterey and Santa Lucia Ranger Districts.
Water: Water from hose bib at Forest Service structures at ride start is safe to drink.
Comments: There are very few services in the area. Be self-sufficient.

Overview: After a tough climb to a ridge, this ride offers great vistas to the west and the east, including views of both Lopez and Santa Margarita lakes. As an out-and-back trip, it's fire road the whole way, or you can continue and descend some twisty, fast and fun singletrack to the old Rinconada Mine site. You can leave a vehicle here for a shuttle ride or fashion a loop. A loop requires a 6.5-mile pavement section between Rinconada Mine and the town of Pozo. I prefer to park at Rinconada Mine and get the pavement section over with first. The advantage of parking in Pozo is that you can get food and drink at the saloon—if it's open. (It's supposedly open Thursday through Sunday, but I was there on the Friday of Memorial Day weekend and it was closed.)

Getting There: From San Luis Obispo, take Highway 101 north to Highway 58 toward Santa Margarita. Continue through town and turn right over the railroad tracks. When Highway 58 forks left just past the cemetery, go straight onto Pozo Road. Take Pozo Road for 10 miles to the clearly signed Rinconada Mine trailhead on the right. Park here for the loop ride or leave a vehicle here for the one-way ride.

To start the loop from Pozo or for the out-and-back ride, continue 7 miles past the Rinconada Mine trailhead to the town of Pozo. Park at the ranger station on the right. Hi Mountain Road is clearly signed and there is an information board with OHV maps here.

Route: Head up Hi Mountain Road. It soon turns to dirt and passes a gate (locked during bad weather) at 0.6 mile. At 0.9 mile, you cross the Salinas River. Normally an easy crossing, it was running thigh-high during the winter of '98.

From here you start climbing in earnest, following a creek, first on your right, then on your left. At 1.5 miles, you cross a cattleguard and pass a Forest Service sign. Keep climbing until a brief downhill at 2.2

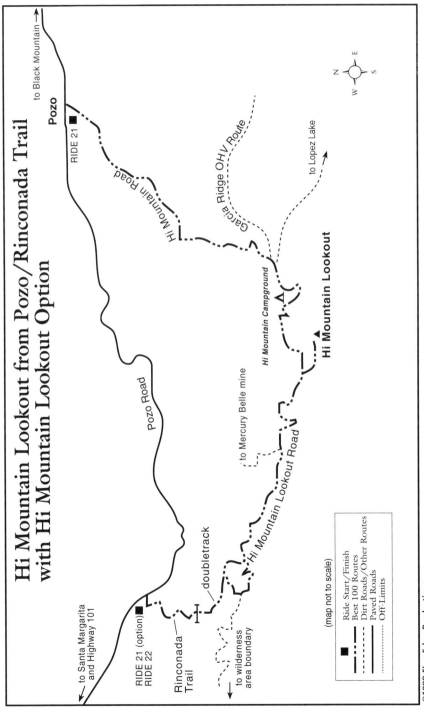

Hi Mountain Lookout from Pozo/Rinconada Trail
with Hi Mountain Lookout Option

miles. Resume climbing. At 3.5 miles, you cross another cattleguard. Just beyond, you crest Hi Mountain summit (2,080').

Here there is a 4-way intersection. Hi Mountain Road (30S05) continues straight, eventually dropping to Lopez Lake. Garcia Ridge OHV Trail goes left. You turn right (west) onto signed Hi Mountain Lookout Road (30S11).

Most of the work is over at this point and you can enjoy the views to the north and then to the south as the road wiggles its way from one side of the ridge to the other.

At 4.3 miles, you pass oak-shaded Hi Mountain Campground—pit toilets but no water. This makes a nice rest stop if you're tired. If you're up for it, continue climbing for another 1.5 miles. At just under 6 miles, you reach the turnoff to Hi Mountain Lookout. Go left, up past the gate to the lookout (3,198'), reached at 6.3 miles.

While there is much broken glass and the Forest Service sign is pockmarked with bullet holes, the view from the lookout more than makes up for these blemishes. Dating from the early part of this century, the tower is the southernmost fire lookout in the Santa Lucias. From here you can see Huasna Valley, Cuesta Ridge and the Santa Lucia Wilderness Area.

Munch a snack and ponder your options. You can return the way you came for a fast, virtually all-downhill conclusion to your adventure or backtrack to Hi Mountain Lookout Road and continue west toward Rinconada Mine.

To head toward Rinconada Mine, turn left onto Hi Mountain Lookout Road and descend. Yee-hah. You sweep through several broad corners, passing the trailhead for the Mercury Belle Mine at 7.5 miles. Keep descending until 8.8 miles where you start a gradual but steady climb.

Ride start for Hi Mountain

Salinas River crossing on Hi Mountain Road

Stay on the main road at 9.3 miles, ignoring the road on the left. A mile later, 10.3 miles, you reach a Y-intersection. Once again, go right. Begin a steep 0.5-mile hump up the doubletrack. At 10.8 miles, take the singletrack on the right. At 11 miles, it ends at a doubletrack. To the left is a locked gate. You go right and downhill.

Enjoy! This is the fast and fun Rinconada Mine Trail. Follow the metal trail signs (fork left onto the singletrack) as you pitch, roll and swerve down, down, down to the Rinconada Mine. The fun is over all too soon when you reach the parking area at 12.5 miles. If you left a vehicle here, your ride is over. If you left your vehicle at Pozo, pass through the parking area and descend to Pozo Road. A right turn and 6.5 miles of pavement pedaling will return you to your car.

22 Rinconada Trail with Hi Mountain Lookout Option

Distance: 5 miles; 11 miles with lookout option.
Difficulty: Strenuous; technical.
Elevation: 1,000' gain/loss; Hi Mountain Lookout option would add another 1,000 feet of gain/loss.
Ride Type: Lollipop loop on singletrack and dirt roads.
Season: Year-round; can be hot in summer.
Maps: Santa Margarita Lake; or SLO Adventures' Mountain Biking Eastern San Luis Obispo County; or Los Padres National Forest: Monterey and Santa Lucia Ranger Districts.
Water: None. Bring plenty.
Comments: There are very few services in the area. Be self-sufficient.

Overview: A good choice for the intermediate or advanced rider who enjoys technical climbing and descending, this route involves a very steep singletrack climb, some rough 4WD track and a scenic section of fire road. You also have the option of continuing out and back to Hi Mountain Lookout.

Getting There: From San Luis Obispo, take Highway 101 north to Highway 58 toward Santa Margarita. Continue through town and turn right over the railroad tracks. When Highway 58 forks left just past the cemetery, go straight onto Pozo Road. Take Pozo Road for 10 miles to the clearly signed Rinconada Mine trailhead on the right.

Route: Head up the trail. There's no getting around the fact that this is a tough, steep climb. It's also technical in spots. Conditioned riders may ride much of it, but cleaning it would be an achievement.

Route-finding is easy as several rusty metal signs (they say "trail") help direct you. At 1.0 mile, follow the signs and zig to the right, then zag to the left. Two more signs point the way onto a doubletrack. Take the doubletrack, still climbing, to the gate at 1.5 miles. You will be returning via the singletrack on the left just before the gate. For now continue around the gate.

The doubletrack leads to a small, grassy saddle. Continue across the saddle to a rough 4WD track, marked by a trail sign. This is a steep descent, exceptionally rough and rocky. There's not much of a line as you bounce—one way or another—your way down toward Hi Mountain Lookout Road (30S11). There are a couple of other tracks through the area, but a trail sign directs you onto singletrack. Near its end, the singletrack bends to the left. You should see the road below you as well as a water tank. There's also another metal trail sign at the bottom. The track deposits you on 30S11 at just under 2 miles.

Go left onto 30S11. The road climbs moderately in a series of rollers, some steeper than others, as it contours along the northern boundary of the Santa Lucia Wilderness. Enjoy the views, first to

Hi Mountain Lookout

the south and then to the north, as you make your way to an intersection at 2.8 miles. Here a right turn will take you to Hi Mountain Lookout, 3 miles and roughly 1,000 feet of climbing away (see the previous ride). To complete the loop, go left.

If you choose to go left, you begin a steep 0.5-mile hump up a doubletrack. At 3.3 miles, take the singletrack on the right. This is the trail you passed just before the gate on the way up the Rinconada Trail. At 3.5 miles, you're back at the first doubletrack with the gate to your left. Go right and downhill. Enjoy descending what you worked so hard to climb earlier. It's a lot more fun in this direction, huh? All too quickly you're back at your car at 5 miles.

23 Fernandez Trail Loop

Distance: 19 miles.
Difficulty: Strenuous; technical.
Elevation: 2,800' gain/loss.
Ride Type: Loop on pavement, dirt road, singletrack and motorcycle trail.
Season: Year-round, but can be muddy in winter and scorching in summer; best in spring.
Maps: Camatta Ranch, Pozo Summit; or SLO Adventures' Mountain Biking Eastern San Luis Obispo County; or Los Padres National Forest: Monterey and Santa Lucia Ranger Districts (Fernandez Trail not shown); Forest Service OHV map (Fernandez Trail not shown).
Water: None. Bring epic amounts as this can be a very hot ride. Creek water (may be dry in summer) should be filtered.
Comments: This is a remote area. Be prepared. This is also a very popular OHV area—be alert for motorcycles and the like.

Overview: Wow. Thanks to a recent wildfire and the inundation of El Niño, this area has exploded with spring wildflowers in recent years. The 1998 season was a bumper crop—the best wildflower ride I think I've ever done. Add to that some of the best singletrack in the county, a waterfall, and a beautiful narrow canyon and you've got arguably the nicest ride in the area.

Of course there is a price to be paid. There is more than enough climbing on the route, and the fire left the area virtually shadeless. Don't even think about riding out here in August. The trail can also get overgrown, and I got a lovely case of poison oak here.

Getting There: From San Luis Obispo, take Highway 101 north to Highway 58 toward Santa Margarita. Continue through town and turn right over the railroad tracks. When Highway 58 forks left just past the cemetery, go straight onto Pozo Road. Continue on Pozo Road for 17 miles to the town of Pozo. Pass through town and through a 90-degree left turn followed by a sharp right turn. When Pozo Road makes another 90-degree right, continue straight on the unsigned but paved road. About 2.5 miles past this intersection, go right on Navajo Grade Road (29S02). Continue just up the road to the Turkey Flat OHV staging

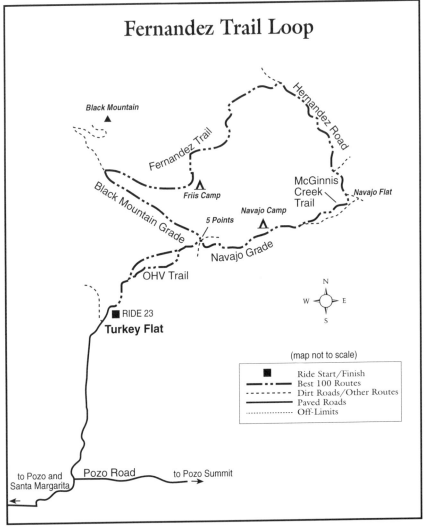

Fernandez Trail Loop

Black Mountain

Fernandez Trail

Black Mountain Grade

Friis Camp

5 Points

OHV Trail

■ RIDE 23
Turkey Flat

Hernandez Road

McGinnis
Creek
Trail

Navajo Flat

Navajo Camp

Navajo Grade

(map not to scale)

N
W ⟡ E
S

■ Ride Start/Finish
—··— Best 100 Routes
------ Dirt Roads/Other Routes
——— Paved Roads
·········· Off-Limits

to Pozo and
Santa Margarita

Pozo Road

to Pozo Summit →

©1999 Fine Edge Productions

area. Park here. There is an information board and pit toilets, as well as a nice shady oak to park under.

Route: From the staging area, head up the paved Navajo Grade Road. At first the grade is very gradual, but it grows steeper as you make your way to the "5-Points" intersection, accompanied by the sight and sound of McGinnis Creek far below you.

At 2.6 miles, you reach 5-Points, where two roads and an OHV trail join the paved road. All of them head down—except the paved road (Black Mountain Grade) which heads *very* steeply up. I'm sorry to say that the paved road is what you need to take. Grunt and groan your way up. Fortunately the steep pitch doesn't last too long.

Next, the road rolls along with a couple of steep uphill and downhill pitches. Overall you continue to gain elevation. You can appreciate the extent of the wildfires in the area as all of the surrounding hills are still pretty barren.

At 5.1 miles, you come to a singletrack, the Fernandez Trail, on your right. It's in a bend in the road at the bottom of a downhill. A small sign (might be obscured by brush) reads: *Friis Camp, 2 miles.* Take it.

It's mostly downhill, narrow, sometimes overgrown, but pretty smooth and almost always fun. You can hear Friis Creek burbling below you, and at one point you have a view into a side canyon with a waterfall.

At 6.8 miles, you reach Friis Camp. Following the trail through here is a little tricky. Go through the camp and pick up the singletrack at the far end of the parking area on the left. There's a small metal gate here

View of waterfall from Fernandez Trail

designed to block vehicle access. The Fernandez Trail is closed to motor vehicles, including motorcycles, but I saw evidence that this prohibition is sometimes ignored.

The next section of trail closely follows the narrow streambed. There are several stream crossings before the trail climbs above the water. You're in a skinny canyon which, in the spring, is choked with wildflowers. There were so many flowers to look at and views of rock and water that I literally rode off the trail trying to take it all in.

The trail bends away from the creek and climbs steeply around three switchbacks. These are followed by three descending switchbacks. An-

other steep climb tops a small pass at 8.3 miles. Stay on the singletrack as it crosses a fire break. In general the section of trail beyond Friis Camp seems to see more horse use and is thus rougher and more chewed up.

At 9 miles, fork right to follow the creek. You can see Hernandez Road on your left and slightly above you. Continue on the trail past another metal vehicle stop until the trail runs into Hernandez Road. Go right. There is some descending along here, but mostly it is a moderate climb.

Just under 11 miles, a road joins from the left; ignore it. Half a mile later, cross a cattleguard and pass a small house on a rise on your left. At 12.2 miles, you intersect McGinnis

Fernandez Trail

immediate right into the staging area and followed the fence along the area's perimeter, you would run into the trailhead. The trail pretty much follows the creek and deposits you onto McGinnis Creek Road at 14.3 miles, where you go right.]

If you take McGinnis Creek Road, it is flat or climbs moderately to Navajo Camp, 15.2 miles. Past the campground you begin a steep climb, much steeper than you probably want to deal with at this point in the game. It gets worse—steeper and looser—the closer you get to the 5-Points intersection. Above and to your right you can see powerlines and another road converging at the intersection and can gauge how far you have to go. When you hit a really steep left-hand corner, you're almost there. There's actually an oak tree which provides a tad of shade at the top, 16.2 miles.

Head downhill on paved Navajo Grade Road. This is fast and furious but there are two good reasons not to get going too fast: first, the road is open to motor vehicles; second, for more technical fun there is a single-track on your left at 17.0 miles. (If you're tired, take the paved road.)

The singletrack heads steeply uphill and was pretty overgrown last time I rode it. You'll probably have to do some pushing here. When the trail tops out at a powerline tower, bear right down a couple of super steep pitches. These will test how far you can get off the back of your bike as

Creek Road. Left is a sign: *Toward Highway 58.* You turn right and take McGinnis Creek Road to Navajo Flat OHV staging area, less than a mile away. Here oak trees provide some of the ride's only shade, making it a good choice for a food stop or rest break.

Once you've refueled and rehydrated, you have a choice to make. You can continue on the road to Navajo Camp or you can opt to take the more difficult McGinnis Creek motorcycle trail. 16E14 has lots of whoops and stream crossings but no big climbs or descents. [The trail, if you choose to take it, is clearly signed but a little difficult to find. As you approach Navajo Flat, if you made an

well as your braking ability. You soon see some Route and Trail signs. Follow them to make your way down this OHV route. (It basically parallels the road.) The trail gets less steep and more fun as you go, with quite a few whoops. But it's still pretty steep and technical (think ruts) and no place for beginners or those who are pooped out from the ride.

When the OHV trail ends at the pavement, turn left and continue downhill to Turkey Flat, reached at 19 miles.

24 Pine Mountain Loop

Distance: 25 miles.
Difficulty: Strenuous; technical.
Elevation: 3,000' gain/loss; high point 3,600'.
Ride Type: Lollipop-shaped loop on dirt roads and trails.
Season: Year-round; can be brutally hot in summer.
Maps: Pozo Summit, La Panza; or SLO Adventures' Mountain Biking Eastern San Luis Obispo County; or Los Padres National Forest: Monterey and Santa Lucia Ranger Districts; or Forest Service OHV map.
Water: Don't count on finding any clean water sources. Bring all you will need—and then some.

Overview: This is no three-hour tour. Plan on an all-day adventure. This is by far the toughest ride in this chapter because of its length, difficulty, remoteness and technical challenge. It features three major climbs, with the third one being the toughest, as well as innumerable other smaller ups and downs. If those don't do you in, the infamous "Stair Steps" will (a technical descent through boulders). The paybacks are a feeling of achievement, spectacular views from Pine Ridge into the Machesna Wilderness and of the Castle Crags, and an opportunity to see California condors if you're lucky.

Getting There: From San Luis Obispo, take Highway 101 north to Highway 58 toward Santa Margarita. Continue through town and turn right over the railroad tracks. When Highway 58 forks left just past the cemetery, go straight onto Pozo Road. Continue on Pozo Road for 17 miles to the town of Pozo. Pass through town and through a 90-degree left turn followed by a sharp right turn. At the Parkhill Road intersection, 1.5 miles from town, go right to stay on Pozo Road. Less than 3.5 miles from town, go left at the San Jose-Avenales Ranch Road intersection. About 0.5 mile later, look for a dirt parking area just before a concrete ford.

Route: Cross the bridge at the ford to continue on Pozo Road. The pavement soon gives way to a wide, dirt road as you make the climb toward Pozo Summit. This is a fairly consistent grade, gaining 1,100 feet over 5 miles, but there are enough short, steep pitches to keep you grunting.

At the summit, you pass the Pine Mountain Trail (16E01) on your right. You will be returning via this trail to complete the Pine Mountain Loop. The Las Chiches Trail is on the left. For

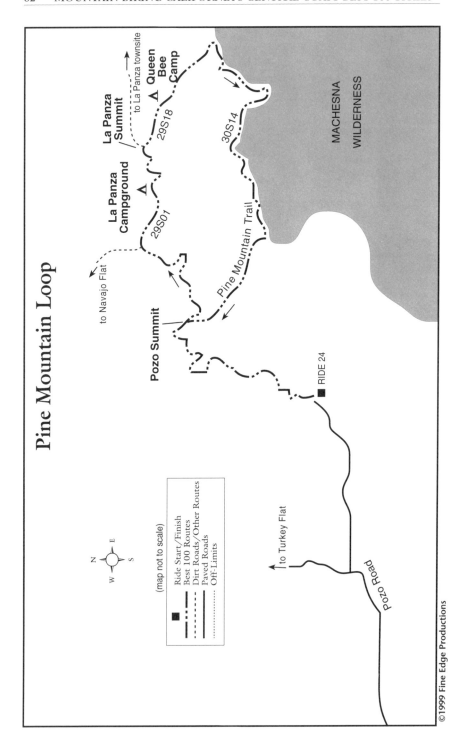

Pine Mountain Loop

©1999 Fine Edge Productions

now, continue on Pozo Road and enjoy the 3-mile downhill that awaits.

Near the bottom, you come to an intersection with Navajo Grade (29S02) on your left. Continue to the right on Pozo Road (29S01) and begin your second climb. This one is shorter, just under than 3 miles, and gains 600 feet. Since you're all warmed up from that first 5-mile climb, this one should be no problem, right? Just keep telling yourself that.

One mile into the climb, you pass shady La Panza Camp on the north side of the road (your left). Two miles later, you reach 2,500-foot La Panza Summit. Here road 29S18 goes right toward Queen Bee Camp. (A left would take you toward Highway 58 and, 3 miles from the summit, to the remains of the gold rush town of La Panza. But this is best left for another day as it would add 6 miles to an already long, tough ride.)

You need to take 29S18. Go right and head downhill across the cattleguard and through the camp. (*Note*: If you're camped here, you can ride this loop from here; it would eliminate the 5-mile climb to Pozo Summit.)

Within 0.5 mile you pass Queen Bee Camp on your left and, soon after, Chester Springs on your right. (There's a water trough here.) You get just a little more downhill before the real work begins. All the climbing you've already done has merely been preparation for the ascent of Pine Mountain Ridge.

Just shy of 13 miles, you reach a fork. Veer right onto Pine Mountain Road (30S14) and prepare to suffer. The climbs vary from steep to steeper and steepest, and the trail surface from loose to very loose. You gain about 1,100 feet over 3.5 miles. You may begin to wonder whose idea this was in the first place, or why you even attempt this masochistic sport. Bowling begins to sound like a preferable leisure-time activity.

Fortunately the views and the photo opportunities make excellent excuses for stopping. Pine Mountain Road follows the northern boundary of the Machesna Wilderness here. (No bicycles allowed on any trails dropping to the south.) You can see the Castle Crags to the southeast and Machesna Mountain due south. In fact, you can see most of the San Luis Obispo backcountry from your airy perch.

While you don't actually summit Pine Mountain on this route, you do top out at about 16.5 miles on a high point (roughly 3,600') on the ridge. At the junction with Pine Mountain Trail (16E01), veer downhill to your right. The road pretty much turns into the trail, as an old fence and locked gate block the left fork.

Now comes the fun part, depending on your definition of fun. If you're totally worked by now, you may not enjoy the technical challenge ahead. Think rocks. Lots of them. If, however, like me you're a bit sick, this will be your just reward for all the climbing you've done. The Stair Steps start about a mile down the trail.

Be forewarned: It's not all downhill. I never said it would be. After the initial drop, the trail actually follows a ridge of its own for part of its 2.5 miles before dropping to Pozo Road. If you can take your eyes of the trail long enough, about 1.5 miles along the trail (when you come out on the open ridgeline) you can see the Temblor Range to your right (east). (See Ride 26 for more abut these mountains.)

Back at Pozo Summit on Pozo Road, you need to hang a left to return to your car. Remember that first 5-mile climb? It's now a downhill. Ahhhh.

Huasna Valley

The Huasna Valley marks the southernmost tip of the Santa Lucia Mountains. The hills are much less rugged and steep here than to the north. A single ridge, Pine Ridge (2,700'), marks the northern boundary of the valley. Don't confuse this ridge with Pine Mountain Ridge in Ride 24. The terrain in the valley is as gentle and rolling as that ridge is precipitous and angled.

Huasna Valley is also an important watershed for the Santa Maria River; both the Huasna River and Arroyo Seco Creek flow into it.

There is much private land and lots of cattle here. Be sure to respect private property and to leave all gates as you found them. Many of the ranches in the area have been handed down through several generations and the landowners can be territorial.

Home to some striking and unusual rock formations, the valley has several Chumash petroglyphs among the rocks which you visit on this ride. A pastoral dream, the valley is so quiet and peaceful that it's not hard to imagine why the Native Americans chose to hang out here.

25 Huasna Valley Petroglyph Ride

Distance: 5 miles, 7 miles or 28 miles.
Difficulty: Easy to moderate; not technical.
Elevation: Maximum 2,200' gain/loss on the 28-mile route.
Ride Type: Out-and-back on dirt roads and singletrack.
Season: Year-round.
Maps: Caldwell Mesa, Los Machos Hills; or Los Padres National Forest: Monterey and Santa Lucia Ranger Districts.
Water: None.
Comments: There is lots of private land in the valley. *Respect private property!*

Overview: This ride can be done from three different starting points, depending on your desires and on seasonal gate closures. The highlights are the rock formations and petroglyphs on Pine Ridge as well as the view. If you don't think you can make the whole 28-mile route, park at one of the other starting points, as you should definitely make it to the ridge. Why else come all the way out here?

Getting There: From Highway 101,

take the Lopez Lake exit. Continue to the junction with Highway 227 and go right on Lopez Lake Road. At the junction with Huasna Road, turn right. Continue on Huasna Road, following the signs to Huasna. Pass by the turnoff to the old Huasna townsite. Park off the side of the road just before the wooden bridge over the Huasna River.

This is the starting point for the 28-mile ride, but if you want to get to closer starting points, continue on Huasna Road. You pass several signs

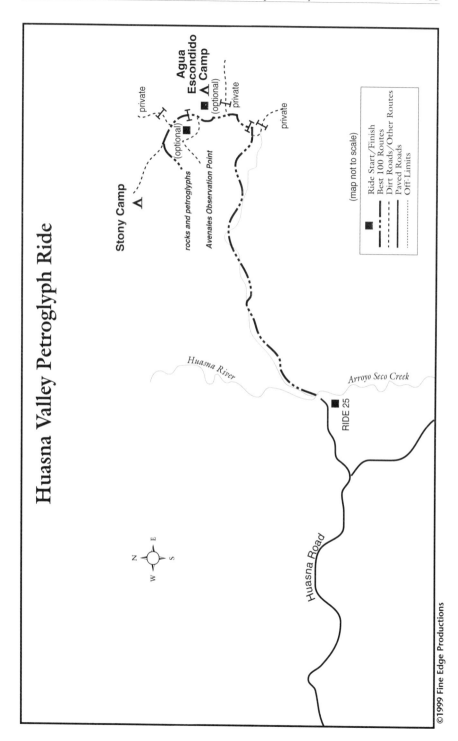

Huasna Valley Petroglyph Ride

noting private property and at least half a dozen cattleguards and stream crossings. At 9 miles, you come to a fork in the road; the right fork leads to private property and is blocked by a locked gate with a No Trespassing sign. Continue to the left.

Almost immediately you come to a seasonal gate. If it's closed, you will have to backtrack to the nearest legal parking—all the way back at the bridge. Unless it's been raining, it should be open and you can continue.

At 10.5 miles, you reach yet another cattleguard. Cross it and ignore the road on your right. The next road on your right, just up the hill, leads to Agua Escondido Campground, the starting point for the 7-mile option.

Or you can stay on the road for another mile to the turnoff for the Avenales Observation Point on your left. There is a parking area near the Forest Service signs.

Route: For the 28-mile route, follow the "Getting There" directions above. On a bike, the terrain is generally easy, although you are gaining elevation the whole time.

Less than 0.5 mile beyond the third parking spot near Avenales, you reach another gate. This one is locked, and someone has welded a No Trespassing sign onto it. According to the Forest Service map, there is a private parcel here. However, the road you are on is county- and/or Forest Service-maintained road (depending where you are), and you have the right to ride here. Just be sure to stay on the road and behave yourself. (I ran into this same problem, only worse, in Big Sur.) The gate does successfully block auto access to Stony Creek Campground, a jumping-off spot for the Garcia Wilderness.

About 0.5 mile later, go left at the fork onto Stony Creek Road. The road to the right leads to more private property and is also gated. Follow Stony Creek Road for one mile until you see a row of metal posts lining the north (right-hand) side of the road. Look for a single-track through the grass on your left. Take it as it drops down to and crosses a stream.

At the fork on the other side, veer right. Soon the trail splits into a singletrack and a doubletrack. It can be a bit confusing through here as there are also some cattle tracks. Either fork will lead onto Pine Ridge. After a brief climb, you enter a meadow, Garcia Potrero. It is both a surprise and a delight to pop up into this grassy meadow where you are greeted (maybe startled would be a better word) by pines and jutting rocks.

Follow the trail to those rocks. Find a convenient place to leave your bike and continue on foot. The rock formations are fun to explore and this is where you'll find the Chumash petroglyphs as well. If you enjoy these, check out Ride 26 for even better examples of Native American rock art.

Finally, if you hike out past the backside of the rocks, you can get a view off the ridge and across the whole Huasna Valley. When you're done gazing and exploring, get back on your bike and return the way you came.

Carrizo Plain
By Mickey McTigue

For something entirely different, try the little-known and remote Carrizo Plain Natural Area in the far southeast corner of San Luis Obispo County. Midway between Bakersfield and Santa Maria, this arid flat valley boasts 85 miles of low-traffic dirt roads and 15 miles of paved roads ideal for the bicycle traveler.

A yearly average of 8-10 inches of rainfall drains from the surrounding mountains out onto the valley floor and makes its way to Soda Lake. The Carrizo Plain is a large depressed area with no outlet, so the water that drains into the lake leaves only by evaporation. The salts remain and the surface is a brilliant white. But in winter this 3,000-acre lake bed receives enough water to attract great numbers of migratory birds. Hawks, eagles, owls and meadow songbirds spend the winter on the plains while thousands of lesser sandhill cranes and other waterfowl flock to the lake.

The San Andreas Fault is visible along the east side of the plain where stream channels are offset hundreds of yards to the north. Working with wildlife and conservation agencies, the Bureau of Land Management has reintroduced tule elk and nearly 300 pronghorn antelope which can sometimes be seen on the west side. Also on the west side at Painted Rock are Native American pictographs, one of the most elaborate Native American rock art sites in North America.

26 Carrizo Plain Loop

Distance: 72.6 miles.
Difficulty: Moderate in good weather; long distance, but good roads and no long, steep hills; not technical.
Elevation: 3,000' to 1,917'; 1,083' differential.
Ride Type: Two-day ride on dirt roads and pavement.
Season: Spring and fall best; spring wildflowers can be spectacular.
Maps: Reward, McKittrick Summit, Simmler, Panorama Hills, Painted Rock, Chimineas Ranch, Fellows, Ballinger Canyon, Cuyama, Maricopa, Elkhorn Hills, Wells Ranch, Caliente Mountain.
Water: Bring all the water you need; it is far better to overestimate your needs than to underestimate them.
Comments: This is a very remote area with little traffic. The weather can change fast in the winter, and rain could leave you stranded in mud. The summers are very hot and on these treeless plains there is almost no shade. There are no stores, no gas stations and no water available in the reserve. Nearest services are at the BLM Fire Station, Washburn Road; in an emergency, call 911 or 805-861-4119; for business, call 805-861-4110 or 861-4236. Other services are found in Maricopa or Taft.

Overview: The Carrizo Plain is a long narrow valley with Soda Lake Road running the length of it. To the east, at the base of the Temblor Range, is the Elkhorn Plain which is separated from the Carrizo Plain by the low Panorama Hills and farther south by the Elkhorn Hills. The Elkhorn Road runs the length of this very narrow and parallel plain. Elkhorn Plain is higher than the Carrizo Plain and from several places along the road you can see out across the Carrizo Plain, especially on the northern half. These roads are not connected by cross roads except near each end, making a long ride.

With a start/finish at Reyes Station, the whole loop is 72.6 miles. If you ride the 5 miles up to the primitive camping area at the Selby-Arco pad and back to Soda Lake Road, you have a total of 82.6 miles. Carrying all your camping gear and the necessary 3 or 4 gallons of water is more than most people are willing to do.

An alternative is to leave the second day's water and camping equipment in a vehicle parked at the Painted Rock Visitor Center. Park the second vehicle at Reyes Station, ride northwest through the Elkhorn Plain, south across the Carrizo Plain on Simmler Road to Soda Lake Road and the Visitor Center. First day's mileage would be 42.6 miles. Drive 5.8 miles to the camping area and the next morning drive back to the Visitor Center. Park the car and ride 30 miles southeast on Soda Lake Road through the Carrizo Plain back to Reyes Station. For a one-day ride, just ride the part that interests you.

Getting There: From Highway 101, just north of Santa Maria, take State Highway 166 east 65 miles through the Cuyama Valley to the junction with State Highway 33. Continue east 4.7 miles to the signed Soda Lake Road on the left (north) at Reyes Station. This 76 gas station is the last one on your way to the reserve.

From Interstate 5 south of Bakersfield, take State Highway 166 west for 24 miles to Maricopa and then 9.3 miles southwest to Reyes Station and Soda Lake Road. Park along Soda Lake Road near Reyes Station at Highway 166 or at Painted Rock Visitors Center on Soda Lake Road, 30 miles northwest of Reyes Station.

When you park at these places, check with someone there to make sure your car is not in the way and let them know where you are going and when you will return. A good time to bring up parking arrangements is while making a purchase of gas or souvenirs or making a donation. It's a small price to pay to have someone watching out for you.

Reyes Station to Painted Rock Visitor Center: This is a 42.6-mile ride, based on parking a camping vehicle at the Visitor Center. Start from Reyes Station and ride northwest on paved Soda Lake Road passing treeless, grass-covered, rolling hills. You descend and pass a salt-rimmed sag pond formed where the land sinks into the San Andreas Fault. The road is built right next to the fault as you can see while you climb up from the sag pond, cross the county line and drop down to another sag pond. On the north end of this pond, at 3.5 miles, you turn right (east) onto the signed Elkhorn Road.

This graded dirt road climbs very steeply in places but only gains 250

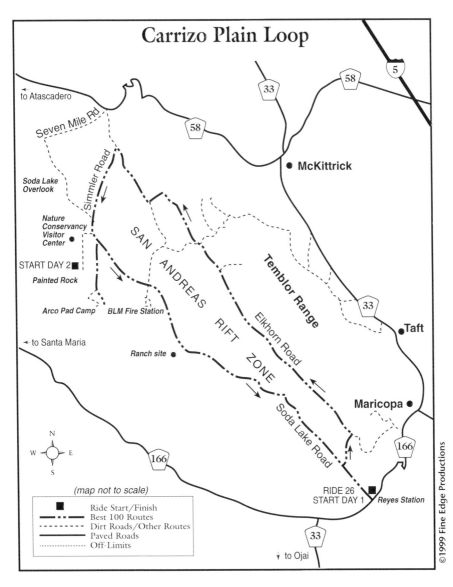

Carrizo Plain Loop

to Atascadero

Seven Mile Rd

Simmler Road

Soda Lake Overlook

Nature Conservancy Visitor Center

START DAY 2 ■
Painted Rock

Arco Pad Camp   BLM Fire Station

to Santa Maria

Ranch site ●

SAN ANDREAS RIFT ZONE

Elkhorn Road

Soda Lake Road

Temblor Range

McKittrick ●

Taft ●

Maricopa ●

Reyes Station

RIDE 26
START DAY 1

33

58

58

5

33

33

166

166

N
W ─ E
S

(map not to scale)

■	Ride Start/Finish
	Best 100 Routes
	Dirt Roads/Other Routes
	Paved Roads
	Off-Limits

to Ojai

©1999 Fine Edge Productions

feet in 1.1 miles to the high point of the ride at 3,000 feet. The descent east starts out steep but moderates when the road switchbacks twice and levels out where you circle around the south side of a large corral at 5.9 miles from Reyes Station. There is a good view northwest along this part

of the Elkhorn Plain while you ride northeast 0.8 mile to the junction with Elkhorn Grade Road. Turn left.

The elevation at the junction is 2,406 feet. In the next 24 miles, you go from 2,300 feet to 2,452 feet, and at the end of the plain you drop back to 2,354 feet. The scene is not a long, seemingly endless plain, but is broken up by low hills and washes that cross at right angles, breaking the ride into interesting segments. In each section, the terrain changes slightly as do the plants. You pass many fences, cattle guards, water tanks and corrals; after a while you may notice a pattern—about one set of each occurs every mile. There are many side tracks remaining from ranching operations, but you should keep to the main road that heads mostly northeast.

At 25.6 miles from Reyes Station, you come to the signed Crocker Grade Road on the right that climbs about 700 feet in 1.9 miles to Crocker Summit at 3,213 feet. Keep to the left and continue on Elkhorn Road across a deep gulch. On the other side is another junction. (The road to the left (west) follows the water course you just crossed through the Panorama Hills down to the Carrizo Plain. There it joins with the San Diego Creek Road, which heads straight south to Soda Lake Road just opposite Washburn Road.)

Take Elkhorn Road on the right for another 5.1 miles, crossing more gulches and climbing over low hills before coming to the end of the Elkhorn Plain. Here, at 31 miles from Reyes Station, elevation 2,354 feet, you turn west and descend a narrow canyon to Carrizo Plain. At 32 miles, the road turns north where a less-traveled road joins in from the south. You climb gradually, crossing several washes where debris has been strewn across the plain by flash floods. Go 0.4 mile past the power lines to the junction with Simmler Road at 36 miles. Highway 58 is 3 miles ahead to the north.

Turn sharp left and descend on Simmler Road back to the south,

crossing under the power lines again. Simmler Road is less traveled and has some closed gates that you must close behind you. This road crosses the plain on a ridge that separates Soda Lake on the north from some smaller lakes to the south. The top of this ridge is fairly flat, but the sides have steep slopes down to the lakes on both sides of the ridge. This is a surprise; from a distance, the area around the lake appears to be almost flat.

After 5.8 miles, you come down off the ridge and Simmler Road ends at paved Soda Lake Road, 41.8 miles, elevation 1,917 feet. Go south on Soda Lake Road 0.8 mile to the dirt road on the right; this leads to the Nature Conservancy's Painted Rock Visitor Center.

To get to the Selby camping area, go southeast on Soda Lake Road 0.7 mile from the Painted Rock Visitor Center drive. Take the dirt road right (south) 4 miles to a fork and take the left fork 1 mile to the Arco oil exploration pad where you may camp.

Painted Rock Visitor Center to Reyes Station: At 30 miles, this segment has shorter mileage and about a third of the way is paved, making this day an easier ride except for the net elevation gain of 917 feet. About 300 feet of downhill that you have to make up again gives a total climb of around 1,200 feet. Almost all of it is gradual and not very difficult. The Carrizo Plain is much wider and flatter than the Elkhorn Plain.

Heading south on Soda Lake Road from Painted Rock Road, at 5.8 miles, you cross a cattle guard at the intersection of Soda Lake and San Diego Creek roads on the north and Washburn Road to the south. The BLM fire station is 2.5 miles south on Washburn Road. The KCL ranch site, 5 miles farther southeast on Soda Lake Road, was to be a developed campground until it was found to be a significant archeological site.

Soda Lake Road stays on the west side of the plain where most of the farming and ranching activities took place. Over time I expect almost all of the buildings, water tanks, and fences will be removed to restore the area to pre-settlement conditions.

After about 20 miles on the west side, the road crosses the plain and starts climbing on the east side next to the Elkhorn Hills. When you come to the paved part of the road, there is one more short steep uphill, and then a long steep downhill to where Elkhorn Road forks east. Continuing on Soda Lake Road, you pass the sag ponds and the county line, and climb the last hill to Reyes Station.

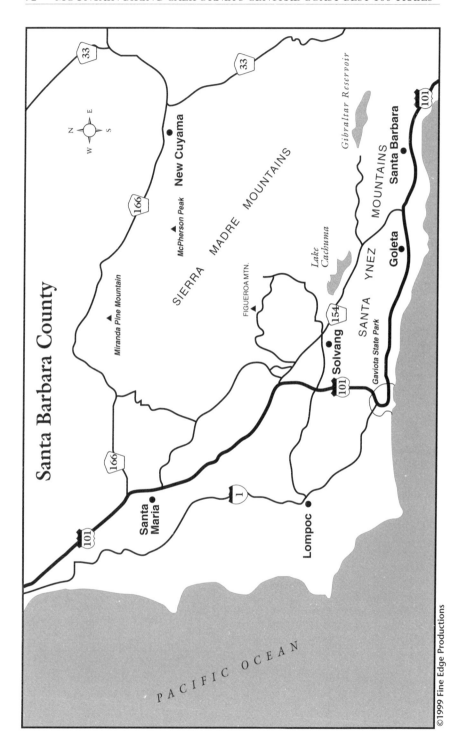

CHAPTER 3

Santa Barbara County

by Mickey McTigue,
Don Douglass, Jamie Griffis
and Delaine Fragnoli

Santa Barbara County, west of Los Angeles and Ventura counties, is the epitome of Southern California. Mountains tumble to a strip of palm-lined sand under almost perpetual sunshine. Ocean breezes keep temperatures down so you can enjoy a variety of recreational activities year-round.

The Pacific Ocean borders the south and west sides of this roughly rectangular county. The abrupt turn of the coastline at Point Conception, the barrier of mountains, and the Channel Islands just offshore all serve to block the wind and smooth out the waves, creating a micro-climate considered the best in California. No wonder most of the population lives on the narrow strip of the south coast, 5 miles long and 25 miles wide, that lies between the mountains and the ocean.

Much of the west county is rural cattle- and horse-grazing land interspersed with vineyards. The Los Padres National Forest takes up about one-third of the county, primarily in the east and northeast sections. The center of the forested area is divided into large wilderness areas (off limit to bikes); mountain bicycle routes are located around their edges.

In the southern part of the county, major land features are aligned in an east-west direction. Parallel to the beach and only 4 to 6 miles inland, a formidable, steep-sided, continuous ridge separates the south coast from the rest of the county. This mountain wall has peaks rising above 4,000 feet and runs from the Ventura River to Point Conception. It is broken only at Gaviota Creek where Highway 101 engineers used a tunnel to carry the highway through the narrow canyon.

The south side of the barrier ridge is known as front country and everything to the north in the eastern half of the county is known as backcountry. This high ridge made access to the backcountry difficult, first for the Native Americans, and later for settlers who improved earlier trails. By the 1930s, roads had been built and now, during dry weather, it is possible to drive into parts of the backcountry. Because people could now drive over the range, travel on some trails was reduced and they were abandoned. The remaining trails are now used more heavily as recreation increases.

The rides in this chapter begin with the fire roads and trails of southeastern Santa Barbara County, covering the front country access trail up Romero Canyon and the roads and trails along the upper Santa Ynez River. Four auto-accessible camps, two hot springs, fishing and swimming in the river, and isolated trail camps make this a popular area. Enjoy all this plus mountain biking rides that range from easy to very difficult.

On the north side of the front range on State Highway 154, the lower Santa Ynez River Canyon can be accessed via Paradise Road. This paved road leads upstream past several campgrounds and many forest trails and dirt roads open to bicycles.

Twenty-five miles northwest of the city of Santa Barbara, Figueroa Mountain, overlooks the Santa Ynez Valley on the south and the San Rafael Wilderness to the north. Campgrounds on the mountain or on the east and north sides are available. The nearby town of Solvang offers plenty of distractions if you're tired of riding. Ride here in the spring, summer and fall. In winter, snow and mud are sometimes a problem.

In the remote north-central part of the county, about 27 miles from Santa Maria over narrow paved and dirt roads, is the La Brea Canyon/Pine Canyon area. You can do day rides here or stay at one of the campgrounds. This is a good spot for those looking for less strenuous routes. Miles of nearly-level road wind through canyons lined with meadows, and oak and sycamore trees beckon you around the next bend. Although best in spring, the area is also pleasant in the fall. Summer can be very hot. The road is closed to car traffic in wet weather, but winter can be a fine time to ride here if the road isn't muddy and the streams are not high.

Camino Cielo/Upper Santa Ynez River

This front country is most easily accessed from Santa Barbara. There are three ways to get here: via East Camino Cielo Road off Highway 154 (San Marcos Pass Road); up paved Gibraltar Road to East Camino Cielo Road; or by bike up Romero Road to Camino Cielo. East Camino Cielo Road is paved up to Romero Saddle, 5.8 miles east of the upper end of Gibraltar Road (where Romero Road comes up).

The area boasts challenging ridge roads as well as nicely graded dirt ones. There are a number of front range trails south of East Camino Cielo, but we do not recommend them. They are steep and rocky and have been the center of numerous conflicts with hikers, equestrians, private landowners and others. Some trails—such as Rattlesnake Canyon (not to be confused with Rattlesnake Canyon in the La Brea Canyon section)—have been closed permanently, while others may be closed in the future. In addition, several trails are poorly defined and require local knowledge and the permission of private landowners. You are generally safe in riding on the Edison maintenance dirt roads which contour across the front range and connect many of the trails in question. Make local inquiry for the latest information.

The trails to the north of Camino Cielo are more relaxed, generally easier to ride and more interesting, and there is less chance of conflict with other trail users.

Ruins at top of East Camino Cielo/Upper Santa Ynez

Jamie Griffis

27 Romero Road

Distance: 13.2 miles.
Difficulty: Moderate; somewhat technical.
Elevation: 850' to 3,100'; 2,250' gain/loss.
Ride Type: Out-and-back on dirt road and singletrack.
Season: Year-round; winter rain may force closure.
Map: Carpinteria.
Water: Area campgrounds have no water. Any stream water should be treated. You may be able to find water at the USFS Pendola Station.

Overview: Romero Road has become a popular bicycle route. One of the few front range trails that is rideable uphill, it provides a good route to the Santa Barbara backcountry with connections to the major roads and trails. Since most of this trail is within 3 miles of the beach, the views

Romero Road

East

Romero
Saddle

Camino   Cielo

Romero Canyon

N
W — E
S

to Toro Canyon

RIDE 27 ■

Bella Vista Drive   Bella Vista Drive

Romero Canyon

East Valley Road

(map not to scale)

■   Ride Start/Finish
— ■ —   Best 100 Routes
- - - -   Dirt Roads/Other Routes
———   Paved Roads
· · · · ·   Off-Limits

Sheffield Drive

← to Santa Barbara   101

to Ventura →

©1999 Fine Edge Productions

south over the coast to the ocean and the Channel Islands are especially good. The south-facing slopes provide little shade but ocean breezes moderate the high summer temperatures.

Formerly a vehicle route for access

to water projects in the backcountry, the road has eroded so much that now it is essentially a trail. Heavy rains in early 1995 caused many rockfalls and washouts that left boulders the size of small cars in the trail and showed just how dangerous these

JUNCAL ROAD
← UPPER SANTA YNEZ CAMP   2½
← MURIETTA DIVIDE   4
  JUNCAL STATION   1½ →
  JUNCAL CAMP   3½ →
  LOS PADRES NATIONAL FOREST

Trail sign and view from Juncal Road

Jamie Griffis

mountains are during storms. A volunteer effort reopened the trail; later, grading restored the doubletrack from the gate to the first saddle.

Getting There: Exit Highway 101 at Sheffield Drive and head north toward the mountains through Montecito. Where Sheffield Drive ends at East Valley Road (Route 192), turn left and then almost immediately take the next right onto Romero Canyon Road. Follow this paved road as it winds up into the foothills and joins Bella Vista Drive. Turn right and, 0.3 mile farther as you cross the canyon, look to the left to the locked gate at Romero Road. Park alongside Bella Vista Drive. Make sure your wheels are off the pavement and you are not blocking the fire road.

Route: From the gate at Bella Vista Drive, Romero Road (5N15) climbs somewhat steeply in the canyon, cross-es a creek over a concrete bridge, turns east and crosses a second creek without a bridge. (On the other side of the creek, a hiking trail starts north along the creek and keeps to the canyon bottom until it crosses Romero Road high up in the canyon. *Caution:* This hiking trail is not suitable for bicycles and should not be ridden.)

Past here, Road 5N15 (more like a doubletrack) climbs moderately to the east out of Romero Canyon, circling around a foothill. You reenter Romero Canyon at a saddle where a road to the right leads down to private homes in Toro Canyon. Keep left here and continue climbing on the east side of the canyon where regrading stops and the road turns into a singletrack for the rest of the route.

A small stream flows from the east and crosses the trail 3.3 miles from the gate. The hiking trail mentioned earlier (unsuitable for bikes) crosses 5N15 again at 3.9 miles and can be seen climbing with switchbacks above. Continuing along Romero Road, climb west around two south-facing ridges before heading north and crossing back into Romero Canyon again. At this point the trail narrows considerably and there may be quite a bit of shale to negotiate along with the grade. Past this divide, the trail levels and it is an easy ride to Romero Saddle on the Santa Ynez Ridge. The road ends at a prominent concrete cistern next to paved Camino Cielo Road (5N12).

You can return the way you came or connect to several other routes from here. For example, you can go east past Juncal to Ojai or Big Caliente Hot Springs and return.

Option: A loop can be completed by heading west on paved Camino Cielo for 2.8 miles to Cold Springs Trail (26W10). Cold Springs Trail drops south opposite Forbush Trail (same number) to the north. There's a cement water tank here. This 3-mile singletrack descends the East Fork Cold Springs drainage. Turn left at the powerline road and take it down through Hot Springs Canyon. Continue through Montecito east to the Romero Road trailhead.

28 Romero Saddle to Juncal Camp

Distance: 5.3 miles one way; 10.6 miles out and back.
Difficulty: Easy to moderate, with some rough spots; not technical.
Elevation: 1,200' gain/loss.
Ride Type: One-way or out-and-back on dirt road; part of many possible loops.
Season: Year-round; winter can be muddy and access gate may be closed.
Maps: Carpinteria, Hildreth Peak.
Water: Area campgrounds have no water. Any stream water should be treated. You may be able to find water at the USFS Pendola Station.

Overview: This long, sometimes steep descent has a short uphill at Blue Canyon Pass, followed by another descent east of the pass. Your goal, Juncal Camp, is a large, shady campground where you can turn around—it's more work on the way back—or continue northwest to Mono Camp or east toward Murietta Divide.

Getting There: Take State Highway 154 to San Marcos Pass and, at the summit, turn east onto Camino Cielo Road. Continue east to Romero Saddle where the pavement ends. This is marked by the low spot of this portion of the ridge and by one of the USFS concrete rain reservoirs on the right. To the right of the tank, beyond a yellow gate, is the upper trailhead of Romero Road (see previous ride description).

Or you can reach Romero Saddle from Santa Barbara proper by means of Gibraltar Road. Just past the Santa Barbara Mission, turn right on Mountain Drive and head uphill past a large rock wall on the right. This route turns into State Highway 192

Romero Saddle to Juncal Camp
Juncal Camp to Mono Camp

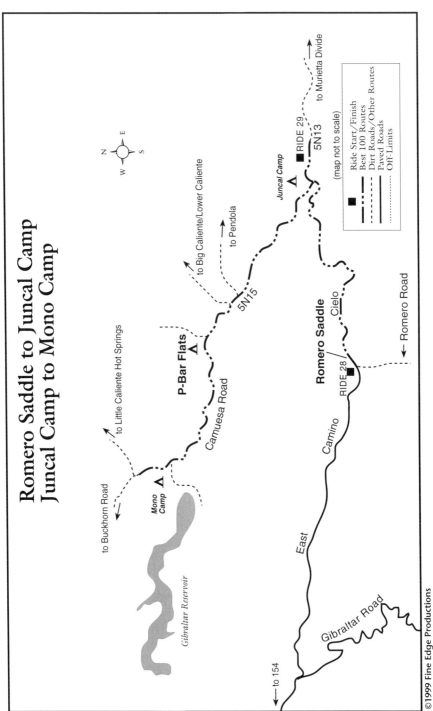

at Foothill Road. Stay on Highway 192 (Mission Ridge) until you reach the filtration plant (painted green) at mile 1.4. In front of the plant, turn left onto Mountain Drive. Soon after, at the three-way intersection, take Gibraltar Road and head right (not a hard right). Continue on Gibraltar Road until its end at Camino Cielo. Go east (right) 5.8 miles to Romero Saddle. Park here.

Route: From Romero Saddle, follow the dirt road to the east. Here it crosses over to the north side of the ridge and starts a mostly downhill contour to the Santa Ynez River. *Caution:* The road is gravel, used by high-speed motor vehicles, and is subject to rock falls.

At 1.3 miles, there is a trailhead on the right at a brown gate—Toro Saddle/Divide Peak Road. 5N12 continues to the right, while the main road takes the number of Romero Road, (5N15). You continue straight on 5N15.

Just over a mile later, the road enters a shady canyon where water usually flows. This can be used as a protected bivouac area if necessary. Pass directly under high tension wires at 3.2 miles.

At a cement bridge, mile 3.8, the road starts to climb. This is Blue Canyon. Blue Canyon Trail starts 100 feet up on the left at the trail marker signed 26W12, just to the west of Blue Canyon Pass.

At 5.3 miles, you cross the Santa Ynez River on a concrete ford. *Caution:* Algae grows on the cement and it's very slippery. Try to follow the tire tracks carefully through the water or get off and walk. Juncal Campground—a large campground in a well-shaded area—is located on the north side of the river. There are several tables, fire pits and pit toilets here. Flies and insects can be bothersome in early summer.

From here you can retrace your route, continue east on Juncal Road (5N13) (see Ride 31), or head west on 5N15 toward Mono Camp (see the next ride).

29 Juncal Camp to Mono Camp

Distance: 15.4 miles.
Difficulty: Easy for 5 miles; moderate hills beyond.
Elevation: 300' gain/loss.
Ride Type: Out-and-back on dirt road; part of many possible loops.
Season: Year-round; winter rain may force closure.
Maps: Carpinteria, Hildreth Peak.
Water: Area campgrounds have no water. Treat river water; water may be available at Pendola Station.
Comments: Camino Cielo is closed during wet weather. Beware of fast motor vehicles and their dust when you're riding.

Overview: An easy ride, this riverside road is the best way to experience nature here. The quiet travel and unrestricted views allow you to hear and see things others miss. Early morning and late afternoon are the best times to ride. An extra treat is the trip to the Little Caliente Hot Springs.

Getting There: Auto access to the Upper Santa Ynez River is by paved Camino Cielo Road. Take State Highway 154 to San Marcos Pass and at the summit turn east onto Camino Cielo Road. From Santa Barbara, go up Gibraltar Road and meet Camino Cielo at the ridge top. Go east on Camino Cielo past Romero Saddle and the top of that trail, where the pavement ends. Go 5.3 miles to Juncal Camp next to the Santa Ynez River on this good graded dirt road. (You can ride this section if you wish—see previous ride— but there is a lot of climbing on your way back.) You can park in turnouts along the road and at various camps. Be sure not to block access.

Route: From Juncal Camp, Camuesa Road (5N15) heads west past oaks and sycamores on the north side of the river, and is fairly level for 0.75 mile. In the next mile, you climb over two hills with a canyon in between. These are short hills, but the elevation gives you an overview of the area.

After descending the second hill, you have more level cycling to the junction with Agua Caliente Road, 3.2 miles from Juncal Camp. USFS Pendola Station is visible on the right about 200 yards up that road. (It is an easy 2.5 mile-ride up Agua Caliente Road to the hot spring that is piped into a rectangular concrete tub set in the ground.)

From Pendola Station, take Camuesa Road west, crossing Agua Caliente Creek just past the junction. The large Mid-Santa Ynez Camp is on the left at 3.4 miles; the smaller

P-Bar Flats Camp is on the right at 4.3 miles. The P-Bar Jeepway comes down a ridge and joins Camuesa Road just east of the camp. Continue west on Camuesa Road over rather flat terrain past the camps along the north side of the river.

At 4.9 miles, Blue Canyon Trail is a doubletrack on the left that crosses the river. Camuesa Road (your route) leaves the riverbank and climbs over a series of ridges, dipping into side canyons in between. You pass over the first saddle at 5.4 miles, the second at 6.3 miles, and the last at 6.9 miles (elevation 1,875 feet). Now it's all downhill to Mono Camp at 7.7 miles.

[**Side trips:** Explore the area. Mono Camp is the last camp you can drive to and it makes a good base camp or parking spot for riding in the area or deeper into the backcountry. A short trail from the northwest side of the camp leads to the Mono Debris Dam with its vertical waterfall. Just 0.2 mile past the camp on Camuesa Road, a right fork leads east and north 1.0 mile to Little Caliente Hot Springs. From the turn-around loop, take a footpath 50 yards to the right to a nice cement hot tub with deck. Beyond the loop, Mono Road leads north along Mono Creek.

If you want to continue west on Camuesa Road past Mono Camp, go past the hot springs turn-off. Where Indian and Mono creeks come together there are several concrete fords through the water. There is a locked gate just past the Indian Canyon trailhead, 1.3 miles from Mono Camp.]

When you've finished exploring, head back the way you came for a pleasant out-and-back ride.

30 Toro Saddle Road/ Divide Peak Road

Distance: 4 miles one way to Toro Saddle; 12 miles one way to Divide Peak Road; 18-mile loop with Franklin Canyon Trail.
Difficulty: Toro Road, easy to moderate; Divide Peak, more strenuous with some steep pulls.
Elevation: 350' gain to Toro Saddle; 1,590' gain to Divide Peak; lots of ups and downs.
Ride Type: Out-and-back on dirt road; loop possible with (25W09).
Season: Year-round, but winter can be muddy.
Maps: Carpinteria, White Ledge Peak.
Water: None

Overview: A popular designated motorcycle route, Toro Saddle Road/Divide Peak Road provides extended ocean and coastline views to the south. The road gets more difficult the farther east you go, so you can turn back whenever you've had enough. There's also a difficult loop option via an unmaintained singletrack.

Getting There: Follow the directions for the previous ride to Romero Saddle. Continue past the saddle for 1.3 miles. There is a parking area to the left (motorcycle central!) where the main road turns left. Signed and gated 5N12 goes south and uphill into thick chaparral. Park here.

Route: Your route is Toro Saddle Road (5N12). This road twists and turns up a ridge and across Upper Escondido Canyon to Toro Saddle on the Santa Ynez Ridge. Once on the ridge you are about 1000 feet above the Doulton water tunnel which carries water from Juncal down to Santa Barbara.

At 4 miles, you reach Toro Saddle. Here Divide Peak Road (24W08) climbs very steeply, 650 feet in a little over a mile. Bicyclists headed east will enjoy the next 2.5 miles because the riding is much easier,

with a descent of 250 feet. This pattern is repeated again less severely with first a 350-foot climb in one mile, and then a descent of 50 feet in 1.5 miles to a saddle at the head of Franklin Canyon Trail.

Loop Option: An 18-mile loop can be completed by taking Franklin Trail (25W09) down to Juncal Road (5N13). The trail is brushy, rough and unmaintained, but great for adventurous types. Look for the trail crossing the crest 5 miles from Toro Saddle. The trail angles back and left under a powerline heading down into Franklin Canyon. It switchbacks down to Alder Camp, 1 mile from the top. Trail's end is another mile farther at Jameson Reservoir and Juncal Road. Go left here and head downhill to meet up with 5N15 at Juncal Camp. From there, it's a 4-mile climb back to Toro Saddle Road.

Instead of the loop option, continue on Divide Peak Road 5 miles farther to Divide Peak. The road rises and falls over all the peaks on this ridge, gradually working to a high point at Divide Peak (4,707 feet). From here you will probably want to retrace your route back to your car.

Other Options: You could continue east for another 0.5 mile to an old trail, called Monte Arido Trail in some old sources, which leads down

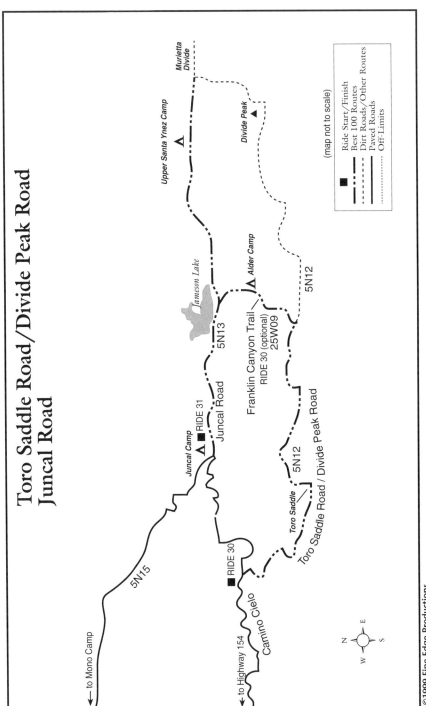

Toro Saddle Road/Divide Peak Road
Juncal Road

to Murietta Divide. It's not maintained but is passable if you're willing to portage your bike a bit. You could also try riding Ocean View Trail which continues east for a mile or so but gradually fades on the ridge top.

31 Juncal Road

Distance: 7.5 miles one way; 15 miles out and back.
Difficulty: Easy to moderate, with some steep hills.
Elevation: 424' gain, Juncal Camp to Jameson Reservoir; 1,100' gain to Upper Santa Ynez Trail Camp; 1,600' gain to Murietta Divide.
Ride Type: Out-and-back on dirt roads; several loop options possible.
Season: Best in spring and fall; winter can be muddy, summer can be hot.
Maps: Carpinteria, White Ledge Peak.
Water: In creek at Upper Santa Ynez Trail Camp—treat all water!

Overview: This nice rolling fire road can be used to fashion a loop with Toro Saddle Road/Divide Peak Road (see Ride 30) or with the very difficult Pendola and Monte Arido roads (not described in this book). It can also serve as a good warm-up spin or family ride. It is pretty easy up to the lake and somewhat more difficult from there. Beware of goathead thorns in the drier months.

Getting There: Follow the directions for Ride 29 to start from Juncal Camp.

Route: Find the start of 5N13 at the gate at the east end of Juncal campground. Pass the locked gate and cross a concrete-lined creek ford. The first mile is an easy, nearly level ride in Santa Ynez Canyon past oaks and sycamores, meadows and chaparral. Soon the road climbs, then switchbacks with more climbing until suddenly you have a view of

Juncal Dam and the caretaker's house.

Keep right (west) past the road down to the dam. More climbing, and then finally the road levels out with a view over the dam and lake. At 3.2 miles, there's a fork in the road with a sign for Franklin Canyon Trail. This road goes down into Alder Creek and, near the head of a metal flume, joins the Franklin Canyon Trail (25W09). There is water here during most of the year, but it should be treated.

Road sign on Juncal Road

Jamie Griffis

View from Franklin Canyon Trail

Continue past this fork on Juncal Road for a steep climb of about one mile and then a descent back to the creek bed in Juncal Canyon. On the west side of the road, just before the canyon bottom, at 4.6 miles, a spring flows most of the year. Beyond this spring the road is rougher with steeper climbing. It's two miles, 6.5 miles total, to Upper Santa Ynez Trail Camp. The camp has a year-round stream, shade trees, table and firepit. *Caution:* Poison oak grows along the

sides of the creek.

Continue on for one more mile and a very steep climb to Murietta Divide (7.5 miles). This is a crossroads where Monte Arido Road (see the Ventura chapter, Ride 83) leads north, 5N13 continues east down Murietta Canyon toward Ojai, and a very steep, rough trail 24W08 leads south up to Divide Peak Road. The best and easiest option is to return the way you came.

32 Agua Caliente Road

Distance: 5 miles.
Difficulty: Easy.
Elevation: 400' gain/loss.
Ride Type: Out-and-back on dirt road.
Season: Year-round.
Map: Hildreth Peak.
Water: Treat water from the creek. Potable water may be available at Pendola Station.
Comments: Be alert—the road is open to motor vehicles.

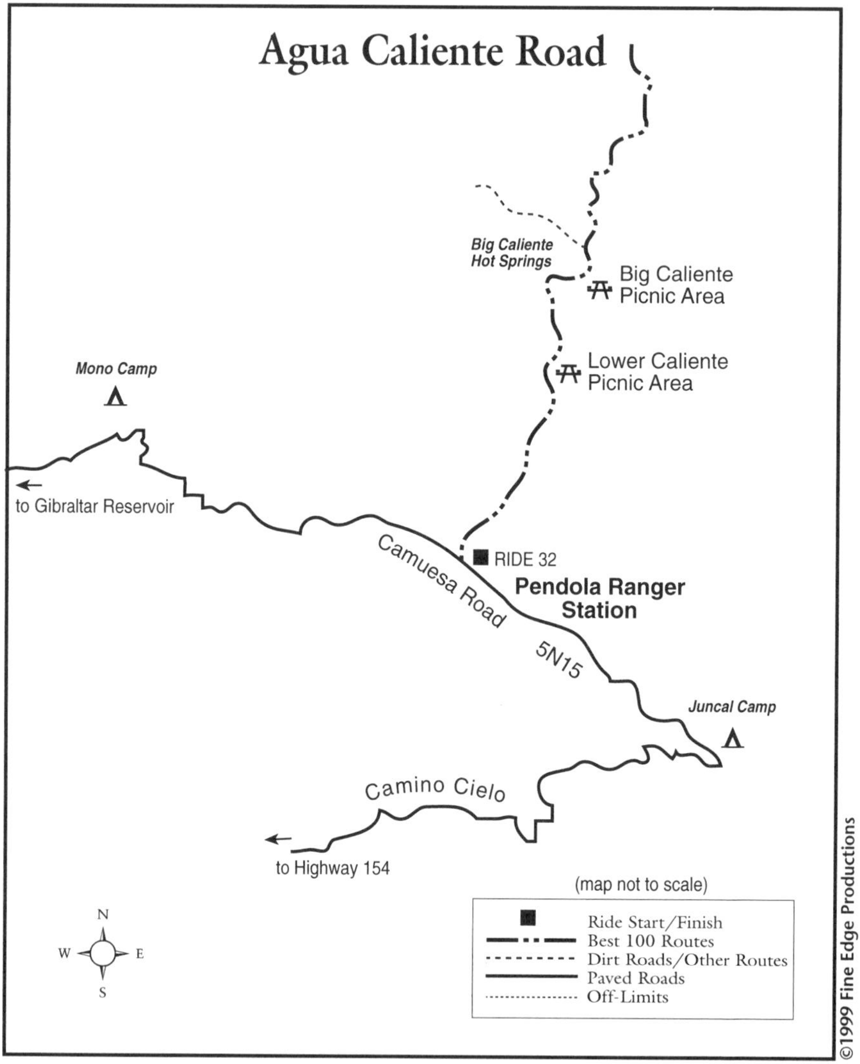

Agua Caliente Road

Big Caliente
Hot Springs

🎋 Big Caliente
Picnic Area

🎋 Lower Caliente
Picnic Area

Mono Camp
⛺

← to Gibraltar Reservoir

Camuesa Road

■ RIDE 32

**Pendola Ranger
Station**

5N15

Juncal Camp
⛺

Camino Cielo

← to Highway 154

(map not to scale)

■ Ride Start/Finish
━━ Best 100 Routes
- - - Dirt Roads/Other Routes
───── Paved Roads
········· Off-Limits

N
W ⊕ E
S

©1999 Fine Edge Productions

Overview: Since this ride is so short, you can use it as a reward for a day's hard riding elsewhere in the canyon. This easy road is in good condition as it follows a stream among oak and sycamore trees.

Getting There: Take either Highway 154 (San Marcos Pass Road) or Gibraltar Road to Camino Cielo and go right (east) past Romero Saddle.

At Juncal Camp, go northwest on Camuesa Road (5N15) for 3.2 miles to Pendola Station. Park here.

Route: From Pendola Station, it's 2 miles to Lower Caliente Picnic Area on the east side of the road. 0.5 mile farther on you find the Big Caliente Hot Tub where a pipe from the hot spring brings hot water to a rectangular concrete tub set in the ground.

Little Caliente Hot Springs, Agua Caliente Road

Jamie Griffis

A valve regulates the amount of hot water and thereby the temperature of the water in the tub. Nearby are changing rooms made of concrete block and a pit toilet. This is a day-use area only—no camping. Turn around here (2.5 miles).

[**Side trip:** If you want to get in a few more miles before your soak, explore a bit farther up Agua Caliente Canyon to where the road ends at a parking lot. Trail 25W06 continues on up a ridge in the canyon, passing east of a debris dam. Water falls over the dam into a large pool below. Above the dam, the trail drops back into the canyon bottom and heads north for about 2 miles along fairly level terrain.]

33 North Cold Springs Trail/ Forbush Flat

Distance: 6 miles on North Cold Springs Trail; 2 miles on Forbush Trail; all one way.
Difficulty: Moderate downhill; somewhat technical.
Elevation: 2,000' loss.
Ride Type: One-way; several loops possible.
Season: Year-round, but winter can be muddy.
Maps: Santa Barbara, Little Pine Mountain.
Water: At waterfall of north branch; none on south branch. Treat all water.

Overview: This trail features lots of switchbacks and water under an oak canopy as it makes its way along Mono Creek and across the Santa Ynez River.

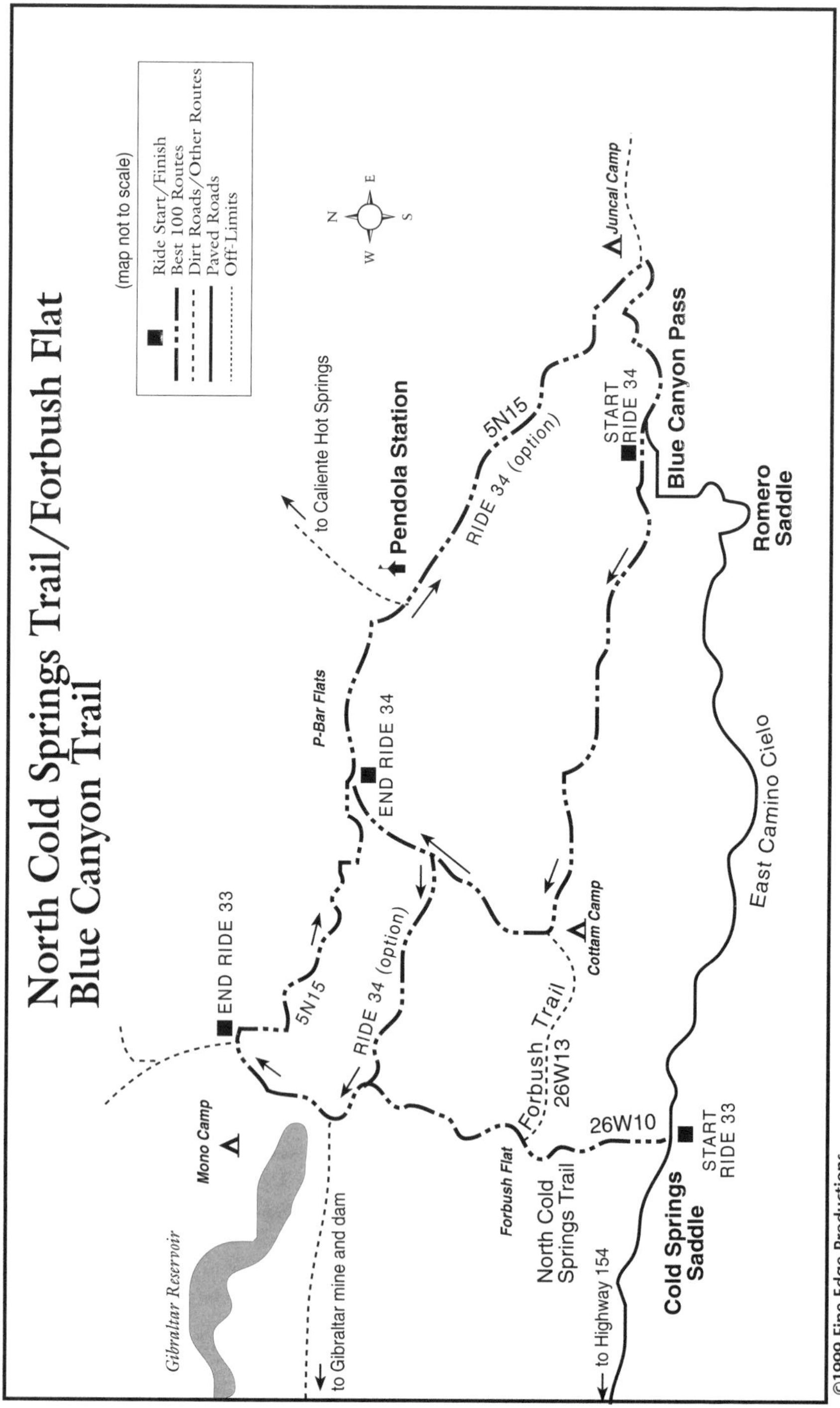

North Cold Springs Trail/Forbush Flat
Blue Canyon Trail

(map not to scale)

Ride Start/Finish
Best 100 Routes
Dirt Roads/Other Routes
Paved Roads
Off-Limits

N
W — E
S

to Caliente Hot Springs

Pendola Station

5N15

RIDE 34 (option)

△ *Juncal Camp*

START
RIDE 34

Blue Canyon Pass

Romero Saddle

P-Bar Flats

END RIDE 34

East Camino Cielo

END RIDE 33

5N15

RIDE 34 (option)

△ *Cottam Camp*

Mono Camp △

Gibraltar Reservoir

Forbush Trail
26W13

26W10

Forbush Flat

START
RIDE 33

North Cold
Springs Trail

Cold Springs Saddle

to Gibraltar mine and dam

to Highway 154

©1999 Fine Edge Productions

"Trail Daze," Cold Springs Trail

Getting There: Take Gibraltar Road to East Camino Cielo, or take Highway 154 to East Camino Cielo and go 11 miles to the top of Gibraltar Road. Here a brown sign lists place names with directions and distances. Continue east 3.2 miles to Cold Springs saddle, marked by a concrete water tank on the hill south of the road. 26W10, Cold Springs Trail, heads both north and south from here. (If you want to explore the south branch, you're better off making a loop with Romero Road (see Ride 27). The following route describes North Cold Springs Trail, heading north from Cold Springs saddle to Forbush Flat. Across the road is the start of North Cold Springs Trail (the one you want).

Route: North Cold Springs Trail descends 1,050 feet in 1.75 miles of steep switchbacks from Upper Gidney Canyon to Forbush Flat. Watch for a wash-out and trail realignment about

0.3 mile from the trailhead. Most of the trail is in good condition, with almost no rocks and not too many "surprise" steep sections.

One hundred yards before For-bush Flat, in an oak grove, you will see a steep, less-traveled trail that branches left (west) toward Forbush Camp. (Unless you want to visit the campsite, avoid this trail.) The main trail goes right around the east side of a small hill. (At the east side of Forbush Flat, if you want to visit the camp, another short trail leads west to Forbush Camp. This camp—under large oaks next to a meadow—has two tables and three fireplaces. Gidney Creek is usually dry here.)

Gidney Canyon veers west, blocked on the north by a steep, rocky ridge that rises right up out of Forbush Flat. Past the camp turnoff described above, the main trail (North Cold Springs Trail) switchbacks down so steeply that, for a short way, you have to walk.

Jason Houston

Cold Springs Trail

to the tree-filled Mono Canyon river bottom. After a short, steep and rocky "walk-only" descent, the trail switchbacks down to the river. The ride is fun here under oak trees. You reach the canyon bottom (1.0 mile from the ridge), where there are small pools of water.

For 0.25 mile, the trail follows the east side of the creek in a narrow, rocky part of the canyon. Water flows here over the rocks, creating small noisy cascades. The trail crosses this creek at the top of a large waterfall. Minerals in the water have formed a series of semicircular dams across the creek, the largest of which is a pool 10 feet across and 5 feet deep. This dam forms the face of a 20-foot waterfall covered with small plants through which the water trickles.

On the west side of the canyon, the trail comes to a more open area. Gibraltar Trail (5N18) goes west to Gibraltar Lake past the old Sunbird mercury mine. It can be brushy, but is passable. (In fact, this would be the easiest bike passage from the upper to the lower Santa Ynez River.)

From the Gibraltar Trail junction, head 0.5 mile down North Cold

[**Side trip:** You can add another 2 miles if you take Forbush Trail (26W13) at the bottom of this hill; it descends east 2 miles in Forbush Canyon to Cottam Camp in Blue Canyon. This trail can be seen overgrown with brush down the north side of Forbush Canyon.]

Where North Cold Springs Trail climbs the steep ridge north of Forbush Flat, large shell fossils can be seen. The view from the top of the knife-edge ridge is down a small canyon and across Santa Ynez Creek

Springs Trail to the Santa Ynez River crossing. The trail crosses to the north side of the river and plunges into a jungle of trees and plants. For the next 1.0 mile, it keeps to the east of Mono Creek and is level, except occasionally where it climbs over steep hills.

After crossing a small meadow, where secondary side trails head north, the main trail turns east, then west, and climbs up to Camuesa Road (5N15) just east of Mono Campground. (If you camped at Mono Campground, it is a moderately easy ride out to the Santa Ynez River and back—about 2 miles round-trip—on North Cold Springs Trail.)

Blue Canyon Trail, Upper Santa Ynez River

Jamie Griffis

34 Blue Canyon Trail

Distance: 6 miles; 13-mile loop with Cameusa Road (5N15).
Difficulty: Challenging and technical.
Elevation: 600' loss.
Ride Type: One-way on singletrack or part of loop with dirt road.
Season: Year-round, but winter can be muddy.
Maps: Carpinteria, Hildreth Peak.
Water: In creek; be sure to treat it!

Overview: Mountain bike riders can plan and enjoy many different types of trips on Blue Canyon Trail. Some parts in the upper half are very rough, requiring you to carry your bike while climbing steep hills. Because of this, bicycle campers should ride in from the lower end to Cottam Camp (moderate) or Blue Camp (a little more difficult). To ride all the way through Blue Canyon, start at Blue Canyon Pass at the upper end and head mostly downhill.

Getting There: The trailhead is at Blue Canyon Pass on 5N15, 3.8 miles past Romero Saddle. There's parking here for about three cars. (If you're planning to loop it, you can continue on 5N15 to Juncal Camp, Pendola Station or P-Bar Flats.)

Route: From the trailhead, the trail follows the north side of Blue Canyon for the first mile. It's a little rough and there are some rocky areas. There should be water at the first stream crossing and most of the way to Cottam Camp, though it may be dry in summer. Treat all water.

Keep to the south side of the creek for 0.6 mile as the trail passes over some rough spots on its way to Upper Blue Canyon Trail Camp. This former walk-in camp has weathered the ravages of heavy winter rains poorly and, for all intents and purposes, no longer exists. It's just a wide spot in the willows past a deep gully with rusted old stove parts stacked up to the side.

The trail gets progressively rougher, with steep climbs around cliffs next to the stream. You may have to walk and carry your bike up, as well as down, in some places, and there are many stream crossings. At times you may have to search to find the trail beyond the water crossings. The Santa Ynez has gotten a lot of rain in recent years and reclaimed the lower parts of the trail here and there.

At 2.5 miles, a powerline road drops steeply to join the trail. The trail soon improves as it passes Blue Canyon Trail Camp. This excellent camp—just off the trail among sycamore trees and almost hidden from the trail—can be easy to miss. Look for the camp just east of the north-south opposing canyons that drain into Blue Canyon at the mid-point, 3 miles in from either end of Blue Canyon. Next to the north canyon is a large gray pyramid rock, over 100 feet high, that stands as a sentinel. There are three stoves at this camp between the trail and the creek. The creek north of camp almost always has water.

For the next mile, the riding is greatly improved. At Cottam Flat and Camp, there are two nice sites with tables and stoves under oak trees next to the creek (dry in summer). Cross this creek, head directly north, and look for the trail climbing on the east side of Blue Canyon which turns north here, cutting through the ridges to Santa Ynez Creek. This narrow trail widens; 0.4 mile from Cottam, just past an eastern branch which dead ends, there is a dangerous drop-off. *Caution:* This sudden drop cannot be seen from above until you are quite near.

The trail becomes a doubletrack down into a flat canyon bottom where it crosses two usually dry creeks. At a wire fence, you come to a good road. Ride one mile northeast, crossing Santa Ynez Creek twice, to the junction with 5N15. Here you are 1.5 miles west of P-Bar Flats Camp. *If you decide to do the loop,* go right on 5N15 for 6 miles back to your car at Blue Canyon Pass.

Option: Another option is to continue past Cottam Camp on the dirt road to an overgrown trail to the bottom of North Cold Springs Trail (26W10). Cross the river to find Mono

Trail alongside the north bank of Mono Creek. The trail continues 1.5 miles through willow thickets to emerge at Mono Camp at the end of 5N15. Here you could continue up to Caliente Hot Springs (see Ride 32) or return east on 5N15 for 8 miles to your car at Blue Canyon Pass.

35 Camuesa Road/ Buckhorn Trail Loop

Distance: Loop trail, 23.7 miles; 18 miles out and back.
Difficulty: Difficult; strenuous.
Elevation: 2,200' differential.
Ride Type: Loop on dirt road and singletrack or out-and-back on singletrack.
Season: Year-round; summer can be hot and winter can be muddy.
Maps: San Marcos Pass, Little Pine Mountain.
Water: Buckhorn Creek; treat all water.

Overview: Riding under the trees along the creek in Buckhorn Canyon provides a pleasant contrast to the usual chaparral in this area, especially during hot weather. Downstream, after it joins Indian Creek, Buckhorn Creek has many pools and more open vegetation. Fine for sunning and swimming when the water is flowing, Buckhorn Creek can be dangerous in periods of high water.

Expert riders should make a loop by riding up Camuesa Road and down the length of Buckhorn Trail. Less-experienced cyclists should ride from the bottom of Buckhorn Trail near Mono Camp. That way they can ride out-and-back as far as their energy allows.

Options: You could also arrange a shuttle by starting at Upper Oso Camp (see the *Paradise Road/Lower Santa Ynez River* section) and picking up at Mono Camp. Or you could do the whole loop from Upper Oso Camp. The disadvantages of starting there are that you add about 9.5 miles and you have to do some tough climbing on Camuesa Road late in the ride.

Getting There: Take State Highway 154 to San Marcos Pass; at the summit, turn east onto Camino Cielo Road. Or you can go up Gibraltar Road from Santa Barbara and meet Camino Cielo at the ridge top. Go east on Camino Cielo and pass Romero Saddle where the pavement ends. It is 5.3 miles to Juncal Camp. From there, continue on Camuesa Road (5N15) another 7.7 miles to Mono Camp.

Route: From Mono Camp, head west on Camuesa Road (5N15). At 1.0 mile a sign on the north side of the road marks the lower end of the Indian Canyon/Buckhorn Canyon Trail (27W12). You will finish your ride by coming down this trail. For now, continue past a second sign, reading: *Camuesa Road: Hidden Potrero - 7 miles; Upper Oso - 14 miles; Mono Camp - 1 mile; Pendola Station - 6 miles.* About 100 yards later, go around the locked gate.

Begin a 1.5-mile climb followed by a 1.1-mile descent. Then the real work starts with a 5-mile, 1000-foot

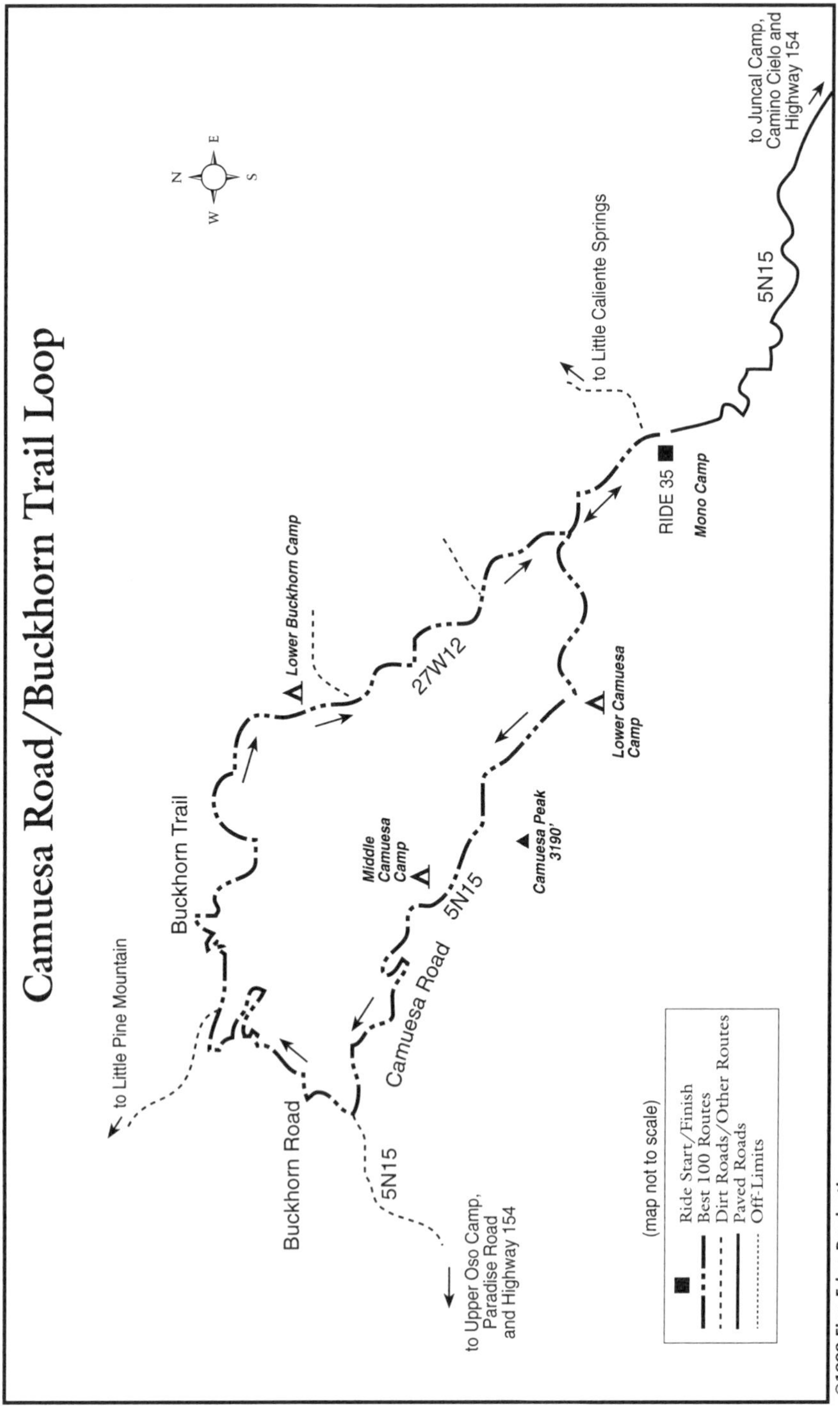

Camuesa Road/Buckhorn Trail Loop

to Juncal Camp,
Camino Cielo and
Highway 154

5N15

to Little Caliente Springs

RIDE 35
Mono Camp

Lower Buckhorn Camp

27W12

Buckhorn Trail

Lower Camuesa
Camp

Middle
Camuesa
Camp

Camuesa Peak
3190'

5N15

Camuesa Road

to Little Pine Mountain

Buckhorn Road

5N15

to Upper Oso Camp,
Paradise Road
and Highway 154

N
E
W
S

(map not to scale)

Ride Start/Finish
Best 100 Routes
Dirt Roads/Other Routes
Paved Roads
Off-Limits

© 1999 Fine Edge Productions

climb. It gets steeper toward the end with a series of switchbacks. Along the way you pass a pipe which feeds spring water into two open water tanks beside the road. Near the tanks is Middle Camuesa Trail Camp on the north side of the road.

About 2.5 miles past the trail camp, an old road climbs out to the site of Camuesa Peak lookout. If you don't feel like you're getting enough of a workout, you can ride the 2 miles (about 300' gain) up to the peak. The view is worth the effort.

From the turnoff to Camuesa Peak, it's just under 2 miles, 10.5 miles total (not including Camuesa Peak), to the road's high point (2,797 feet) and the junction with Buckhorn Road.

Gibraltar Mine, Red Rock Canyon/Gibraltar Dam Trail

Jamie Griffis

Take Buckhorn Road north (right). Although not level, the first 1.6 miles is fast, with up-and-down grades that deposit you 150 feet lower than the junction. Next you have a steep 1-mile climb up a south-facing bluff where on a hot day the sun is cruel. On the north side, past this bluff, the road is not as steep as it passes through the shade of oak trees. Out around another ridge you pass Buckhorn Trail (27W12) below on the right. The trail starts a little farther up the road, marked by a sign, 4.3 miles from the Buckhorn Road/ Camuesa Road junction and 14.7 miles total.

Buckhorn Trail descends moderately at first along a ridge, but soon becomes steep and enters a series of switchbacks, dropping 1,400 feet in 1.75 miles! This is not a good place for stunts—walking may be advisable as you are a long way from help. Once in the canyon, the trail does little real descending except when it crosses the creek, which it does often. The overgrown remains of Upper Buckhorn Camp may be seen 2.2 miles down the trail. Another mile and you reach the little-used old Lower Buckhorn Trail Camp. Water may be found here or in nearby Indian Creek; treat all water.

Continue on the trail. After you pass the junction with Pie Canyon Jeepway (6N24), you find a fine trail camp under large oak trees beside Indian Creek. For the next 4.2 miles, the trail heads southeast along Indian Creek with little elevation change. The only real difficulty is posed by rocky sections, especially those at stream crossings. The eastern trailhead is reached at Camuesa Road, 1 mile west of Mono Camp. A left turn takes you back to camp.

If you decide to ride Buckhorn Trail as an out-and-back from Mono Camp, be sure to avoid the trails and roads which head east toward Pie Canyon Jeepway, a rather unattractive area for cycling.

36 Angostura Pass Road

Distance: 6 miles.
Difficulty: Moderate to strenuous; not technical.
Elevation: 2,000' gain/loss.
Ride Type: One-way on dirt road; several loops possible.
Season: Year-round, but winter can be muddy.
Maps: Santa Barbara, Little Pine Mountain.
Water: None.

Overview: The descent of Angostura Pass Road is an exhilarating freefall and worth the effort of climbing back up to Camino Cielo. It can also be connected with several roads and trails in the following section for longer loops.

Getting There: Angostura Pass Road (5N25) is located off East Camino Cielo, 0.7 mile west of paved Gibraltar Road (also 5N25), or 9 miles east of San Marcos Pass.

Route: At the Angostura Pass saddle on Camino Cielo, look for a dirt road beyond a gate to the north, near a No Shooting sign. The gate reads: *No motorcycles, no trail bikes.* Head down this road.

At 0.2 mile, a trail sign reads: *Tunnel Trail.* This is a very steep singletrack which starts to the left. From this point, Angostura Road is relatively fast and well graded with some loose rocks and occasional ruts. It is maintained as an access road to Gibraltar Reservoir.

At 2.1 miles, watch out for small stream crossings. You pass through a shady canyon at 3.0 miles, and past sandstone outcroppings at 4.7 miles. Where you cross under high-tension lines contouring to the west, you can see Tunnel Trail as it follows the ridge down into Devils Canyon. *Caution:* The road is steep here, watch excessive speed.

At 5.1 miles, cross the ridge where you have a good view of Gibraltar Dam and the log booms above the dam. Sometimes you can see a large floating dredge on the lake. Carp up to a foot long are said to live in the reservoir. At 6.0 miles, Angostura Pass Road ends at Paradise Road (5N18), also known as Gibraltar Dam Road.

Options: At this point, you have a wealth of options if you choose to extend your ride. You could go left

Angostura Pass Road

to Paradise Road

END RIDE 36
to Gibraltar

to Arroyo Burro Road

27W19
Matias Trail

Angostura
Pass Road
(5N25)

Devils
Canyon
Trail

27W21

East Camino Cielo

START RIDE 36
Angostura Pass

to Romero Saddle

N
W — E
S

Gibraltar Road

(map not to scale)

■ Ride Start/Finish
— · — · Best 100 Routes
—————— Dirt Roads/Other Routes
- - - - - - Paved Roads
················ Off-Limits

to Santa Barbara ↓

©1999 Fine Edge Productions

here to continue to the dam and Red Rock Canyon (see Ride 37), or go right on Gibraltar Trail (also known as Old Mine Road) which then connects to Mono Canyon and the rest of the Upper Santa Ynez River area.

There are several other options by which you can connect Angostura Pass Road to other roads and trails. It could be done as an out-and-back addition to the Red Rock/Gibraltar Dam ride (see Ride 37). Or you could fashion a loop by turning off of Angostura Pass Road onto Matias Potrero Trail (27W19) (see Ride 39), taking the trail to Arroyo Burro Road

(Ride 38), climbing that road to Camino Cielo, and finally, hanging a left along Camino Cielo back to your car.

Or, for an 11.5-mile loop, you could take Matias Potrero Trail from Angostura Road, then take Devils Canyon Trail to Gibraltar Road, and finally Gibraltar Road back to Angostura Road for the climb to Camino Cielo. *Note:* Matias Potrero Trail is unsigned; look for it on the left 2 miles down Angostura Road from Camino Cielo. The junction with Devils Canyon Trail is 1.5 miles down Matias Potrero Trail.

Paradise Road/Lower Santa Ynez River

The Lower Santa Ynez River has some of the easiest and most pleasant mountain bike riding in this area of the coast. The Santa Ynez River runs all year and has many fine swimming holes. Shade is abundant and the campsites along Paradise Road have water, tables and convenient camping. Whether you stay a day or a week, you can explore the river bed and have strenuous, scenic workouts with the many rides described. The area has many different recreational possibilities, and the Los Prietos Ranger Station can give you detailed information on biking opportunities and current conditions; we recommend a quick check with them.

Access to this part of the Los Padres National Forest is via Paradise Road off of Highway 154 (San Marcos Pass Road).

37 Red Rock/Gibraltar Dam Trail

Distance: Loop is 7 miles; out-and-back to mine is 13 miles.
Difficulty: Easy to moderate; not technical.
Elevation: 750' gain/loss.
Ride Type: Loop ride on fire road and river trail; out-and-back on fire road with mine option; or add mine out-and-back to loop.
Season: Best in spring and summer; winter can be muddy.
Map: Little Pine Mountain.
Water: From creek; treat all water.
Comments: The trail changes each year, especially after a hard winter. Some years, particularly in spring, it can be more of a portage than a ride. If that sounds like too much work, you can ride out-and-back on the upper road.

Overview: The basic ride is east on 5N18 to the dam. From there, you can continue eastward to the mine, or drop to the river and loop back to the parking area on the river trail. This enjoyable loop has water crossings and opportunities for swimming in spring and summer, including the gorgeous Red Rock hole. The out-and-back to the old Sunbird Mercury Mine adds some fun singletracking to a great year-round ride.

Getting There: From Santa Barbara, take Highway 154 north for 11 miles to Paradise Road (5N18). Follow Paradise Road to its end and park in the picnic area there.

Route: If you just want to ride up to the swimming holes in Red Rock Canyon, ride from the day-use parking area at the end of Paradise Road to the river trail behind the metal gate, and head north up the canyon following an old wagon road.

For the loop, exit the parking lot to the south and head left uphill to a gate. The Gibraltar Dam Road (also 5N18) climbs above the parking lot and up to a ridge overlooking the Santa Ynez Canyon. This is the preferred way to go to the dam and beyond.

On this road, you climb moderately to a ridgetop with great views of the swimming holes in Red Rock Canyon and the mid-mountain area. (*Option:* A fabulous little singletrack comes in about 0.25 mile up the road on the right at a left-hand switchback. This is a nice option for your return ride if you decide to go back on 5N18 rather than the river trail. It would be mostly a push to take the trail up from here. It's easier ridden from its upper end at the saddle just past where Gibraltar Road levels out. Past the high point of the road, it drops steeply into Devils Canyon onto the bottom of Gibraltar Dam. Devils Canyon Trail (27W21) rises sharply out of the canyon bottom at the apex of the last turn, to the right.)

To complete the basic loop, go left toward the creek here and cross the river to the river trail. (A right up to the dam is a nice diversion and the way to go to add the mine route; see *Mine Option* below.) Take the river trail as it crosses below the dam and heads downstream. This crossing is often strewn with "babyheads" (cantaloupe-sized stones) that

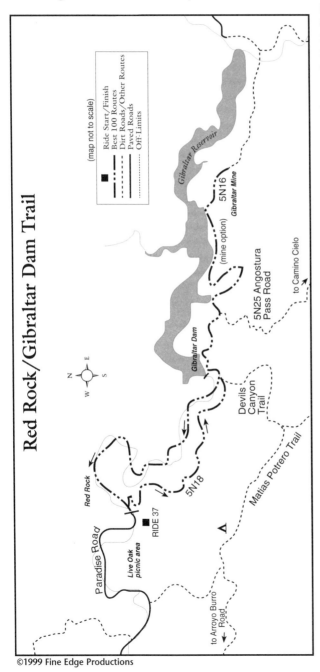

Red Rock/Gibraltar Dam Trail

(map not to scale)

Ride Start/Finish
Best 100 Routes
Dirt Roads/Other Routes
Paved Roads
Off-Limits

Gibraltar Reservoir

5N16
Gibraltar Mine

(mine option)

to Camino Cielo

5N25 Angostura Pass Road

Gibraltar Dam

Devils Canyon Trail

Matias Potrero Trail

Red Rock

5N18

RIDE 37

Live Oak picnic area

Paradise Road

to Arroyo Burro Road

Top of Arroyo Burro Road overlooking the lower Santa Ynez River

Jamie Griffis

make the riding difficult and challenging. In fact, many of the stream crossings will be so blessed—so get used to it! The river trail continues down the canyon with intermittent fast riding on the oak-shaded bluffs along the river and slow, torturous river crossings when it's easier to carry your bike than to try and ride. The sandstone cliffs plunge steeply down into the river past numerous rock outcroppings, examples of the faulting and folding processes which created this canyon.

After passing through oak and willow forests, about 1.5 miles up from the parking area, you come to one of the finest and most inviting pools anywhere. There are many long, deep pools here, the largest of which is over 100 yards long! Reeds and willows along the ponds draw waterfowl and small animals. If you're alert, you may spot wildlife in the quiet pools.

You continue to ford the river, negotiating fords which may or may not be rideable, depending on the previous season's weather. The last 0.25 mile of trail is strewn with gravel and rocks and follows an old wagon road back down to the parking/day use area.

Mine Option: For the longer option out to the old mine, climb the steep gravel road to the top of Gibraltar Dam and head right (east). As you approach the dam, keep clear of it and its equipment. Trespassing and loitering are prohibited. You pass the dam keeper's residence on the right. Next to a water tank on the left is a gate that is passable on the left. The main road, Angostura Road (5N25), goes east on up to the ridge and El Camino Cielo. Go around the gate and descend a rutted fire road. Cross Gridley Creek and climb to the west up an eroded road that is mostly a singletrack. You top out with a view of Gibraltar Reservoir. Continue 2.4 miles to the old mine works.

The USFS has posted warning signs around the site due to the possibility of mercury waste materials in the mine tailings. (They can be toxic, and even make you crazy like the Mad Hatter!) Also, there is some concern about the integrity of the old buildings.

The trail continues past the diggings to the left and toward the Mono Creek drainage. Turn around when you're ready and head back to the dam. This is the point where you can go left up the high road, 5N18, with the inviting little singletrack on your way down, or make the loop by going right on the river trail, with all that water and the swimming holes waiting for you. You choose.

38 Arroyo Burro Loop

Distance: 11 miles.
Difficulty: Moderate; trail is technical.
Elevation: 1,600' gain/loss.
Ride Type: Loop on singletrack and dirt road.
Season: Year-round, but winter can be muddy and summer can be hot.
Maps: San Marcos Pass, Little Pine Mountain.
Water: In Santa Ynez River and in creek; treat all water.
Comments: *Caution:* Beware of shooting activities along the east side of Arroyo Burro Road. Watch for poison oak on the trail.

Overview: Certain sections of the Arroyo Burro Trail are like a greenhouse, the plants forming a tunnel through which you ride. You also have the option of going to some swimming holes.

You can do this loop from either Paradise Road or Camino Cielo. We recommend starting at Paradise Road. That way, you get the fire road climb over with first, then finish with a singletrack downhill.

Getting There: To start at Paradise Road, take Highway 154 (San Marcos Pass Road) to Paradise Road and go east for 5 miles to the Lower Oso Picnic Area. Park here. You could also begin at Live Oak Picnic Area, farther east on Paradise Road.

To start at Camino Cielo, drive 5.5 miles on East Camino Cielo east of Highway 154. Arroyo Burro Saddle is a low point on the ridge several miles west of the radio repeaters on La Cumbre Peak. Arroyo Burro Road is past the shooting area to the northwest at a brown gate. You can also come up Gibraltar Road to Camino Cielo and turn left (west) for 5 miles.

Route: Take Paradise Road east for less than a mile, then turn right toward White Oaks Camp. Cross the river and head up Arroyo Burro Road (5N20). After 2.8 miles of climbing, you pass the signed Matias Potrero Trail (27W19) on your left.

From here, you have about 3 miles to the top at Camino Cielo. The Arroyo Burro Trail (27W13) takes off to your right 0.1 mile south of Camino Cielo. It's on the left in a shallow drainage—you have to look carefully to find it; however, 50 feet down the trail a metal sign reads: *Arroyo Burro Trail, White Oak Camp, Santa Ynez River Road 4 miles.*

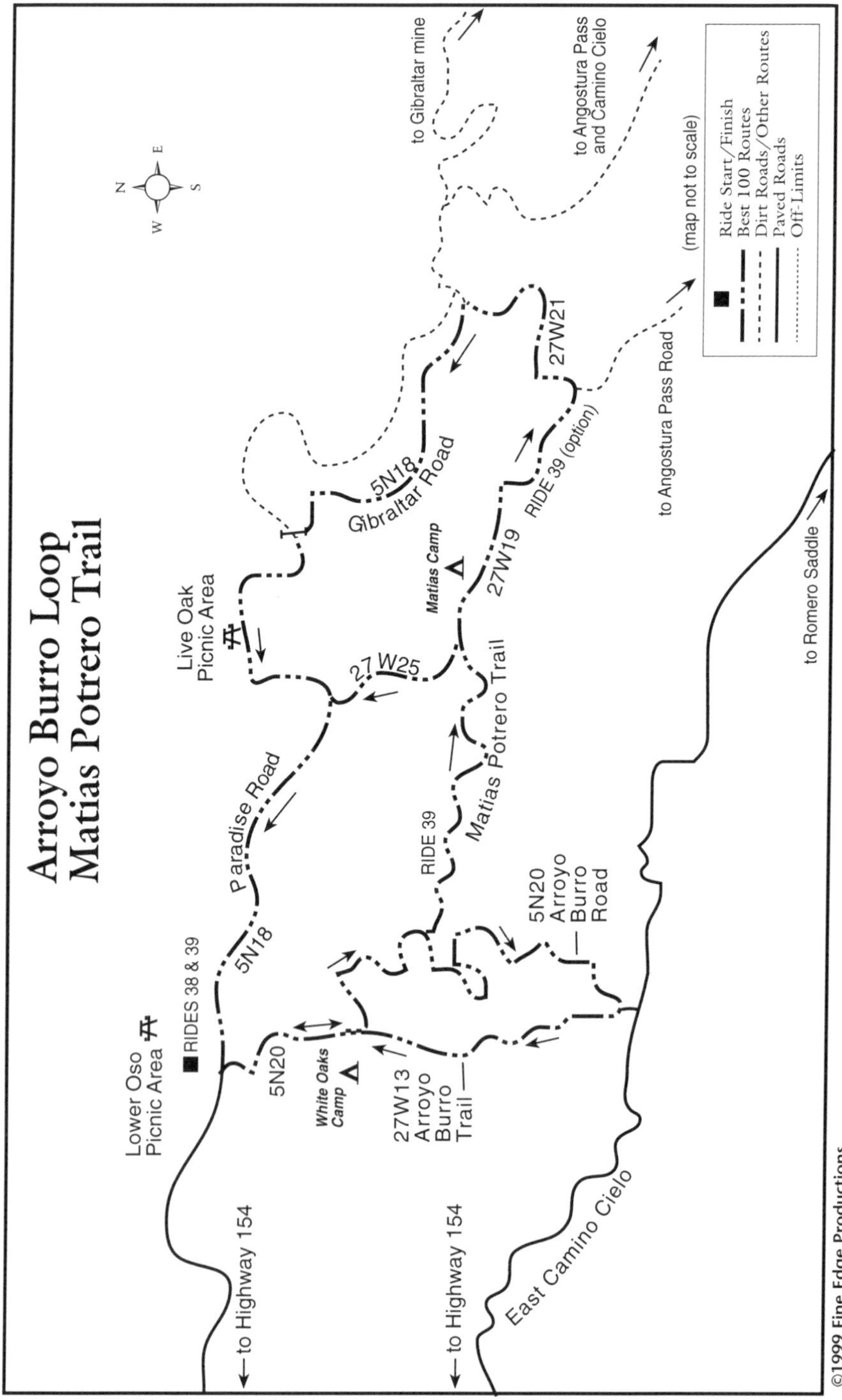

Arroyo Burro Loop
Matias Potrero Trail

to Gibraltar mine

to Angostura Pass
and Camino Cielo

N
W   E
S

(map not to scale)

■ ▪—▪—▪ Ride Start/Finish
— ▪ — ▪ — Best 100 Routes
— — — — Dirt Roads/Other Routes
———— Paved Roads
········· Off-Limits

to Angostura Pass Road

27W21

5N18
Gibraltar Road

RIDE 39 (option)

27W19

Matias Camp

Live Oak
Picnic Area

27 W25

Matias Potrero Trail

Paradise Road

RIDE 39

5N20
Arroyo
Burro
Road

RIDES 38 & 39

5N18

Lower Oso
Picnic Area

5N20

White Oaks
Camp

27W13
Arroyo
Burro
Trail—

to Highway 154

to Highway 154

to Romero Saddle

East Camino Cielo

©1999 Fine Edge Productions

The Arroyo Burro Trail starts out in chaparral but soon enters an area of ferns and other plants growing under trees. About 1.2 miles down the trail, a small creek from the east crosses the trail. Below this creek, the trail follows a pattern of good trail that leads away from the creek bed and then suddenly comes to a very steep "walk-only" descent over boulders. This is repeated with variations so often that you never really dare to let go on the good sections.

At 2.4 miles on the trail, go right across the stream, then left on Arroyo Burro Road. High voltage lines cross over Arroyo Burro Road and the trailhead here.

Continue down Arroyo Burro Road for about a mile to the river. From here, you can head upstream to find some swimming holes. After a break and a swim, head down Arroyo Burro Road to Paradise Road. A left turn takes you back to your car.

39 Matias Potrero Trail

Distance: Loops of 10.5 miles and 18 miles.
Difficulty: Difficult; technical with some steep, rough spots.
Elevation: 1,900' to 3,000' with lots of ups and downs.
Ride Type: Loop on dirt road, singletrack and pavement.
Season: Year-round, but winter can be muddy.
Map: Little Pine Mountain.
Water: None.

Overview: Matias Potrero is a horizontal band of meadowland situated between Arroyo Burro Road (5N20), and Angostura Road (5N25), 4 miles east. Its location, half-way down the steep north slope of La Cumbre Peak and cut by many narrow, parallel canyons, makes it an unusual potrero (meadow).

Matias Potrero Trail traverses the mountain side through English rye grass. The grasses are so thick and tall that, in some places, the trail is hidden from view and shows only as a dark line ahead. The trail, so level-looking on maps, actually descends into and climbs out of every narrow canyon it crosses. Although the elevation doesn't change much, these 100- to 300-foot climbs add up.

The trail is the main part of an interconnected trail and road system that allows you to chose many different loops or connected trail rides in the area. As long as you don't have to be somewhere at a particular time, it's possible to make up a route as you go on these short trail sections.

Getting There: Take Highway 154 (San Marcos Pass Road) to Paradise Road and go east for 5 miles to the Lower Oso Picnic Area. Park here. (You could also begin at Live Oak Picnic Area, farther east on Paradise Road.)

Route: Take Paradise Road east for less than 1 mile and turn right toward White Oaks Camp. Cross the river and head up Arroyo Burro Road for 2.8 miles. Look for the signed Matias Potrero Trail (27W19) on your left above a grassy saddle. From here, the trail crosses five canyons in 2.5 miles and meets trail 27W25 on a ridge under some powerlines.

For the 10-mile loop, turn left onto trail 27W25, actually a powerline road, which descends steeply north along a ridge, dropping 510 feet in one mile to the Santa Ynez river and to paved Paradise Road. This trail comes out at a brown gate marked: *Fire Road, do not block.*

Caution: This last section of the trail is very steep. The trail drops directly down to Paradise Road, 0.25 mile below Live Oak Day Use Area, 50 yards above where the road splits in two sections around a tree in the middle of the road. Go left to take Paradise Road back to your car at Lower Oso, or go right if you parked at Live Oak.

For the longer loop, continue east past the junction with trail 27W25. You climb a short hill under the powerlines. From the road here, you can see quite a way east into the next two canyons which are much larger than those to the west. Matias Trail Camp is located down in the first canyon, just a short way from trail 27W25. About 2.0 miles farther east, you reach the junction of Matias Potrero Trail and Devils Canyon Trail (27W21).

(From this intersection, Matias Potrero Trail climbs steeply—950 feet in 1.6 miles—from Devils Canyon to Angostura Road. It is so steep that if you opt for this route, you will push more than you will ride.)

The preferred route is to head left on Devils Canyon Trail (27W21). It heads north, then east, across a ridge before dropping down into Devils Canyon. It then descends in the canyon to Gidney Flat and Gibraltar Road (5N18) below Gibraltar Dam. From here, the easiest route back to your car is to go left on 5N18 to Paradise Road. Continue west on Paradise Road back to Lower Oso Picnic Area. For variations on this return route, see Ride 37.

Note: You can also access Matias Potrero Trail by dropping down from Camino Cielo on Angostura Road or Arroyo Burro Road. It would probably be best to descend Angostura Road, go left on Matias Potrero Trail to Arroyo Burro Road, then left and up to Camino Cielo and your car. (See Rides 36 and 38 for more details.)

40 Aliso Canyon Trail

Distance: 3.5 miles.
Difficulty: Easy to moderate; mildly technical.
Elevation: 200' gain/loss.
Ride Type: Singletrack loop on interpretive trail.
Season: Year-round.
Map: San Marcos Pass.
Water: At Sage Hill Campground.
Comments: This area gets a lot of equestrian use, so be on your best behavior.

Overview: Aliso Canyon Trail is a pretty little ride through riparian and chaparral habitats and can be extended with some pavement, or added to rides originating at Lower Oso Picnic Area for some singletrack excitement.

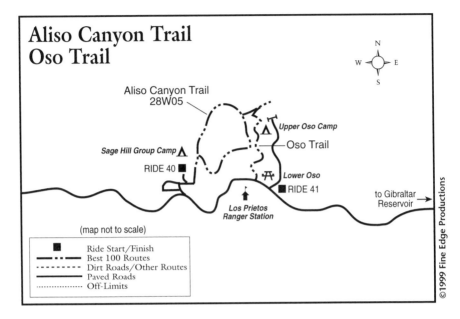

Aliso Canyon Trail
Oso Trail

Aliso Canyon Trail
28W05

Sage Hill Group Camp

RIDE 40

Upper Oso Camp

Oso Trail

Lower Oso

RIDE 41

Los Prietos
Ranger Station

to Gibraltar
Reservoir

(map not to scale)

Ride Start/Finish
━ ･ ━ ･ ━ Best 100 Routes
---------- Dirt Roads/Other Routes
━━━━━ Paved Roads
············· Off-Limits

©1999 Fine Edge Productions

Getting There: Turn off Paradise Road (5N18) at the Los Prietos Ranger Station, 15.1 miles from Highway 101 via San Marcos Pass Road (Highway 154). During the busy season you will need to pay a use-fee at the kiosk here, usually only collected on holidays and Friday through Sunday. It is nominal ($3) and supports maintenance of the recreation area.

Go west beyond the ranger station 0.6 mile to the Sage Hill Group Campground by turning right at the river's edge. Cross the creek bottom, keep right and go to the parking lot (room for 30 cars).

Route: Trail sign near the restroom reads: *28W05 Welcome to Aliso Canyon—we welcome you to come explore with us.* The guided nature trail starting here has a number of stops which point out the unique features of this chaparral environment. Pick up a guide booklet at the right side of the sign to use in interpreting

the natural sites you visit in the one mile up the creek.

The trail starts at the USFS gate (use the bicycle pass-through) and heads up the sandy trail on the west side of the canyon. You may elect to do a one-mile out-and-back, the loop, or continue east from the ridge to come out at Upper Oso Campground next to site #25.

Option 1: If you choose the last route, return to Sage Hill by road from Upper Oso Campground by riding downhill, across Oso Creek, and exiting the campground downhill. At Lower Oso Picnic Area, turn right, cross the Santa Ynez River, and continue back to the Los Prietos Ranger Station and Sage Hill Campground. This would add about 2 paved miles to the basic 3.5-mile loop. You could also add the Oso Trail on your way down from Upper Oso (see following ride).

Option 2: If you wish to start at Upper Oso Campground (less climbing), cross to Campsite #25 on the west side of the campground. Twenty feet left of the picnic table, look for a small trail which heads west (uphill) 50 yards to a fence line with a sign for 28W05. Park to the south in the group parking lot (12-car capacity).

28W05 goes up alongside Oso Creek for about a mile. Then, after much boulder-hopping, it reaches Santa Cruz Trail. If you go left at the fence, you must look for the sidehill connector to Aliso Trail.

41 Oso Trail

Distance: 1 mile.
Difficulty: Easy to moderate; good introduction to singletrack.
Elevation: 200' gain/loss.
Ride Type: Up-and-back on singletrack, or loop with paved Oso Road.
Season: Year-round, but winter can be muddy.
Map: San Marcos Pass.
Water: At Oso Campground and Lower Oso day-use area.

Overview: This fun little trail is off Oso Road just past the bridge over Oso Creek.

Getting There: Park at the Lower Oso Day Use Area off Paradise Road just past the river crossing.

Route: The trail goes left, crosses a small creek, and continues through some small potreros to Upper Oso Campground. You can add a little more trail action by going through the campground and looking for a trail that continues up across a little meadow and heads up to the trees along Oso Creek.

Continuing along this singletrack, you eventually reach 28W05. As noted in the previous ride, this trail meanders along and across Oso Creek, ultimately reaching Santa Cruz Trail (27W09). This cross-trail is about 0.75 mile past Oso Campground. Return the way you came or via Oso Road.

42 Camuesa Road/ Camuesa Connector Loop

Distance: 12-mile loop; Camuesa Peak option adds 6.8 miles.
Difficulty: Moderate to strenuous; moderately technical.
Elevation: 1,800' gain/loss.
Ride Type: Loop on dirt road, singletrack and pavement.
Season: Year-round; winter can be muddy, summer can be hot.
Maps: San Marcos Pass, Little Pine Mountain.
Water: Upper Oso Campground; springs at Hidden Potrero; treat all water.
Comments: This road is open to off-road motorcycles

Camuesa Road/Camuesa Connector Loop

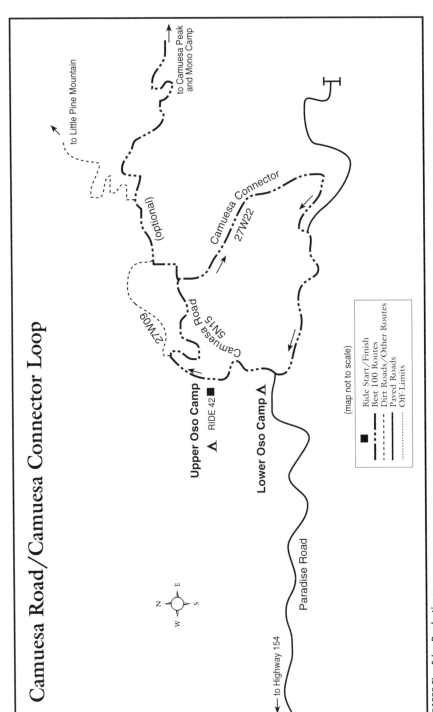

to Little Pine Mountain

to Camuesa Peak
and Mono Camp

Camuesa Connector
27W22

(optional)

27W09

Camuesa Road
5N15

Upper Oso Camp
△ RIDE 42 ■

Lower Oso Camp △

Paradise Road

to Highway 154

N
E
S
W

(map not to scale)

■ Ride Start/Finish
— Best 100 Routes
—··— Dirt Roads/Other Routes
—— Paved Roads
········ Off-Limits

Overview: Camuesa, pronounced Ka-moose-ah, is derived from "gamusa," which means buckskin or deer hide in Chumash. This well-graded road heads east from Upper Oso Campground, climbing and descending the canyon north of the Santa Ynez River to get around Gibraltar Reservoir. Camuesa Road, the area's main access road, has connection points with many other roads and trails.

Getting There: From Paradise Road, take the paved road to the parking area on the northern side of Upper Oso Campground.

Route: Ride around the east side of the locked gate. At this point you enter a narrow canyon hemmed in by rock ledges where there is barely enough room for the creek and the road.

After an easy 0.7 mile, you come to the first switchback. (Santa Cruz Trail (27W09) starts here at a sign listing mileages. This trail is heavily used by horses and hikers so be courteous.) From this junction, Camuesa Road, your route, climbs in a series of steep and not-so-steep switchbacks to a high point on the south side of Oso Canyon.

It is 2.9 miles from Upper Oso to the turn-off for Camuesa Connector Trail (27W22) on the right (south), down and across a meadow. *Option:* About 0.5 mile past Camuesa Connector, the old mine road is on the left. It switchbacks down to 19 Oaks Camp, located off the Santa Cruz Trail. Taking this road down and south back to Upper Oso makes a nice, technical singletrack loop of about 7 miles.

To do the 12-mile loop with Camuesa Connector (27W22), turn right at the meadow. Trail 27W22 climbs over several small saddles and features some tight switchbacks on its way east and down to the Santa Ynez River. *Caution:* There are commercial quantities of poison oak on this trail.

Beyond the first mile, the trail eases considerably. You climb up and down three small mesa-like hills through tall grass and the ever-present poison oak. A hike-a-bike across the rocky streambed leads to paved Paradise Road. A right turn and 3 miles of pedaling take you to Lower Oso. From there, it's another 1.3 miles up to the Upper Oso parking area.

Options: 1) If you decide not to loop it, you could continue up Camuesa Road all the way to Mono Camp (see Ride 35). 2) An out-and-back option would be to go to Camuesa Peak and then catch the Connector Trail on the way back to Upper Oso. At 4.4 miles from the starting gate, you reach Hidden Potrero. This small camp is located on the left and features 2 tables, fireplaces and water piped from a spring of unknown quality. At 4.7 miles, you reach a high saddle and the Buckhorn Road junction to the left. Here you can see Camuesa Road heading east for about two miles, dropping and climbing to another lower saddle. Head right to stay on Camuesa Road.

At 6.4 miles, to the right is an old road that climbs out to the site of Camuesa Peak lookout. It's 2 miles and another 300 feet up to the peak, but the view is worth the effort. You can continue to Mono Camp or backtrack the way you came.

43 Little Pine Mountain

Distance: 23.2 miles.
Difficulty: Moderate; good road but long climb.
Elevation: 1,200' to 4,400'; 3,200' gain/loss.
Ride Type: Out-and-back on dirt roads.
Season: Year-round; winter rain may force closure.
Maps: San Marcos Pass, Little Pine Mountain.
Water: Upper Oso Campground.
Comments: Watch for motor vehicles on this ride. This is a designated motorcycle route and a major backcountry access road for official vehicles. These mountains can be treacherous during the winter. Heavy rain in early 1995 caused a massive landslide that took out the road in five places above the second switchback where the road zigzags up the mountain.

Overview: This is a very popular route due to the good roads and spectacular views. It is a fairly strenuous ride because of the elevation gain, but the variations in grade and terrain keep it interesting. Frequent rest stops also provide opportunities for photography, map reading, and viewing the changing perspective of the backcountry.

Getting There: From Highway 154 (San Marcos Pass Road), drive east on Paradise Road past the ranger station and cross the Santa Ynez River (one-way concrete ford) to Lower Oso Picnic Area. Here take the narrow paved road on the left (north) uphill into Oso Canyon. When you come to the campground, keep right to the Camuesa Road locked gate. Park in the Upper Oso Parking Area, not in the campsites.

Route: The first part of this ride is 4.7 miles up Camuesa Road (5N15) to Buckhorn Road. From the northeast side of Upper Oso Camp, go around the east side of the locked gate. From this point, you head east to enter a narrow canyon hemmed in by rock ledges where there is barely enough room for the creek and a road. After an easy 0.7-mile ride, you come to the first switchback. (Santa Cruz Trail (27W09) starts here and there is a sign listing mileages and a sign-in log for trail users. It is an extremely steep trail, heavily used by hikers and equestrians.)

From this junction, your route, Camuesa Road, climbs the mountainside with five more switchbacks beneath oak trees before traversing the south side of Oso Canyon heading east. Although the climbing is not very steep, the mountain is almost a vertical cliff and the road must have been blasted out of solid rock. This is around the 2-mile mark and here you must be very careful of the edge.

You level out some at 2.9 miles where the Camuesa Connector Trail starts down on the right across a meadow. Here you have crossed to the south side of the ridge and the climbing is easier between the north side of the meadow and the ridgetop. After about a mile, the ridge gets much steeper and the road switchbacks and turns to the north to cross back over to the north side of the ridge.

Where you cross this small saddle, there is a remarkable peaked rock on the left that glistens in the sunlight. Just ahead at 4.5 miles, a trail on the

Little Pine Mountain

▲ Little Pine Mountain

⋀ Happy Hollow

to Lower Buckhorn →

N
W — E
S

Buckhorn Road

Nineteen Oaks ⋀

Road

⋀

to Middle Camuesa →

Hidden Potrero Camp

East Camuesa

5N15

Upper ⋀ Oso ■
RIDE 43

Lower ⋀ Oso

Paradise Road

← to 154

to Gibraltar Reservoir →

(map not to scale)

■	Ride Start/Finish
▬ ▬	Best 100 Routes
------	Dirt Roads/Other Routes
▬▬▬	Paved Roads
··········	Off-Limits

©1999 Fine Edge Productions

left goes down at first and then levels past a fenced bog and on to Hidden Potrero Camp on the east side of the bog. This site has one table and fireplace next to the road at 4.6 miles from Upper Oso.

Only 0.2 mile more and you are at the junction with Buckhorn Road and the high point of East Camuesa Road, 2,797 feet. Take Buckhorn Road north (left). Although not level, the first 1.6 miles is fast, with up-and-

down grades that deposit you 150 feet lower than the junction. Next you have a steep one-mile climb up a south-facing bluff where, on a hot day, the sun is cruel. On the north side past this bluff, the road is not as steep as it passes through the shade of oak trees. Out around another ridge you pass Buckhorn Trail (27W12) below on the right. That trail starts a little farther up the road, marked by a sign, 9.1 miles from Upper Oso Camp.

Buckhorn Road near Little Pine Mountain

The road keeps climbing along the ridge heading west and you soon encounter the first pine trees after a short switchback. You come to Little Pine Mountain Junction next to a concrete rainwater tank. Take the signed road left (southwest) which soon levels out and descends through oak and pine forest to Happy Hollow Trail Camp. This campsite with tables and fireplaces is located in a natural hollow filled with large trees. There is no water here, however; the nearest source is at Little Pine Spring Trail Camp about a mile north on the Santa Cruz Trail.

A short distance west, on a trail that connects to the Santa Cruz Trail, you come out of the trees and can look over the south side of Little Pine Mountain. Far below you can see Camuesa Road; the steep Santa Cruz Trail is closer. Return the way you came up and enjoy the descent! Use safe speeds and watch for other travelers.

West Camino Cielo/Gaviota

The western part of Camino Cielo has more limited riding opportunities than the eastern part due to the large number of ranches and other private holdings both to the north and south of the road. However, it does offer a mostly all-dirt route between San Marcos and Refugio passes. And stunning views! This is an area to explore at your leisure, to gain insight into the wonders of Santa Barbara geology, or just plain have fun.

44 West Camino Cielo

Distance: 20 miles one way.
Difficulty: Moderate; rocky, rough dirt road; long distance.
Elevation: 1,850' gain; 2,220' loss.
Ride Type: Best as shuttle, or ride out and back as far as you like.
Season: Year-round, but winter can be muddy.
Maps: Lake Cachuma, San Marcos Pass, Santa Ynez.
Water: None.

Overview: Plan to ride here on a clear day. The views—across the Santa Ynez Valley and down to Lake Cachuma to the north and along the coast, to Goleta, the ocean and the Channel Islands to the south—cast a spell on you and make you want to return.

Getting There: If you can talk someone into dropping you off at Refugio Pass, you can do a one-way down to San Marcos Pass and make a pretty easy day of it. Otherwise, you need to arrange a shuttle. You can leave one vehicle at San Marcos Pass or, to add the fun downhill on Old San Marcos Pass Road (Highway 192), leave your pick-up vehicle at Tucker's Grove County Park, located on Cathedral Oaks Road between Old San Marcos Pass Road and Highway 154.

To get to the ride start, take Refugio Pass Road north from Highway 101 to Refugio Pass.

Route: From the pass, ride east uphill 5.7 miles on 5N19 to an observatory on Santa Ynez Peak, the highest point of the trip. This narrow, winding road has little traffic; even less when the USFS gates are locked at 1.0 and 1.7 miles.

Past the observatory, West Camino Cielo continues east as a dirt road for 10.3 miles, most of it in long, easy downhill sections on the south side of the ridge. You're in a lot of bright sun, but the ocean breezes hold down the heat.

Radio and microwave antennae are conspicuous on the peaks between the observatory and Broadcast Peak, at 6.5 miles. Downhill from Broadcast Peak, the rough and rocky road requires concentration and slow speed. A small yellow sign: *Closed to motor vehicles,* marks the easy-to-miss Tequepis Trail (29W06), 1.5 miles east of Broadcast Peak on the north side of the road. (See the following ride for a description of this trail.)

The road crosses to the north side of the ridge where it is much improved, with fewer rocks and ruts. It climbs slightly to a rise where you can see a pine basin ahead. A good resting spot, 11 miles from Refugio Pass, this pine grove is probably a remnant of forest left after weather changes almost eliminated these trees.

The next 4 miles have more traffic, with gun enthusiasts target-shooting and a motorcycle area south of the road. A one-mile steep, rocky climb with one switchback puts you at the eastern USFS gate and the paved road to Highway 154. *Caution:* This is a fast downhill, so be aware of traffic. Along the road, 1.0 mile from the highway, notice the large rock with small caves which looks like a grotesque, petrified carved pumpkin.

The eastern end of West Camino

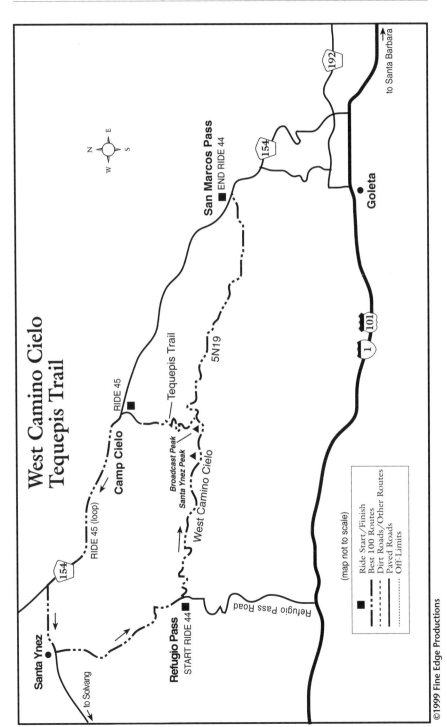

West Camino Cielo
Tequepis Trail

©1999 Fine Edge Productions

Cielo lies on the west side of Highway 154, 0.7 mile south of San Marcos Pass at milepost 25.22. Old San Marcos Pass Road is better suited for bicycle traffic than Highway 154. It comes in across from Painted Cave Road. Steep and pot-holed, it is a blast to ride down with tight, hairpin switchbacks to negotiate. It drops down to Cathedral Oaks Road (Highway 192) just west of Tucker's Grove County Park.

45 Tequepis Trail

Distance: 5.5-mile trail, 32-mile loop.
Difficulty: Moderate to strenuous; trail is technical.
Elevation: As much as 3,300' gain/loss.
Ride Type: Up-and-back on singletrack; loop with paved and dirt roads, singletrack; shuttle option.
Season: Year-round, but summer can be hot and winter can be muddy.
Maps: Santa Ynez, Lake Cachuma.
Water: None.
Comments: Camp Cielo is operated by the Ventura County Camp Fire under permit from Los Padres National Forest. The camp personnel are friendly, but you should ask permission to pass through their area. Respect their private property and their activities. Please do not interfere or loiter. For permission to cross their property, call the Camp Fire Headquarters in Oxnard at 805/485-3417.

Overview: It's best to ride down the Tequepis Trail; however, you can start or end anywhere in the loop. If you leave your car at a lower elevation, you can coast back downhill should the going be tougher than you expected. The routes described below are the out-and-back and a west loop. An east loop is possible by parking at Highway 154 and the lower Tequepis trailhead. Go east on Highway 154 and take Old Pass Road up to San Marcos Pass and then to West Camino Cielo. Head west on Camino Cielo to Tequepis Trail and down to your car. A shuttle is also possible by leaving one vehicle at the lower Tequepis trailhead and driving a second vehicle to Refugio Pass.

Getting There: The most difficult trailhead to find on this scenic loop is the lower Tequepis trailhead. One-half-mile east of Lake Cachuma Recreation Area (about 11 miles west of San Marcos Pass), turn south (left if you're headed west) off Highway 154 at the Camp Cielo sign. The road immediately becomes a bumpy dirt road going uphill. Proceed up past several private camps—all posted: *Keep Out.*

A half-mile from Highway 154, the road becomes a single lane. Within 1.1 miles, and just after crossing the stream bed, look for a small parking area (room for six cars) and the Tequepis Trail sign. This area is located just below Camp Cielo's wooden gate. The sign at this point is confusing. Do not take the fire road to the right but stay on the paved trail. About 100 yards past the swimming pool, as the road switchbacks right up to the camp headquarters, a larger USFS sign says: *Camino Cielo 4 miles.* The trail is the dirt road which continues up the canyon past the camping huts.

Route: *For the out-and-back,* start at the lower Tequepis trailhead. Above the camp, follow the trail as it climbs steeply up the north side of Broadcast Peak. Beware of water pipes and support cables which cross the trail. The trail passes the canyon waterfall, and striking views of Lake Cachuma and the surrounding country increase as you go. *Note:* Several service trails branch off to the right of Tequepis Trail. Stay on the main trail which climbs upward and generally is the left one going up the lower canyon. The trail tops out on the Santa Ynez Ridge at West Camino Cielo, 0.25 mile east of the easternmost radio antenna of Broadcast Peak.

You could turn right and head down Camino Cielo and north on Refugio to Highway 154, but if you've struggled up Tequepis you might as well ride back down! Enjoy!

For the west loop, start at the lower Tequepis trailhead. Backtrack to Highway 154 and head west toward Solvang. *Caution:* The shoulder of Highway 154 is narrow and cars travel at high speeds on this stretch.

At the junction with Highway 246, turn left toward Solvang and make your way to Refugio Pass Road in the town of Santa Ynez. Head south (left) on Refugio. This is a pleasant pedal, 7.6 miles up to Refugio Pass at 2,254 feet. (In fact, novice riders can have a nice ride by starting in Santa Ynez and riding up to the pass and back.) On your way to the pass, you cross the Santa Ynez River on a bridge and splash through a few crossings of Quiota Creek. The road is paved for about 5 miles then becomes dirt.

There is a pretty oak grove at the top of the pass and a junction with West Camino Cielo (paved). Go left. Along this part of West Camino Cielo, several peaks have radio antennae. Broadcast Peak is 6.5 miles from Refugio Pass and 13.5 miles from San Marcos Pass. There are no major antennae east of Broadcast Peak.

The upper Tequepis trailhead can be difficult to find; it is located 1.5 miles east of Broadcast Peak near an old Closed to Vehicles sign located on the north side of the road. The trail climbs shortly through brush to the north side of the ridge and turns west before starting downhill. You can see switchbacks below you from this point. The trail follows the very steep ridge directly north of Broadcast Peak.

About 2.5 miles down the trail, another trail branches east. Keep left, continuing down into Tequepis Canyon. Soon after crossing the creek, you enter Camp Fire Camp Cielo property. Be sure and phone ahead for permission to pass. Your car should be waiting for you at the bottom of the road, off Highway 154, at 32 miles.

46 Gaviota State Park

Distance: Varies.
Difficulty: Easy to moderate.
Elevation: 640-foot gain from north parking lot to tunnel overlook.
Ride Type: Various loops on dirt roads and trails.
Season: Year-round; winter can be muddy
Maps: Solvang, Gaviota.
Water: In campground and Las Cruces parking area.

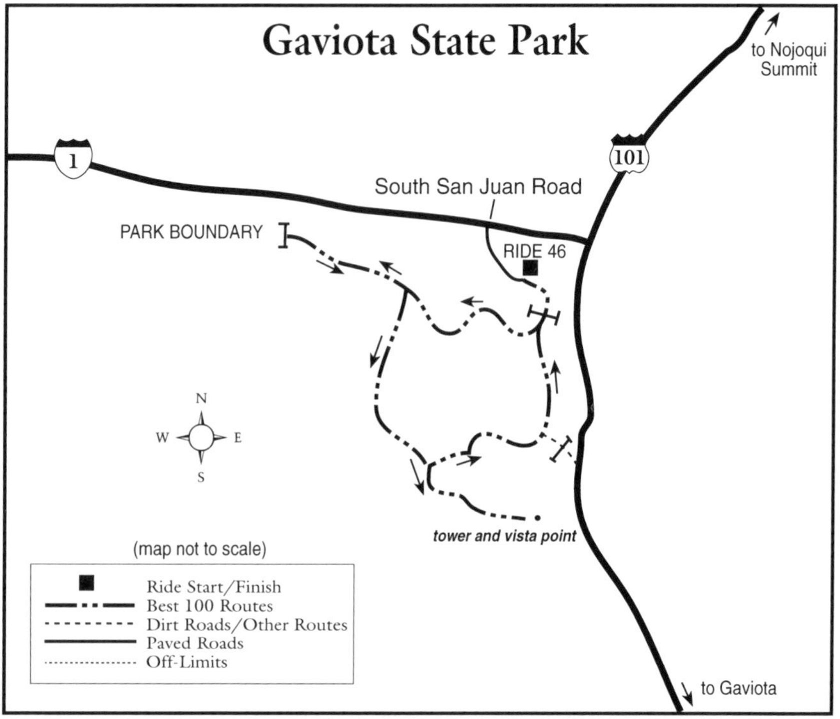

Gaviota State Park

to Nojoqui Summit

South San Juan Road

PARK BOUNDARY

RIDE 46

1

101

N
W — E
S

(map not to scale)

tower and vista point

■   Ride Start/Finish
— ·· —   Best 100 Routes
- - - - -   Dirt Roads/Other Routes
———   Paved Roads
·············   Off-Limits

to Gaviota

©1999 Fine Edge Productions

Overview: Gaviota State Park, 36 miles west of Santa Barbara, is located on both sides of Highway 101, extending from the beach north to Highway 1. The State Beach Campground is well known and very popular. Less well-known are the hot springs in the northeastern part of the park and the roads from there up into Las Padres National Forest to Gaviota Peak and beyond. (See the following ride.)

Almost unknown is the Las Cruces Unit in the northwestern part of the park. Here 6 miles of graded roads pass through grass and oak-covered hills. Summer ocean breezes and fog cool the air. The dominant wind which can be very strong is

from the north. You can see evidence of the wind's direction by the way the oaks grow in exposed places—all downwind. The park rangers are encouraging bicycle riding here.

Getting There: Take the Highway 1 exit off U.S. 101, 2 miles north of the Gaviota State Park entrance. Head west (toward Lompoc) 0.6 mile to the San Juan Road south, passing El Rancho Arbolado on the right. There is a school west of here, but you go east to a new parking area with restrooms and water. This lot services the Las Cruces Adobe as well as the trails in the hills above. Park here.

Route: Head up the hill to your

right. There is a fire gate with a sign: *Fire Road—keep clear.* You can ride a 4-mile loop in either direction that connects with two spur roads, each about a mile long. Riding the whole loop with spurs is 8 miles.

To ride in a counterclockwise direction starting from the gate, keep right, pass a gas pipeline valve assembly on the left, and start a fire road climb that gains about 480 feet in 1.25 miles. This climb occurs in three stages with a level rest area in between. At the top is the first junction. Here a less-traveled spur road with grass growing in the middle starts right (north) and continues on the south side of a ridge, leading to the western boundary of the park—a nice 1.0-mile ride that ends at a gate. Return the same way to the fork. *Caution:* Beware of waterbars—ditches cut across the road to drain water off the hillsides.

To continue the loop, follow the main road south, climbing very steeply up a short hill. Here you should see a road descending to the south. There are gas and oil pipeline signs along here. Two more climbs and descents, and after 1.25 miles on this ridge, the road turns left (east). This starts a sometimes steep descent with deep waterbars.

Under oak trees, 0.2 mile below the ridge, the road forks again. Here, the second spur, Tunnel Overlook Road, begins. It climbs to the right (south), switchbacks to the east, and follows a ridgetop out to the end at a radio tower. A small opening in the brush east of the tower leads out to a rock cliff. Here there's a dizzying view almost straight down to Highway 101. (If you're afraid of heights, the Gaviota Tunnel should be avoided—it's really scary in the fog, with the sound of nothing but traffic below.) Back to the main loop road is about 0.7 mile.

Back at the fork, head downhill (north), then east on a twisting steep downhill with more deep waterbars. After a short, easy climb around a hill, more downhill leads to the highway. Near a large highway bridge, this road ends at another gate. Past this gate a paved drive enters Highway 101. *Caution:* Don't go this way unless you are riding south on the highway.

To get back to your starting point, follow a pipeline road north which starts just where the main dirt road turns and heads steeply downhill past some gas installations near the gate. At first the road is not very apparent, but it is the only road parallel to the highway. If you stand next to the gas devices and look uphill, the way back is to the right where the road turns left.

Follow this poor road back to the north gate (0.75 mile). At 0.2 mile, this road leaves the pipeline near a huge fallen oak and heads downhill to the right a short way. Paralleling the highway again, the road gets easier as it crosses a field of tall weeds and joins the road on which you started near the north gate. This road is more of a trail here and can get very rutted after winter rains. Looking back at the trail from the main road, you can hardly tell the roads from the weeds: the main road heads south from the level area just before the fenced gas pipeline valve assembly. Turn right on the road to return to your car.

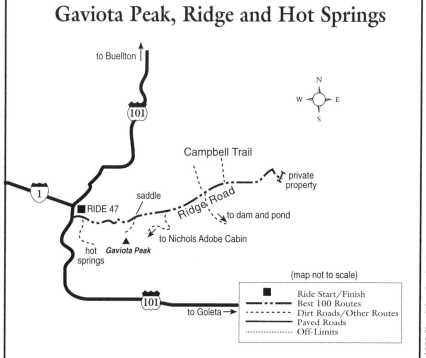

Gaviota Peak, Ridge and Hot Springs

47 Gaviota Peak, Ridge and Hot Springs

Distance: 0.5 mile to the hot springs; 3.5 miles to Gaviota Peak; 5 miles along ridge road; all one way.
Difficulty: Moderate to strenuous; not technical.
Elevation: 2,400' gain/loss.
Ride Type: Out-and-back on dirt roads and trail.
Season: Year-round, but winter can be muddy.
Map: Solvang.
Water: None.

Overview: There are three ride options in the northeast section of Gaviota State Park which can be combined in different ways. Whether you ride up to Gaviota Peak or out on Gaviota Ridge—or both, a stop at the hot springs on the way back is a must. Or you can add the quick jaunt to the springs onto other rides in the area.

For years the hot springs were semi-private, visited by those in the know who were willing to trespass to soak in the hot pools. Now they are owned by the State and very popular. A hot soak is just the cure for all the trail dust and aches and pains of climbing Gaviota Peak. State law requires clothing.

Gaviota Pass, Gaviota State Park

Getting There: Take the Highway 1 exit from U.S. 101, drive east to the frontage road and turn right (south). The parking area is at the end of this road. You will be asked to pay a fee at the self-registration box. There is an outhouse here as well. This is a day-use area only—no overnight parking.

Route: At the south end of the parking lot a marked trail heads steeply uphill beyond a fire gate. There is an unmarked road up about 0.25 mile from the gate that branches south around Gaviota Peak. (Exploring this road yielded some nice singletrack and could be fun if the climb to the peak is too arduous.)

Take the left fork; at 0.4 mile, near a water pump and creek crossing, the main road turns left and the hot springs trail takes off to the right. There should be a sign here for the hot springs, which are uphill, sometimes steeply, through lush growth—including massive quantities of poison

oak. At the end of this trail you find your reward: an upper pool (semi-hot) and a lower, larger pool (warm). But, first—the peak!

Keep left on the road to climb Gaviota Peak.

One mile from the parking lot, you pass around the north side of an unsigned gate. After many switchbacks, at 1.7 miles, a USFS sign announces entry to the Los Padres Forest. There are good views here out over the Santa Ynez Valley. Continue climbing in the uppermost part of the north-sloping canyon to the ridgetop east of Gaviota Peak. This road joins Gaviota Ridge Road at a deep saddle with Gaviota Peak on the right (west), then continues a very steep climb for another 0.2 mile. At the peak, there is a register in a can under a cairn.

Enjoy the view. When you're ready, backtrack to Gaviota Ridge Road. (If you're pooped, you can now head back to the trail to the hot springs that you passed earlier.) If not, the ridge road has such great views on clear days it's worth the climb. With boats, ships, oil platforms and the islands, the view can be downright distracting. From Gaviota Peak, you can ride the ridge road 5 miles east, climbing to a high point of 2,850 feet and ending at private property at 2,600 feet. Ride this area when it's too hot in the backcountry. Because of its elevation and proximity to the ocean, flowers bloom "out of season" here.

[**Side trip:** There is a partially brushed-out but passable old trail that leads southeast to the site of Nichols Adobe Cabin. The cabin site near a spring is shown on USFS maps and is accessible by a spur road which branches south from the ridge road, 1.2 miles east of Gaviota Peak.]

The road along the ridge, east from the peak, repeatedly climbs and descends steeply. This turns an easy 350 foot net elevation gain into a difficult struggle. At 1.8 miles from Gaviota Peak, the Campbell Trail (signed) descends northwest from another deep saddle. Just opposite this trailhead, a road descends south a short way before turning east, passing a dam and pond. Another hard climb brings you to the high point of the ridge road. Just south of the beacon peak, you can see a poor road that heads north and passes west of this peak before descending steeply on a ridge toward the northwest.

Continuing on the ridge road, you now enter an area of oak groves with few steep hills. This is the most pleasant part of the road and gives excellent views of the Santa Ynez Valley and Solvang. Farther east, the road descends through a very rough and rocky area that you must climb back up to return. Might as well turn back here since you cannot travel through to Refugio Pass Road across the private land ahead. The only return route is the way you came. You've definitely earned a soak in the hot springs now!

Figueroa Mountain

Figueroa Mountain, 25 miles northwest of Santa Barbara, sits on the north side of Santa Ynez Valley. This wide pastoral valley with rolling, grass-covered hills and scattered oak trees is in sharp contrast to the steep, rugged mountains to the north. Several small communities provide services in the valley, and the Danish town of Solvang is a tourist favorite.

Figueroa Mountain (4,528 feet) is a large mountain with several adjoining peaks. It forms an east-west ridge running from Cachuma Saddle seven miles west to the Los Padres National Forest boundary. With its steep meadows, scattered trees and chaparral contrasting with large dark outcroppings of rock, the mountain presents a striking image from the south.

Figueroa Mountain is reached from the west via Figueroa Mountain Road (7N07), a narrow paved road that provides auto access to the entire length of the ridge. Dirt side roads lead to picnic areas and Figueroa Mountain lookout. Figueroa Mountain Road heads north from Highway 154 out of Los Olivos just opposite Grand Avenue. The town of Los Olivos lies 2.5 miles east of U.S. 101 on Highway 154. For 7 miles this

View from Figueroa Mountain Road

road passes through rolling grass-lands, past ranches and meadows with large oak trees. It then climbs—some-times steeply—6 miles to Figueroa USFS Station. Recent rain damage has made the road surface rough and there are occasional detours around washed-out sections. Past the USFS station to Cachuma Saddle on 7N07, it is 8 more paved miles.

You can also reach Cachuma Saddle from the south via mostly paved Happy Canyon Road (8N09). Take the Armour Ranch Road north from Highway 154, 5 miles west of Lake Cachuma, just past where you cross the Santa Ynez River. At 1.3 miles, turn right (east) onto Happy Canyon Road (county road 3350 at this point). Within another 1.1. miles, Baseline Road comes in from the left. You keep right on Happy Canyon. Heading north through the scenic oak-studded canyon, the road gets progressively narrower. Old oaks,

sun-bleached barns and quiet pastoral scenery take you back in time—a truly lovely area! Nine miles from Highway 154, the road suddenly starts to climb through pine, oak and chaparral, and you encounter more grasslands on the slopes before drop-ping into Cachuma Canyon. Because of a short unpaved section, there may be seasonal gate closures. Fourteen miles from Highway 154, you come to Cachuma Saddle and the USFS Station there at the junction with Figueroa Mountain Road.

Sunset Valley, north of Figueroa Mountain, is accessible by auto from Cachuma Saddle via paved Sunset Valley Road (8N09). Between Sunset Valley and Figueroa Mountain, as well as west of the mountain, there are several roads and trails which make a variety of riding experiences possible. Drive-in camping is available at Cachuma, Davy Brown, Nira and Figueroa campgrounds.

48 McKinley Mountain

Distance: 11.2 miles.
Difficulty: Moderate to strenuous.
Elevation: 3,100' to 6,100'.
Ride Type: Out-and-back on dirt road.
Season: Year-round, but winter can be muddy.
Maps: Figueroa Mountain, San Rafael Mountain.
Water: McKinley Camp may have water.
Comments: This area is a major entrance to the San Rafael Wilderness (bikes prohibited) and is frequently used by equestrians. Yield to horses.

Overview: McKinley Mountain is reached via Cachuma Mountain Road (8N08). This is a well-maintained dirt road, although there is a bit of climbing involved. You can turn around at any time and coast most of the way back to Cachuma Saddle. This area is one of the highest places where you can ride a bike in Santa Barbara County, and the views of the San Rafael Wilderness are outstanding.

Getting There: Begin at Cachuma Saddle. You can park there or west of the water tank to the right of the locked gate.

Route: Take the dirt road east (directly across Sunset Valley Road (8N09) from the Cachuma USFS station). At 1.3 miles, as you climb up a west ridge of Cachuma Mountain, you start to get views of the back-

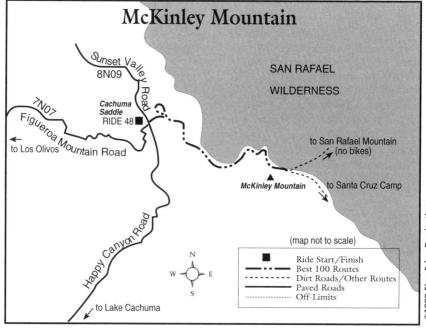

country. The large heavy pine cones along the route with sharp tips (flat alert!) grow on Digger pines. At 2.3 miles, you reach a saddle with good views. The peak ahead is Cachuma Mountain which you pass on the northeast side. There is a water catch basin on the east side of the saddle. At 2.9 miles, you curve around the north side of Cachuma Mountain and the road levels out a bit and turns south. The road designation changes here from 8N08 to 28W01. The San Rafael Wilderness boundary parallels the road on your left.

As you cross a saddle on the ridge to the southeast side of Cachuma Mountain, 3.4 miles, there are good views of Lake Cachuma. The ridgetop along here offers panoramic views of Manzana drainage and Hurricane Deck on your left, and the Santa Ynez drainage on your right. At

3.7 miles, you pass a water tank and drop slightly, heading east along the ridge. At a flat area on the south side, about 300 yards east, there's a single pine tree; this spot could be used as a primitive campsite.

Small pines and firs appear at 5.4 miles. As you cross the saddle, you leave the trees and re-enter the chaparral among large white boulders. At 5.6 miles, the trail turns to the northeast and climbs very steeply over sandstone, crossing behind the north side of Mt. McKinley (6,182 feet). East of McKinley the trail turns left toward San Rafael Mountain (no bikes allowed in Wilderness Area). The old trail, 6N14, continues along just outside the Wilderness boundary to Santa Cruz Camp and Little Pine Mountain.

Head back the way you came.

49 Sunset Valley Road

Distance: 6.5 miles one way.
Difficulty: Easy paved road; more strenuous and technical loops possible.
Elevation: 3100' - 1900'; 1,200' differential.
Ride Type: Out-and-back on paved road; loop options possible (not described in this ride).
Season: Year-round.
Maps: Figueroa Mountain, Bald Mountain.
Water: At Davy Brown Camp.
Comments: Hunters, hikers, campers, fishermen and picnickers make this a busy road most of the time. Be cautious and courteous at all times.

Overview: Sunset Valley Road gives paved auto access to Sunset Valley, Davy Brown and Nira camps, as well as to many trails and roads, some of which enter the San Rafael Wilderness—off-limits to bikes. By riding up the paved road and back down the trails, loop trips that avoid steep trail climbs are possible. Above Sunset

Valley, the steep slopes are covered with chaparral, the canyon bottoms and valley floor with large oaks, pine and sycamores.

Getting There: Start at Cachuma Saddle.

Route: Head north on Sunset Valley

Jason Houston

Sunset Valley Road

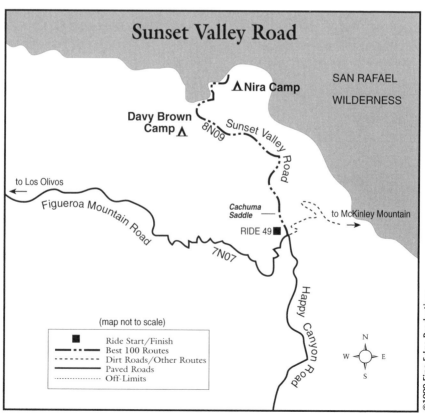

Jason Houston

Sunset Valley Road

Road (8N09). Distances to the various trailheads are as follows: White Rock Canyon Trail (29W05) on the left (west) at 0.9 mile; Sunset Valley Trail (no number) on the left (west) at the sign at 1.5 miles; Munch Canyon Trail (29W04) on the left (south) at 3.3 miles; Davy Brown Camp on the left (south) at 4.0 miles; Fir Canyon Trail (29W03) on the left (south) from the west end of Davy Brown Camp; Catway Jeepway (8N03) on the left (west) at 4.2 miles. Nira Camp is located a little over 6 miles from Cachuma Saddle at the end of Sunset Valley Road.

You can ride out-and-back as far as you like on any of these trails, or see the following ride descriptions for loop possibilities.

50 White Rock Canyon Trail

Distance: 3.5-mile trail; 8.3-mile loop.
Difficulty: Moderate to difficult.
Elevation: 4100' - 2900'; 1200' differential.
Ride Type: Loop on paved road and trail.
Season: Year-round, but winter can be muddy.
Map: Figueroa Mountain.
Water: None.

Overview: This loop is best done clockwise from Cachuma Saddle. It features a visit to an old chrome mine works. *Caution:* Mines are dangerous and old ones can be deadly

Getting There: Begin at Cachuma Saddle.

Route: Climb to the west up paved Figueroa Mountain Road (7N07) for 3.7 miles. Here East Pinery Road (8N32) starts to the right (north) opposite Ranger Peak. Follow this good dirt road 0.2 mile, keeping an eye out for the White Rock Canyon Trail (29W05). The upper part of the trail starts among trees and tall brush, and here on the north side of Ranger Peak it is steep. This doubletrack is on the east side of East Pinery Loop, downhill from a point a few hundred yards down from Pinery.

After descending from an old chrome mine, the slope levels and the trail crosses some small meadows. This trail leaves White Rock Canyon and enters a small narrow canyon for the final descent to Sunset Canyon Road (8N09). Turn right, uphill, on the road and ride the 0.9 mile back to Cachuma Saddle and the USFS Station.

White Rock Canyon Trail

Jason Houston

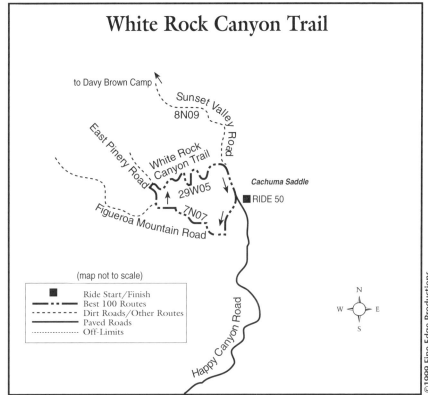

White Rock Canyon Trail

to Davy Brown Camp

Sunset Valley Road
8N09

East Pinery Road

White Rock Canyon Trail

29W05

7N07

Figueroa Mountain Road

Cachuma Saddle
■ RIDE 50

Happy Canyon Road

(map not to scale)

■ Ride Start/Finish
▬ ▬ ▪ ▬ Best 100 Routes
--------- Dirt Roads/Other Routes
▬▬▬▬ Paved Roads
················ Off-Limits

N
W ⊕ E
S

©1999 Fine Edge Productions

51 Sunset Valley Trail (a.k.a. Fish Creek Spur)

Distance: 4 miles, 6 miles or 7 miles.
Difficulty: Easy; mildly technical.
Elevation: 2900' - 2200'; 700' differential.
Ride Type: Loop on paved road and trail.
Season: Year-round, but winter can be muddy.
Maps: Figueroa Mountain, Bald Mountain.
Water: None.
Comments: Beware of sharp turns and numerous low-cut stumps and roots which cross the trail.

Overview: Sunset Valley Trail is an easy and pleasant 2-mile downhill which parallels Sunset Valley Road to Fish Creek Divide. The trail meanders through oaks, pine and chaparral. You can do this ride from three points. From Davy Brown Camp, it is about a 6-mile loop. You can also park in a turnout near the lower trailhead for a 4-mile loop. Or you may begin at Cachuma Saddle for a 7-mile loop.

Getting There: You can start at Davy Brown Camp, from the turnout along Sunset Valley Road, or at Cachuma Saddle.

Route: If you do this trail as a discrete ride, it's probably best to start at Davy Brown Camp or Sunset Valley Road. That way you can ride up the paved Sunset Valley Road and return downhill on the trail.

However, most riders will probably add this trail to other routes in the area, using it as an alternative to the paved road. For that reason, the following

Jason Houston

Sunset Valley Trail

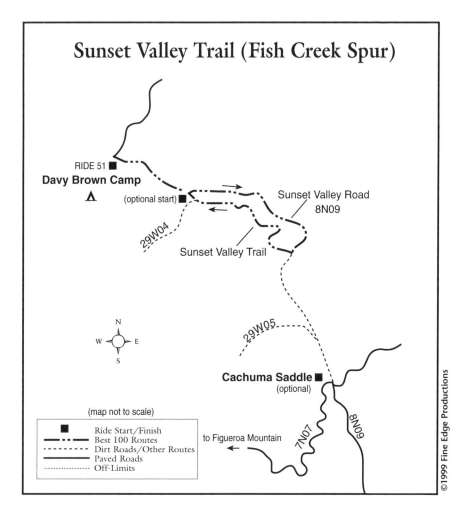

Sunset Valley Trail (Fish Creek Spur)

RIDE 51 ■
Davy Brown Camp

A   (optional start) ■

Sunset Valley Road
8N09

29W04

Sunset Valley Trail

N
W ─◆─ E
S

29W05

Cachuma Saddle ■
(optional)

(map not to scale)

■   Ride Start/Finish
▬▬▪▬▪ Best 100 Routes
------------- Dirt Roads/Other Routes
▬▬▬ Paved Roads
.... Off-Limits

to Figueroa Mountain
←

7N07

8N09

©1999 Fine Edge Productions

description begins at Cachuma Saddle.

Head north on Sunset Valley Road (8N09). The trail takes off just below a little saddle 1.5 miles below Cachuma Saddle. It is signed: *29W04 - Sunset Valley Trail 2.5 miles; Davy Brown Camp 3.0 miles.* This singletrack biases west and north along a small sidehill. The first 0.5 mile is a narrow, well-graded trail which drops down into a U-shaped canyon and follows a doubletrack jeep trail through the deeply-shaded bottom. Recent fires in the area may make the trail difficult to follow, but you are never far from Sunset Valley Road.

At 3 miles, you come to a large V-shaped turn. You can turn around here, or turn right and cross an informal and usually rutted picnic area and pick up Sunset Valley Road. A third choice is to bear left and follow the Munch Canyon Trail (29W04), an old mining road and good spur with a singletrack trail, which connects to Pinery Road for a moderately strenuous second loop. (See the following ride for more details.)

52 East Pinery Road/ Davy Brown Trail

Distance: 11.4 miles.
Difficulty: Strenuous; moderately technical.
Elevation: 4100' - 2200'; 1900' differential.
Ride Type: Out-and-back or loop on dirt and paved roads and singletrack.
Season: Year-round, but winter can be muddy.
Maps: Figueroa Mountain, Bald Mountain.
Water: None.

Overview: From Figueroa Mountain Road, just north of Ranger Peak, narrow East Pinery Road (8N32) heads north along a tree-covered ridge. This can be a pleasant out-and-back ride in itself or the beginning of a loop ride down to Sunset Valley Road (8N09).

Getting There: Any loop ride incorporating East Pinery Road should start either in Sunset Valley or at Cachuma Saddle. That way most of the climbing is on pavement and is fairly straightforward.

Route: From Cachuma Saddle, take Figueroa Mountain Road (7N07) up the switchbacks to Ranger Peak and find East Pinery Road (8N32) taking off to the north. Take Pinery north to its end at a little loop. From the loop, a fast spur trail drops down to intersect the Munch Canyon Trail (29W04). It can be overgrown and fairly technical with rocks and ruts on its way down to Sunset Valley Road (8N09). Look for a singletrack trail (unmarked) on the east side of the Pinery loop which contours down to the north.

If you go left when the spur trail hits the Munch Canyon Trail, you reach Davy Brown Trail (29W03). This connector intersects 29W03 about halfway down its meander through beautiful Fir Canyon. Surrounded by big cone spruce, maple and oak, it is easy to lose yourself in the magical solitude. But the trail is tough enough to require your attention.

Jason Houston

Davy Brown Trail

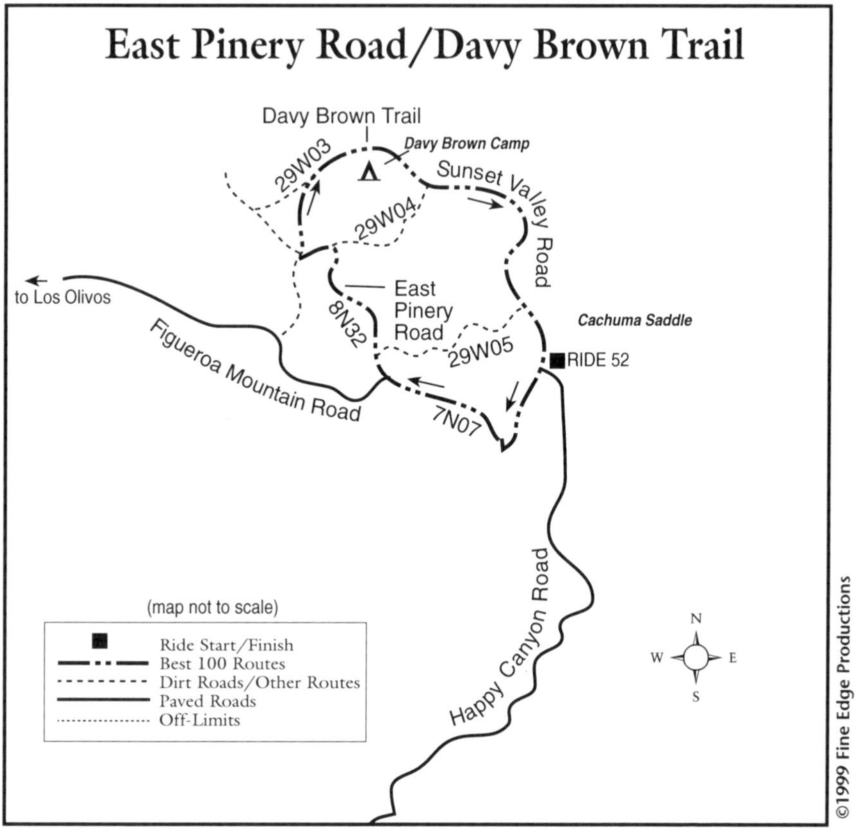

East Pinery Road/Davy Brown Trail

Davy Brown Trail

29W03

Davy Brown Camp

Sunset Valley Road

29W04

to Los Olivos

Figueroa Mountain Road

8N32

East Pinery Road

Cachuma Saddle

29W05

RIDE 52

7N07

(map not to scale)

■ Ride Start/Finish
━━ ● ━━ Best 100 Routes
━━━━ Dirt Roads/Other Routes
------ Paved Roads
·········· Off-Limits

Happy Canyon Road

N
W ─◇─ E
S

©1999 Fine Edge Productions

Just past the Munch Connector, you pass Black Willow Canyon Trail on the left which eventually heads up to Zaca Ridge Road (8N01/ 8N02). Davy Brown Campground and Sun- set Valley Road are reached about 2.5 miles beyond the connector. A right up Sunset Valley Road takes you back to your car at Cachuma Saddle.

53 Catway Jeepway (a.k.a. Catway OHV Route/Figueroa Jeepway)

Distance: 8.4 miles.
Difficulty: Strenuous; technical.
Elevation: 4400' - 1900'; 2500' differential.
Ride Type: Out-and-back on dirt road or loop on dirt road and singletrack.
Season: Year-round, but winter can be muddy.
Maps: Figueroa Mountain, Bald Mountain.
Water: None.
Comments: Be aware that this road is used occasionally by motorcycles and four-wheel drive vehicles.

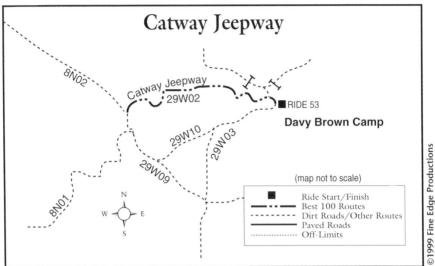

Catway Jeepway

8N02

Catway Jeepway
29W02

RIDE 53

Davy Brown Camp

29W10

29W03

29W09

8N01

(map not to scale)

N
W — E
S

■   Ride Start/Finish
—·—·—   Best 100 Routes
- - - - - Dirt Roads/Other Routes
————   Paved Roads
·············· Off-Limits

©1999 Fine Edge Productions

Jason Houston

Catway Jeepway

Overview: This steep, rocky, rutted road offers a dirt route to Zaca Ridge (see the following ride) for those camping at Davy Brown Campground on Sunset Valley Road.

Getting There: Start at Davy Brown Campground on Sunset Valley Road.

Route: To go west and up-hill from Sunset Valley Road, turn west on an un-marked dirt road in a small meadow just below Davy Brown Campground. Pass a corral; within 0.2 mile, you come to a fork in the road. The road to the right is closed by a locked gate and is signed *Private Property.* Take the left fork (this is Catway Jeepway) through an open gate and over a steep berm. Continue steep-ly uphill. *Caution:* Above the switchbacks, poison oak crowds the trail.

At 2.6 miles, you have your first flat section and a view back down to Davy Brown Campground. At 4.2 miles you reach 8N02.

Options: 1) Turn around and head back the way you came for a screaming downhill. 2) You can continue right on 8N02 (see the following ride for details). 3) *Loop option:* Turn left onto 8N01 and take it toward Figueroa Mountain Road (7N07), 2.5 miles south. If you take this third option, you can choose to descend to Sunset Valley Road via Black Willow and Davy Brown trails. Go left on Black Willow and descend to Davy Brown Trail, where you go left again. This would make an 8-mile loop.

Catway Jeepway

54 Zaca Ridge Road

Distance: 16.4 miles; turn around anywhere for a shorter ride.
Difficulty: Starts out easy and gradually becomes more difficult.
Elevation: Start at 3,440', climb to 4,200', descend to 3,400'.
Ride Type: Out-and-back on dirt roads.
Season: Spring, summer, fall.
Maps: Los Olivos, Figueroa Mountain, Zaca Lake, Bald Mountain.
Water: None.
Comments: Watch for motor vehicles on your ride as the road is closed only during wet weather. Also note that a wildfire in 1993 left many standing dead trees. Keep clear of them as they eventually fall, especially during windy weather.

Overview: This route atop Zaca Ridge is one of the most scenic in the Los Padres National Forest and, except for a few short hills, is not very difficult. The views out over the surrounding countryside are spectacular all along the way, so even a short ride out-and-back is rewarding. The route could be called "Rim of the World Trail" because of its outstanding views—the

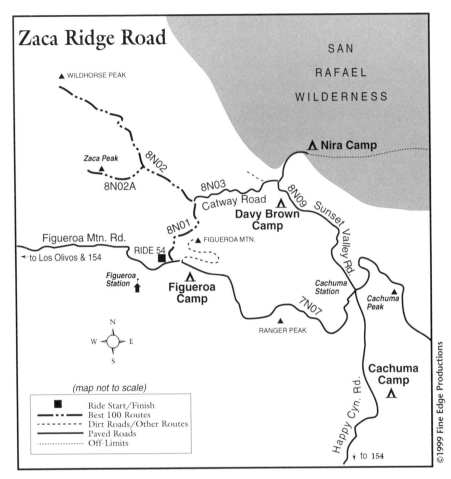

Zaca Ridge Road

WILDHORSE PEAK

SAN RAFAEL WILDERNESS

Zaca Peak

8N02

8N02A

Nira Camp

8N03

Catway Road

8N01

Davy Brown Camp

8N09

Sunset Valley Rd.

FIGUEROA MTN.

Figueroa Mtn. Rd.

RIDE 54

to Los Olivos & 154

Figueroa Station

Figueroa Camp

Cachuma Station

Cachuma Peak

7N07

RANGER PEAK

Cachuma Camp

N
W — E
S

(map not to scale)

Happy Cyn. Rd.

to 154

©1999 Fine Edge Productions

■ Ride Start/Finish
■—·■—· Best 100 Routes
- - - - - Dirt Roads/Other Routes
———— Paved Roads
············· Off-Limits

San Rafael Wilderness below you to the northeast, the Sisquoc River and countless fertile valleys and wooded ridges all the way to the ocean, and Solvang and the Santa Ynez drainage to the south. Pine groves and scattered oaks provide secluded shady spots for picnics, sketching, photography or just taking time to enjoy the natural beauty. Connecting trails make this road your access to much of the country on both sides of the ridge.

Getting There: From the village of Los Olivos, on Highway 154, 3 miles east of Highway 101, take paved Fig-

ueroa Mountain Road north for 12.7 miles to the signed roadhead on the left. Park at the wide turn-around by the seasonal gate—don't block the road.

Route: Zaca Ridge Road heads west from paved Figueroa Mountain Road at the 12.7-mile point and is marked by signs. A large white pipe gate about 100 feet up the road is used for motor vehicle closure during wet weather. Past this gate, 8N01 turns north and with an easy and fairly steady climb traverses the steep western slope of Figueroa Mountain,

The ridge road from Figueroa Mountain to Zaca Peak

Jamie Griffis

mostly through thick forest of pine, fir, and oaks that shade the way. After 2.2 miles, you arrive at a saddle on the ridge north of Figueroa Mountain. From here the view is out over Sunset Valley with Cachuma and McKinley mountains beyond. At this saddle, a little-used doubletrack road is an easy climb to the south for a half-mile to a heli-pad on the hilltop.

The main road turns west and is level around the south side of the next hill on the ridge. At the west side of that hill, you descend to a saddle at about 2.7 miles where a signed road comes in on the right. This is the Catway OHV route to Davy Brown Camp below. Here, the road you are on changes number from 8N01 to 8N02. As you continue west along Zaca Ridge, there is another seasonal gate. Here the road starts to climb the first of two short steep hills, topping out at 3.0 miles. You have a good view of Santa Ynez Valley on the south to the ocean on the western horizon, and north across the San

Rafael Wilderness.

For the next 1.5 miles along the ridge, you drop down to saddles and then climb the hills that follow. At 4.5 miles, you come to a high point on the southwest side of a peak where you can see ahead to Zaca Peak with a road traversing its south side. Surprisingly, the ridge splits right where you are, with the left side going out to Zaca Peak west of you; on the right side, the main road heads northwest, passing Zaca Lake on the north side. As you continue on the right side (northwest), the road descends into heavy forest. At 4.7 miles, there is a fork in the road with a small tree in the middle. [**Side trip:** The road to the left, 8N02A, is the road you saw earlier. It is an easy trip out to the south side of Zaca Peak. A rougher trail beyond that connects to Zaca Lake; don't take this unless you're just dying to visit the lake.]

Beyond here, the main road on the right, 8N02, is tougher going, climbing and descending longer and steeper hills on the ridge heading

Jason Houston

Davy Brown Trail descent

It is 0.8 mile to Cedros Saddle, all moderately steep downhill. Part way down you can see Zaca Lake on the left. Cedros Saddle (almost 6.3 miles) is a shady, tree-filled hollow. (The Sulphur Springs Trail crosses the road at the saddle and is marked by a sign on the north side of the road. It drops steeply down to Zaca Lake on the south and to Manzana Creek on the north.)

Beyond the saddle, the road remains on the ridge more often because the ridge is narrow and less mountainous. You are able to travel faster in both directions due to more level terrain. All along here, you have very good views of Zaca Lake below. You climb a little and pass south of Wildhorse Peak, go through a dip, and come to the road end at a large turn-around at 8.2 miles. (A very rough road goes on from the bottom of the dip but dies out after turning around the hill below.) Head back the way you came in.

northwest toward Wildhorse Peak. A turnout on the right at 5.4 miles has a cliff on the north side and a great view below of Manzana Schoolhouse Trail Camp.

La Brea Canyon/Miranda Pines

Just 27 miles from Santa Maria, this pastoral canyon region, with five drive-in camps and good dirt roads, is an under-utilized area. Most of the year—except during the rainy season—the roads here are open and passable by passenger cars with reasonable ground clearance and careful drivers. This beautiful area, with the wide, 7-mile La Brea Canyon Road, is one of the best for beginning riders. Oak and sycamore groves beside

open grass fields and chaparral provide a varied landscape where it's a delight to ride. The nearly-level road is easy to ride and fun to explore.

More challenging are the trails and steeper roads to the north of the main canyon leading to the Miranda Pines area. Located in the far northern corner of Santa Barbara County, the area south and west of Miranda Pine Mountain has some of the best riding in the county for all skill levels. The roads are in very good condition and the trails—well, where the going gets tough, the tough go riding! But there are some nice campgrounds and good roads for easier riding as well.

Due to its distance from major population centers, this part of the Los Padres National Forest is little used except for cattle grazing—and there's plenty of that. Access to the area is via Highway 33 and Highway 166 from the east, and U.S. 101 and Highway 166 from the west.

55 Colson Canyon Road

Distance: 10 miles.
Difficulty: Moderate.
Elevation: 900' to 2,400'; 1,500' differential.
Ride Type: Out-and-back on dirt road.
Season: Spring, summer, fall.
Map: Tepusquet Canyon.
Water: Colson Camp.

Overview: Colson Canyon Road, the main access route to the La Brea Canyon area, provides entry for mining, ranching and recreational activities. It makes a nice out-and-back venture on its own, or it can be added to some of the following rides for more mileage.

Getting There: At Santa Maria, take Betteravia Road east from Highway 101. Continue 8.4 miles to Santa Maria Mesa Road on your left. It crosses the Sisquoc River, and at 15.3 miles from Highway 101 connects with Tepusquet (Tip-es-kay) Road. Turn left, away from the river, and go up this beautiful canyon 4.5 miles where you turn right (east) onto Colson Canyon Road. Park off the road here.

Route: For 2.7 miles, Colson Canyon Road passes private property before entering the federal forest at a large sign: *Los Padres—Land of Many Uses.* The road follows the canyon bottom, crossing the usually dry streambed many times. For most of its length, Colson Canyon is quite narrow with sheer sides. The road climbs steadily, but there are some very steep sections. Near Colson Camp, the canyon widens with clusters of oaks growing here and there. Colson Camp, 4.1 miles from Tepusquet Road on the north side of Colson Canyon Road, has eight sites with shade oaks, piped water, tables, fire pits and pit toilets. *Please remember to pack out your own trash!*

0.2 mile farther up Colson Canyon Road, you pass the site of the former Colson USFS Station. All that remains are roads, building pads, pipes and telephone lines. Across the road on the north side there is a green water tank and trough. (The trail that starts near the water tank climbs north out of the canyon and turns into an unrideable firebreak, unmaintained trail (31W06).)

Colson Saddle is located 0.5 mile above Colson Camp. Here you have

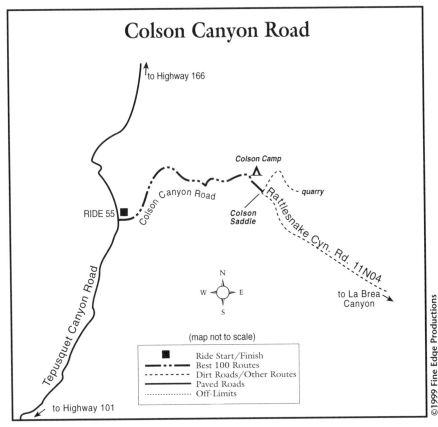

Colson Canyon Road

to Highway 166

Colson Camp

Canyon Road

quarry

RIDE 55

Colson
Saddle

Rattlesnake Cyn. Rd. 11N04

Tepusquet Canyon Road

to La Brea
Canyon

N
W — E
S

(map not to scale)

■ Ride Start/Finish
— · · — Best 100 Routes
- - - - - Dirt Roads/Other Routes
———— Paved Roads
·············· Off-Limits

to Highway 101

©1999 Fine Edge Productions

the first view down into La Brea Canyon and over to the mountains and ridges beyond—an impressive sight. From the saddle, return the way you came for the 10-mile out-and-back. *Options:* You could continue on 11N04 (see Ride 56); for a loop option using Alejandro Trail, see Ride 58.

56 Rattlesnake Canyon Road

Distance: 6.2 miles.
Difficulty: Moderate; mildly technical.
Elevation: 2,400' - 1,030'; 1,370 differential.
Ride Type: Out-and-back on dirt road.
Season: Spring, summer, fall.
Map: Tepusquet Canyon.
Water: Colson Camp.
Comments: Rattlesnake Canyon to La Brea Canyon is open to motor vehicles except during wet winter weather when the gate at Colson Saddle is closed to all vehicles.

Rattlesnake Canyon Road

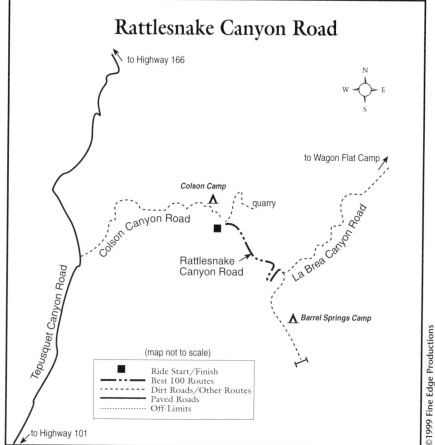

to Highway 166

Colson Camp

quarry

Colson Canyon Road

Tepusquet Canyon Road

Rattlesnake Canyon Road

to Wagon Flat Camp

La Brea Canyon Road

Barrel Springs Camp

(map not to scale)

■   Ride Start/Finish
━ ━ ■ ━   Best 100 Routes
- - - - - -   Dirt Roads/Other Routes
━━━━━   Paved Roads
· · · · · · · · ·   Off-Limits

to Highway 101

©1999 Fine Edge Productions

Overview: This route can be added to the previous ride for a longer trip with more climbing, or it can be used to connect with La Brea Canyon Road for adventures even farther afield.

Getting There: You can start from Colson Camp or Colson Saddle. (See previous ride for more details.) *Note:* you can do the route in reverse, going from Barrel Springs Camp to Colson Saddle. The advantage of this option is that you would do the climb to Colson Saddle on the way out.

Route: From Colson Saddle down, the road stays high up on the north side of the canyon for 1.5 miles and then starts into a series of switchbacks that descend the north ridge of Rattlesnake Canyon into La Brea Canyon. Rattlesnake Canyon Road crosses the usually dry La Brea Creek and ends at La Brea Road at a large sign with directions and distances.

0.2 mile before you reach the bottom of the road, there is a gate in a wire fence to the north. This is the trailhead for Bear Canyon Trail (31W05). There is a sign near the gate in the weeds. (See Ride 59 for details about this.)

0.1 mile farther on, you pass a gate and rough road leading uphill to an old ranch house that is not visible from here. La Brea Creek crosses the road at the bottom in a lush potrero. Across the creek is La Brea Canyon Road heading north and south, with the large forest sign showing directions. You can turn around here. The grade is fairly constant and all rideable uphill heading back.

Or you could turn right and go downstream (south) 1.4 miles to Barrel Springs Camp. This is one of the best camps in the forest with piped-in water, pit toilets, 5 sites with tables and fire pits. The road ends 0.6 mile beyond the camp at a locked white gate marking private property.

57 La Brea Canyon Road

Distance: 16.8 miles.
Difficulty: Easy, not technical.
Elevation: 1,030' - 1,420'; 390' differential.
Ride Type: Out-and-back on dirt road.
Season: Spring, summer, fall.
Maps: Tepusquet Canyon, Manzanita Mountain.
Water: Piped into Barrel Springs Camp.

Overview: La Brea Canyon Road meanders across meadows, in and out of oak groves, and crosses La Brea Creek several times as the canyon gradually narrows. A lovely route in its own right, it can be used to link and loop several other roads and trails described elsewhere in this section.

Getting There: Park at Barrel Springs Camp. From Tepusquet Canyon Road, take Colson Canyon Road to Colson Saddle. From there, descend Rattlesnake Canyon Road (11N04) into La Brea Canyon and the intersection with La Brea Canyon Road. Go right (south) 1.4 miles to Barrel Springs Camp.

Route: Backtrack 1.4 miles north to the junction of Rattlesnake Canyon and La Brea Canyon roads. Continue upstream (north) on La Brea Canyon Road. It is 5 miles from Rattlesnake Canyon Junction to Wagon Flat Camp. Wagon Flat Camp is located on the east side of the road and over-

looks the creek, which flows more here than farther downstream. The stream is the only water source. *Treat all water because of the cattle and up-canyon road crossings.* There are five sites with oak trees, tables, fire pits and pit toilets.

(Just past Wagon Flat Camp (0.1 mile), a rough spur road branches east 0.75 mile to Lazy Camp and the start of Kerry Canyon Trail (see Ride 63). Lazy Camp has two sites with tables and fire pits. This road is in very rough condition and is not suitable for cars.)

La Brea Canyon ends at the junction of Kerry and Smith canyons, mile 8.4. Return the way you came. (The next section of La Brea Road takes off from the fork at Kerry Canyon Trail and goes to a ridge where it joins Horseshoe Canyon Road (11N04) and Miranda Pine Mountain Road (11N03), 3.7 steep uphill miles from Wagon Flat.)

Options: See Rides 60 and 62 for ways to extend your ride.

La Brea Canyon Road

to Highway 166

N
W → E
S

Colson Camp

quarry

Colson Saddle

Colson Canyon Road
11N04

Smith Canyon

Kerry Canyon

La Brea Canyon Road

Wagon Flat Camp

11N04

Rattlesnake / Canyon Road

SAN

RAFAEL

WILDERNESS

Tepusquet Canyon Road

RIDE 57

Barrel Springs Camp

(map not to scale)

■	Ride Start/Finish
—··—	Best 100 Routes
- - - -	Dirt Roads/Other Routes
——	Paved Roads
··········	Off-Limits

to Highway 101

©1999 Fine Edge Productions

58 Alejandro Trail Loop

Distance: 8 miles.
Difficulty: Very difficult; steep and strenuous; experts only.
Elevation: Trail portion drops 1,710' and climbs 500' for a net loss of 1,210'.
Ride Type: Loop on dirt roads and singletrack.
Season: Spring, summer, fall.
Map: Tepusquet Canyon.
Water: Barrel Springs Camp.
Comments: This is the trail of the triple leaves! If you are allergic to poison oak, be warned that upper Alejandro Canyon is choked with the stuff. In some places it grows to a height of 8 feet! We suggest that you ride in spring when the poison oak is not as toxic, and that you wear long gloves, sleeves and tights. You can also use evasive maneuvers—a stick to push the nasty stuff away—to avoid contacting it in the first place.

Alejandro Trail Loop
Bear Canyon Trail

to Buckhorn Ridge

to Buckhorn Ridge

Bear Camp

Bear Canyon Trail

Colson Canyon Road

to Wagon Flat Camp

to Tepusquet Canyon Road

Colson Saddle

11N04

Alejandro Trail

RIDE 59

Alejandro Camp

11N04

Alejandro Trail

RIDE 58

Barrel Springs Camp

(map not to scale)

■ Ride Start/Finish
▪—▪—▪ Best 100 Routes
- - - - - Dirt Roads/Other Routes
———— Paved Roads
·············· Off-Limits

©1999 Fine Edge Productions

Overview: For those not bothered by poison oak, this is an interesting, if somewhat arduous, ride.

Getting There: Park along La Brea Canyon Road south of Rattlesnake Canyon Road or, better yet, at Barrel Springs Camp. From Tepusquet Canyon Road, take Colson Canyon Road to Colson Saddle. From there, descend Rattlesnake Canyon Road (11N04) into La Brea Canyon and the intersection with La Brea Canyon Road. Go right (south) 1.4 miles to Barrel Springs Camp.

Route: From the camp, take La Brea Canyon Road (11N04) north to Rattlesnake Canyon Road (also 11N04) and make the 3.1-mile climb to Colson Saddle. (See Ride 56 for more details.) The Alejandro Trail is marked by a metal sign at the high point of the saddle. It switchbacks 0.3 mile up to a ridge, then climbs another 0.1 mile. From this high point of the trail, you have a good view to the east over Rattlesnake Canyon and the road down to La Brea Canyon. Beware of the steep drop-off into Rattlesnake Canyon along the trail here. Farther downhill, the riding starts out easily enough but soon gets steep, becoming more and more difficult as you encounter rocks and loose gravel.

About 0.75 mile from Colson Saddle, the trail switchbacks steeply down into the head of Alejandro Canyon—so steep, in fact, that walking is advised. At 1.25 miles beyond the saddle, the trail hits the canyon bottom near a water seep. Vegetation changes from chaparral to oak groves where poison oak lurks! After some short steep downhills, the riding improves and becomes fun—except for dodging the poison oak!

About 2.5 miles in from Colson Saddle, the canyon widens and the trail on the east side of the creek enters a grassy potrero (meadow). There are large oaks here as well. A little farther down-canyon, you come to Alejandro Trail Camp. Located east of the creek, the camp is shaded by oaks and surrounded by a barbed-wire fence designed to keep cattle out of the camp—the fence has failed badly! Two tables and fire pits are also here. Farther down the canyon from the camp, there is an old trail which used to branch west up to Tepusquet Peak. It is now overgrown and impassable.

From the trail camp, take the trail which climbs south and then east up out of Alejandro Canyon. Soon after you cross the ridge and descend to the southeast toward La Brea Canyon, the trail forks. The left fork (east) switchbacks steeply down a rocky ridge under oak trees and joins La Brea Canyon Road 0.7 mile north of Barrel Springs Camp. (The right fork continues toward the southeast, joining Difficult Spring Road which descends to La Brea Road 0.1 mile north of the locked gate which marks private property.) Go right (south) on La Brea Canyon Road to return to your car.

59 Bear Canyon Trail

Distance: 5 miles.
Difficulty: Easy to moderate; moderately technical.
Elevation: 1,100' - 1,400'; 300' differential.
Ride Type: Out-and-back on singletrack.
Season: Spring, summer, fall.
Map: Tepusquet Canyon.
Water: Maybe in Bear Creek; treat all water.

Overview: This out-and-back route can be made longer, depending on your penchant for boulder-hopping and portaging. It can also be easily added to Rides 56, 57 and 58.

Getting There: If you're doing the trail by itself, park along La Brea Canyon Road near the intersection with Rattlesnake Canyon Road.

Route: Bear Canyon Trail (31W05) starts on the north side of Rattlesnake Canyon Road (11N04), 0.25 mile above La Brea Canyon Road. The trail is signed here and there is a gate in a barbed-wire fence in the weeds. Near the road the trail is overgrown with brush, but it clears up a bit farther on.

The trail climbs a bit, then drops

down into Bear Canyon past the Webber Ranch buildings. Past the ranch, the trail joins a road on the east side of the creek before narrowing into a trail again. Most of Bear Canyon Trail is used by cattle—so watch where you step. The canyon is narrow and the trail crosses the creek many times, though it is often dry. You are climbing, but the average grade of 120 feet per mile makes it seem almost flat. At 1.0 mile, a large canyon forks east. Keep left (west) for

another 1.5 miles to a second major fork where you find Bear Trail Camp, now little used. You turn around here.

(Beyond Bear Camp, the west fork connects with Buckhorn Ridge Trail. This is a boulder-strewn stream bottom which may or may not be passable depending on prior seasonal rainfall. The east fork noted above is the Bear Canyon Motorcycle Spur Trail (31W14). It is in worse shape than the west fork and would be tough going.)

60 Smith Canyon

Distance: 7.4 miles.
Difficulty: Moderate to difficult; some steep sections.
Elevation: 1,400; - 2,400'; 1,000' differential.
Ride Type: Out-and-back on dirt road; loop possible.
Season: Spring, summer, fall.
Map: Manzanita Mountain.
Water: None.

Overview: Highlights of this ride include the narrow profile of Smith Canyon and the opportunity to see red bark chamiso, the dominant shrub in this one area of the Los Padres National Forest. Uncommon in California, the plant is a native of northern Baja California and grows in only one other part of California— the Santa Monica Mountains.

Although an interesting out-and-back on its own, Smith Canyon could be added to Ride 57 or extended to include Rides 62 and 63.

Getting There: This ride starts at Wagon Flat Campground. Drive up Colson Canyon Road to Colson Saddle. Descend Rattlesnake Canyon Road (11N04) to La Brea Canyon Road. Head left (north) on La Brea

Canyon Road to Wagon Flat. (See Ride 57 for more details.)

Route: This ride begins on La Brea Canyon Road and climbs from Wagon Flat to a ridge where it joins Horseshoe Canyon Road (also 11N04) heading west and Miranda Pine Mountain Road (11N03) heading east.

On La Brea Canyon Road, you enter Smith Canyon and its narrow profile is immediately apparent. The road passes a cattleguard and gate and climbs up the west side of the canyon for a short distance. The canyon opens up a little, the road levels out, and then repeats its narrow, westside climb. At about 1.8 miles, the road crosses Smith Creek and passes a water trough fed by a pipe from the hill-

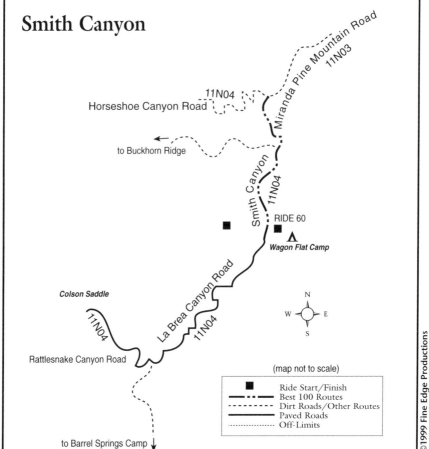

Smith Canyon

11N04
Horseshoe Canyon Road

to Buckhorn Ridge

Miranda Pine Mountain Road
11N03

Smith Canyon

11N04

RIDE 60

Wagon Flat Camp

Colson Saddle

11N04

La Brea Canyon Road

11N04

Rattlesnake Canyon Road

N
W   E
S

(map not to scale)

■ Ride Start/Finish
▬ ▬ ▬ Best 100 Routes
- - - - - Dirt Roads/Other Routes
▬▬▬▬ Paved Roads
·············· Off-Limits

to Barrel Springs Camp

©1999 Fine Edge Productions

side. (As the sign warns, *this water is unsafe to drink!*)

Just past the water trough, the brush on the mountainsides changes suddenly and you can see shrubs with loose red bark hanging in shreds. This is the red bark chamiso.

At mile 2.0, the road crosses back to the west side of Smith Canyon. It then makes a serious climb out of the canyon onto the ridge. Buckhorn Ridge Road (32W01), a 4WD OHV route, starts south from La Brea Canyon Road just as it reaches the ridge top. Follow La Brea Canyon Road along this wide savanna-like ridge as it slopes up and north for 1 mile to join, at mile 3.7, Horseshoe Canyon Road (11N04) and Miranda Pine Mountain Road (11N03). From this point you look down (north) into Pine Canyon toward Cuyama Gorge. You can turn around here and return to your vehicle.

Options: You can continue to the west on 11N04 (see Ride 61) or to the east on 11N03 (see Ride 62). If you go to the east, there's the possibility of looping back on Kerry Canyon Trail (see Rides 62 and 63). That would be a long, tough loop.

61 Horseshoe Canyon/ Buckhorn Ridge Loop

Distance: 7-mile loop; 8 miles out and back on the ridge.
Difficulty: Difficult; technical.
Elevation: 1,200' gain/loss.
Ride Type: Loop on dirt roads and singletrack.
Season: Spring, summer, fall.
Maps: Manzanita Mountain, Miranda Pine Mountain, Tepusquet Canyon, Chimney Canyon.
Water: At Horseshoe Spring Camp.

Overview: Although this loop has plenty of ups and downs and some very steep and technical sections, the views from Buckhorn Ridge and the oak-dotted scenery make it a worthwhile venture for the adventuresome.

Getting There: From Tepusquet Canyon Road, take Colson Canyon Road to Colson Saddle. Descend Rattlesnake Canyon Road from the

saddle to La Brea Canyon Road. Go left (north) on La Brea Canyon Road until it climbs a high ridge where Horseshoe Canyon Road (11N04) goes left (west) and Miranda Pine Mountain Road (11N03) goes right (east). Go left and descend 11N04 for 2.5 miles to Horseshoe Spring Camp, located in a beautiful meadow with large shade oaks. An old stone wall with built-in stairs echoes tales of the

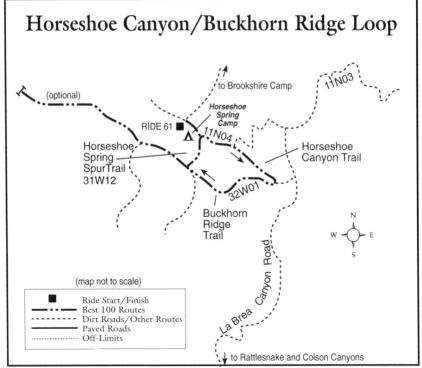

Horseshoe Canyon/Buckhorn Ridge Loop

to Brookshire Camp

11N03

(optional)

Horseshoe
Spring
Camp

RIDE 61 ■

11N04

Horseshoe
Spring
SpurTrail
31W12

Horseshoe
Canyon Trail

32W01

Buckhorn
Ridge
Trail

La Brea Canyon Road

N
W —◇— E
S

(map not to scale)

■ Ride Start/Finish
━━ ‒ ‒ Best 100 Routes
‒ ‒ ‒ ‒ Dirt Roads/Other Routes
━━━━ Paved Roads
· · · · · · · Off-Limits

to Rattlesnake and Colson Canyons

©1999 Fine Edge Productions

Ray Ford

The rolling hills of the Santa Barbara backcountry

past. Three sites with tables, fire pits, and pit toilets are available. Water is piped to the camp. Park here.

Route: From Horseshoe Spring Camp, head uphill on 11N04 back the way you drove in (east). At 0.1 mile, signed Horseshoe Spring Spur Trail (31W12) heads right (south). You will be returning via this trail. For now, continue on 11N04 (the name may change several times).

The road 11N04 climbs past oak trees, then makes a sweeping turn across the canyon and climbs up the north side of the canyon, headed west. The road makes a 180-degree switchback toward the east and just before the next switchback, 0.8 mile from the camp, you see Horseshoe Canyon Trail (no number) on the right. The trail is not signed, but less than 100 feet below the trailhead on the right side of the road there is a red metal triangular sign and, opposite this, a single parking pull-out next to an oak tree.

Take this trail. It climbs 700 feet in 2 miles on its way to the Buckhorn Ridge Trail (32W01). Believe it or not, this is easier than riding the long way around via Horseshoe Canyon Road (remember all those switchbacks you drove down?) to La Brea Canyon Road to the ridge. This trail is 2 miles shorter and has 200 feet less climbing.

When you reach the ridge, go right (west) on 32W01. This is a ridge trail; therefore, it follows the ridge up and down and up again. The climb to the ridge's high point at 2,800 feet is quite steep. (Can you say "push"?) After that, it's more down than up.

About 2 miles along the ridge, you come to Horseshoe Spring Spur Trail (31W12) on your right (north). *Option:* You can descend this trail now or continue on the ridge for roughly 4 more miles. (At that point, Buckhorn Ridge Trail enters private land and you will have to turn around and retrace your route to the spur trail.) This section of the ridge is the most enjoyable part—where it's almost level and you have views south into Bear Canyon, north to Horseshoe and Pine canyons, and west to the Cuyama River Gorge. Here oak trees give shade for rest and picnic stops.

Whether you ride out to the end of the ridge trail or not, the preferred descent back to your starting point is via Horseshoe Spring Spur Trail. Take it to the north off the ridge. (The trails which drop south off the ridge toward Bear Canyon may be impassable depending on the previous season's weather.)

The spur trail switchbacks down and comes in 0.1 mile east and above Horseshoe Spring Camp. The steep north slope here is wooded with small oak trees. The trail is in good condition, but given its steepness, you'll be glad you're riding down and not up it!

Sierra Madre Ridge Road near Painted Rock Camp

62 Miranda Pine Mountain Road

Distance: 20.2 miles.
Difficulty: Strenuous; not technical.
Elevation: 2,400' gain/loss.
Ride Type: Out-and-back on dirt road; loop possible.
Season: Spring, summer, fall.
Maps: Miranda Pine Mountain, Manzanita Mountain.
Water: None.

Overview: This is a long, steep climb, but the views are worth the effort, especially for the conditioned cyclist. The route can be made longer and more difficult if you combine it with Ride 57 by starting at Horseshoe Spring Camp, or you can loop it with Ride 63.

Getting There: From Tepusquet Canyon Road take Colson Canyon Road, to Colson Saddle. Descend Rattlesnake Canyon Road from Colson Saddle into La Brea Canyon and the intersection with La Brea Canyon Road. Go north (left) on La Brea Canyon Road past Wagon Flat Camp and up to the ridge where 11N04 and 11N03 split.

Route: Begin at the junction of La Brea Canyon Road (11N04) and Miranda Pine Mountain Road (11N03). From the junction, take Miranda Pine Mountain Road (11N03) to the northeast. 11N04 drops west toward Horseshoe Spring Camp. It's 3.1 miles up Miranda Pine Mountain Road to Treplett Mountain, a rather steep climb on the west side of the ridge. The going gets very steep where the road switchbacks up the face of the ridge.

After 0.9 mile, you cross a meadow with oak trees and pass a stock pond on the west side of the road. More steep climbing for 0.6 mile

takes you past the point where a side road descends west into a canyon a short distance to Johnson Surprise Spring. The last 1.4 mile to the ridge has some steep parts. Switchbacks do ease the worst part, however.

The ride past the peak is more level and provides views into Kerry Canyon and north to the Sierra Madre Ridge Road. From this point on, the road heads north, descending for 2.6 miles along the east side of Treplett Mountain, then climbing slightly 0.4 mile to Pine Flat. There are no facilities or water at Pine Flat, but this level pine-shaded area is a good resting spot and could be a good campsite. If you were to camp here, however, you would need to secure a fire permit as there are no firepits here.

About 0.1 mile south of Pine Flat, Kerry Canyon Trail (30W02) takes off. A sign reads: *Kerry Camp 3 miles; Lazy Camp 6 miles.* (You could loop back to Wagon Flat via this trail if you're so inclined. See the following ride for more details.)

(From Pine Flat, Pine Canyon Trail (31W02), also called Kerry Canyon/Indian Trail on USFS maps, descends into Upper Pine Canyon. This trail is very hard to follow, very overgrown, and hardly worth the effort you'll expend exploring it. We don't recommend it.)

Continuing on Miranda Pine Mountain Road from Pine Flat, the

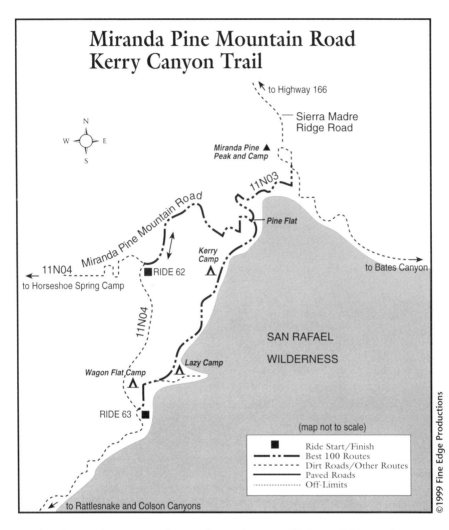

Miranda Pine Mountain Road
Kerry Canyon Trail

to Highway 166

Sierra Madre
Ridge Road

Miranda Pine ▲
Peak and Camp

11N03

Pine Flat

Kerry
Camp
▲

RIDE 62 ■

11N04

to Horseshoe Spring Camp

11N04

to Bates Canyon

SAN RAFAEL
WILDERNESS

Lazy Camp
▲

Wagon Flat Camp
▲

RIDE 63 ■

(map not to scale)

©1999 Fine Edge Productions

■   Ride Start/Finish
━ ∙ ━ ∙   Best 100 Routes
---------   Dirt Roads/Other Routes
━━━━━   Paved Roads
⋯⋯⋯⋯   Off-Limits

to Rattlesnake and Colson Canyons

road twists and turns up the south side of the mountain for the next 3.5 miles. The grade is not very steep, except for a short section about halfway up. This climb would be grueling in mid-summer as there is no shade to speak of. Near the top there is a gate for seasonal road closures.

At the top, on the ridge, there is a five-point intersection: to the east is Sierra Madre Ridge Road (32S13) to McPherson Peak; the center road is Sierra Madre Ridge Road leading

down to Highway 166; southwest, a short road heads down to Miranda Pine Spring, which has a large water tank *(treat all water);* the road heading to the northwest is a steep 0.5-mile climb to Miranda Pine Mountain peak and camp.

You've come this far, so you might as well bag the peak. The camp has three sites with tables, firepits and one pit toilet. Oak and pine trees provide shade. From here, the easiest route is to return the way you came.

63 Kerry Canyon Trail

Distance: 12 miles.
Difficulty: Difficult; with rocky creek crossings.
Elevation: 1,400' gain/loss.
Ride Type: Out-and-back on singletrack.
Season: Spring, summer, fall.
Maps: Miranda Pine Mountain, Manzanita Mountain.
Water: In the creeks. Treat all water.

Overview: Kerry Canyon Trail (30W02) is a designated motorcycle trail, but it is under-used, especially its northern end. It is more easily done as an up-and-back, but could be part of a "killer" loop up La Brea Canyon Road to Miranda Pine Mountain Road to the upper trailhead at Pine Flat and down to Wagon Flat. Or vice versa.

The distance from Pine Flat through Kerry Canyon is 7 miles and you have a 1,400-foot elevation change. By Miranda Pine Mountain Road over Treplett Mountain to Wagon Flat, you climb another 1,000 feet and then descend 1,400 feet over 6 miles. Going up this way is even tougher, with a steep 2,400-foot climb with some sections gaining over 500 feet a mile. Going up Kerry Canyon Trail, you gain a mere 200 feet a mile.

Getting There: To find the lower trailhead, take La Brea Canyon Road to Wagon Flat Camp (5 sites with tables, firepits and toilets). Park here.

Route: Go 0.1 mile north on La Brea Canyon Road to where a road forks right (east) to Lazy Camp (2 developed sites). This road is rough and not suitable for passenger cars. At 0.5 mile on this road, there is a large turnout. The trail is on the left, heading north from La Brea Creek through Kerry Canyon. You pass a spur trail that goes through a gate and up the ridge into the San Rafael Wilderness (closed to bikes) to the abandoned White Elephant Mine (30W29).

Kerry Canyon Trail crosses Kerry Canyon Creek many times on its way up to Pine Flat. Some crossings are washed out and very rocky. Flores Canyon, 1.0 mile above Lazy Camp, is part of a large drainage to the east of Kerry Canyon. At 3.0 miles above Lazy Camp, you come to the site of Kerry Canyon Trail Camp. Where the trail climbs out of the canyon, it becomes steeper, then almost levels out just before joining Miranda Pine Mountain Road, 0.1 mile southeast of Pine Flat.

Continue to Pine Flat for a nice rest stop before your return. *Option*: Take Miranda Pine Mountain Road up to the peak or return the way you came.

Sierra Madre Ridge

As you travel north from the city of Santa Barbara, the mountain ridges are the most visible and distinctive features of the landscape. The ridges are so numerous that on this northward journey, they seem as limitless as ocean waves. Here there are high ridges, low ridges; grass-covered or rocky ridges;

forested, barren or brushy ridges. But in most cases, steep ridges.

Travel far enough by foot or bicycle—it might take you a week—and you would finally come to a 50-mile long ridge cutting across your path. From the crest of this northwest-southeast ridge, called the Sierra Madre Mountains, it is dramatically clear that this is the last ridge. Beyond and far below is the wide, flat Cuyama Valley, and a barren, desert-like land of brown, eroded hills on the distant horizon.

Although the Sierra Madres are an imposing and seemingly impassable maze—too rough and steep and almost inaccessible—there is excellent riding in "them thar hills." While remote and not easy to reach, there are good roads and scenic discoveries that will keep you coming back.

On the other hand, the eastern Sierra Madre Ridge, although 5,000 feet high, is a surprisingly gentle landscape of open potreros (Spanish for meadows), rolling ridge tops, and rather easy grades.

The 50-mile Sierra Madre Ridge Road (32S13), the longest single dirt road in the Los Padres Forest, traverses virtually the whole ridge. It makes an excellent long-distance route with superb views, good road surface and miles of easy grade.

The following section is devoted primarily to describing a point-to-point ride on this road, with suggestions for shorter loops and alternate access points. If you have ever considered long-distance off-road touring, this is the place to do it. *Caution:* Be prepared. Distances are long and water is scarce or non-existent. Thunderstorms are dangerous to those on the high ridges. Snow and ice are common in winter, and spring comes later at these elevations.

64 Old Sierra Madre Road

Distance: 8 miles.
Difficulty: Easy.
Elevation: 500' gain/loss.
Ride Type: Out-and-back on dirt road.
Season: Spring, summer, fall.
Map: Miranda Pine Mountain.
Water: None.
Comments: Do not confuse this road with Sierra Madre Ridge Road, the 50-mile ridge route.

Overview: The highlights of this ride are the views into Pine Canyon and west toward Cuyama River Gorge.

Getting There: From Highway 166, take Sierra Madre Ridge Road up to the southeast, 5.1 miles, to where the road passes from the north side of the mountain to the south side. Old Sierra Madre Road (12N03) is located on the right (south), 2.3 miles west of a peak with many antennae, and 3.3 miles west of Miranda Pine Mountain.

Route: This easy-to-ride road descends from Sierra Madre Ridge Road (32S13) toward the southwest. After crossing a saddle, the road twists and turns upward toward a

Old Sierra Madre Road

↑ to Highway 166

Sierra Madre

to Highway 166
←- - - -

Old Sierra Madre Road

■ RIDE 64

N
W —◇— E
S

(private)

Ridge Road 32S13

(map not to scale)

■   Ride Start/Finish
—·—·—   Best 100 Routes
- - - - -   Dirt Roads/Other Routes
————   Paved Roads
·············   Off-Limits

to Miranda Pine Mountain
↓

©1999 Fine Edge Productions

long grass-covered ridge. Before the road gets to the top of the ridge, it passes around the east side of a hill and climbs through a small saddle to the southwest of that hill.

Here it enters the first of many parcels of private land on the ridge. This road continues on for many miles, eventually coming out onto Highway 166. Avoid trespassing on private land: if it is posted, please turn around and return to your starting point.

65 Sierra Madre Ridge Road

Distance: 56.2 miles; shorter sections possible.
Difficulty: Easy to moderate, not technical; entire route is difficult due to length.
Elevation: 1,500' to 5,700' to 4,500'.
Ride Type: One-way on dirt road as a shuttle; or a self-contained or sagged over-night camping trip; you can do out-and-back portions as well.
Season: Spring is best, autumn second best; avoid the snow and mud of winter and the extreme heat of summer.
Maps: Miranda Pine Mountain, Bates Canyon, Peak Mountain, Salisbury Potrero, New Cuyama.
Water: None. A lack of reliable water sources here is a real problem and is a good excuse for roping a friend into providing SAG support. Carry as much water as is humanly possible.
Comments: Please read this entire ride description before embarking on a through-trip of the ridge road. It is important that you understand which portions of the ridge road are accessible by motor vehicle and what your access and egress options are.

Overview: Now this is the backcountry. Way back. If you ride the entire route, you will visit sites (such as the Chumash rock art at Painted Rock) most people have never heard of, much less seen for themselves. Along the way you have views of the Cuyama Valley to the north and of the San Rafael Wilderness to the south. Beyond Miranda Pine Mountain, the ridge road follows the northern boundary of the wilderness area—bikes prohibited. You can't ride any of the trails dropping to the south as they enter the Wilderness Area.

If you're not up for the whole route, then do sections of it as day rides. Recommended day rides include: out-and-back from Highway 166 to Miranda Pine Mountain; out-and-back from Bates Canyon west to Miranda Pine Mountain; out-and-back from Bates Canyon east as far as you want to go; out-and-back to the east or west from Newsome Canyon/Bull Ridge.

Getting There: There are several access points to Sierra Madre Ridge Road, most from Highway 166. The road's **western terminus** and the best starting point is on Highway 166, 25.6 miles east of U.S. 101, north of Santa Maria, or 36.8 miles west of

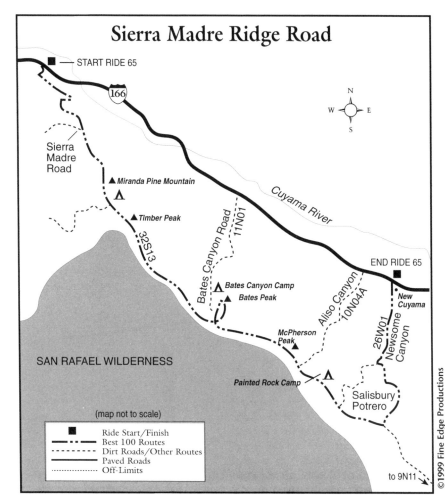

Sierra Madre Ridge Road

START RIDE 65

166

Sierra Madre Road

▲ Miranda Pine Mountain

▲ Timber Peak

32S13

Bates Canyon Road 11N01

Cuyama River

END RIDE 65

▲ Bates Canyon Camp
▲ Bates Peak

Aliso Canyon 10N04A

New Cuyama

McPherson Peak ▲

26W01 Newsome Canyon

SAN RAFAEL WILDERNESS

Painted Rock Camp

Salisbury Potrero

(map not to scale)

	Ride Start/Finish
	Best 100 Routes
	Dirt Roads/Other Routes
	Paved Roads
	Off-Limits

to 9N11

©1999 Fine Edge Productions

Highway 33. Park or drop off in the large turn-out at the top of the hill 0.2 mile toward New Cuyama (north) from Sierra Madre Ridge Road.

The road's **eastern terminus** is only accessible by bike through Santa Barbara Canyon. (See Ride 67 in the following section for details on riding in that way.) If riding west to east (the recommended route described below), the best eastern exit point is through Newsome Canyon into New Cuyama. If you're doing a shuttle, leave your pick-up vehicle in New Cuyama.

The best **mid-way access** point to Sierra Madre Ridge Road is via Cottonwood Canyon Road (County Road 5586) through to Bates Canyon to Bates Canyon Road (11N01). It lets you reach the 23-mile section of road between Miranda Pine Mountain and McPherson Peak. Bates Canyon could be used as a drop-off point, a pick-up point or a mid-trip SAG stop. It's 39.6 miles from U.S. 101 in Santa Maria to Cottonwood Road on Highway 166.

From New Cuyama, Cottonwood Road is 12.2 miles west on Highway 166. Large signs on both sides of Highway 166 give directions to White Oak Station (not in use) and Bates Campground. It is 6.6 miles on narrow, paved road to the campground. The campground's 6 sites have tables, firepits and piped-in water, with two pit toilets and large oak trees for shade. This is an excellent camp, not much used except during deer hunting season.

Note: Vehicle support on the ridge road itself is impossible east of Bates Canyon. Once past Bates, the closest bike-able bail-out point is the trail through Aliso Canyon. If you ride down the canyon (described below), a vehicle could come up-canyon and

meet you at Aliso Park (campground). Aliso Road (10N04A) starts from Highway 166, 2.4 miles west of New Cuyama at the sign: *Aliso Campground 6 miles.* This paved road climbs south 3.8 miles to join Foothill Road where you turn right (west) for about a mile and re-enter Aliso Canyon. The road doubles back north in Aliso Canyon for a short distance past the forest boundary; within 0.8 mile you come to Aliso Campground on the east side of the canyon. Because the trail from the campground to the ridge road is an extremely steep climb, this is not recommended as a way up to the ridge, only as an escape down.

Route: For convenience, this route description is divided into sections which can be done individually as out-and-backs or strung together for longer one-way rides.

Sierra Madre Road to Miranda Pine Mountain: This 9-mile section of the road has the most elevation change of the entire ride, but the 2,400-foot gain spread over 9 miles is not a difficult ride—just long. The road is in good shape and the view is terrific. If you do this section as an out-and-back, you get a good, long downhill at the finish.

The lower section of the road passes through oak groves and grassland on the north side of the mountain for 4.5 miles. As you cross the ridge to the south side, there is a dramatic change in climate and vegetation—drier, warmer, more chaparral and almost no trees. For about 1.0 mile, the road crosses the narrow ridge from north to south and back again, finally ending on the south side before the last 3 miles to Miranda Pine Mountain. 1.0 mile from Miranda Pine Mountain, you can see a peak with white, flat-topped buildings and over a dozen microwave antennas.

Just up the ridge from the "electronic" peak, you enter a grove of pines south of Miranda Pine Mountain. At 4,061 feet, it gives some relief from the hot sun. Miranda Pines Camp is located among these pines on a high spot of the ridge, just east of the peak. It has shade, 3 sites with tables, fireplaces and one pit toilet, but no water. This makes a good rest stop/turn-around point for an out-and-back ride or a potential camping spot for longer ventures. The daytime view is great and the nighttime sky is spectacular.

Farther east, at 9.1 miles, Sierra Madre Ridge Road reaches a five-point intersection. A sharp left and a steep uphill 0.4 mile to the west takes you to Miranda Pines Camp. Straight ahead at the intersection, Sierra Madre Ridge Road heads east for 40 miles or more. A right turn to the south takes you on Miranda Pine Mountain Road (11N03), 3.5 miles to Pine Flat (see the previous section for riding in this area). A sharp right (southwest) at the intersection leads you on a short road that ends at a water tank below Miranda Pine Springs.

Miranda Pine Mountain to Bates Canyon Road: Although this section of Sierra Madre Road is the highest and most remote, it is the easiest riding, gaining 1,300 feet in 13.3 miles. While most other ridge routes follow a particular ridge, climbing up and down every peak, no matter how steep, this road was cut along the side of the ridge and around most of the steep peaks. This evens out the grade, making for a very enjoyable

ride. This section can be added to the previous section or can be done as a westward out-and-back starting at Bates Camp.

From the five-way intersection described above, to Timber Peak, 2.5 miles east, there is a moderate climb of 800 feet with only a few steep sections. Just west of Timber Peak, the road passes through an unusually deep, narrow cut across the ridge. The rocky and rutted road here contrasts with the usually good road conditions.

For 3.5 miles past Timber Peak, the road climbs gradually south-southeast, remaining most of the way on the south side of the ridge, which drops off a little less steeply than the north side. Along the ridge near Spoor Mountain is a large reforestation area where the pines are growing steadily.

At 7 miles, there is a wide spot along the road at a narrow saddle noted on maps as Pines Picnic Area. To the south are the headwaters of the south fork of La Brea and Horse canyons which drain into the Sisquoc River.

The road continues southeast for mile after mile around the 5,000-foot level—good riding and great views! At 11.3 miles, there is a green water tank, near which a long ridge between Horse and Water canyons leads south to the Sisquoc River. This is the present western boundary of the San Rafael Wilderness Area. For the next 24 miles, the Sierra Madre Ridge Road forms the northern boundary of this wilderness.

At 12.9 miles, there's a picnic site on a saddle. To the east, on a ridge north of Guy Peak, the road cutting down into Bates Canyon can be seen. From this point you climb again, and at 13.3 miles (5,200 feet)—just west

Tony Quiroz

Smooth and easy singletrack

descending steeply while crossing over into the center branch of Bates Canyon. Here at 4.3 miles is the former site of Doc's Spring Trail Camp. The spring is a cool resting spot, 1.5 miles from Bates Camp. You cross to the west side of the canyon and descend to the south. After crossing the west branch you come to a seasonal gate and the paved part of the road, 0.2 miles from Bates Camp.

(If you've driven to Bates Camp and are starting your ride from there, head uphill (south) on paved road 11N01. The pavement ends and, 0.2 mile from camp, there is a gate for seasonal closure to motor vehicles. The dirt road continues straight back into the canyon staying west of the stream. The road is moderately steep, except for a few rocky spots. It hits the ridge road at a saddle below and to the west of Guy Peak.)

of Guy Mountain—you come to the junction with Bates Canyon Road (11N01).

To descend to Bates Camp for camping or SAG purposes, take 11N01. You head east around the north side of Guy Peak until the road joins a ridge that connects Guy Peak (5,477 feet) to Bates Peak (4,422 feet). It descends on this ridge to just south of Bates Peak before doubling back to the west and into the east branch of Bates Canyon. In this deep canyon, thick with trees and undergrowth, you come to Cole Spring, 3 miles from the top. This "former" trail camp still has a table near an open water trough.

This road continues to the west,

Bates Canyon Road to McPherson Peak: Beginning at the junction with Bates Canyon Road, this 10-mile segment of Sierra Madre Road passes around the south side of Guy Mountain, climbs past Hot Peak (5,587 feet), and then passes south of Peak Mountain, at 5,843 feet the highest point of the Sierra Madre Ridge Road.

Next you descend to a saddle at 5,400 feet and climb around the south side of McPherson Peak. Here a road branches left and circles around the peak on the south and east side, climbing to the top at 5,747 feet. This was once a lookout site, but it is now occupied by an Air Force microwave station with fuel tanks and generators. McPherson Trail Camp is another 0.4 mile east at a rise on the ridge.

McPhers n Peak to Newsome Canyon: The last part of Sierra Madre Ridge Road is 11.7 miles long and mostly downhill, with a net elevation loss of 1,200 feet. Just east of McPherson Camp, you pass a locked gate and start a steep 1.5-mile descent to the junction with Aliso Trail (27W02), sometimes referred to as Hog Pen Spring Trail. (There is little to recommend this trail as it drops *very* steeply into the canyon. However, if you have had enough or have some kind of emergency, you could use it as a bail-out point. It drops 1,360 feet in 1.5 miles to Hog Pen Spring Trail Camp. (Doesn't that water sound tasty?) Here it turns into a road and continues dropping 2.5 miles to Aliso Campground. A vehicle can meet you here (described in Getting There), or you can continue on 10N04A to Highway 166 where a right turn heads toward New Cuyama.)

For those continuing on the ridge, you have an easy half-mile climb to pass by Hog Peak. You descend again on the rolling ridge road with occasional small climbs. The road makes a final steep descent on a pair of switchbacks as you enter the potreros (meadows) of the Sierra Madre Ridge. As the road levels somewhat, you pass the Jackson Trail to the right (south) which passes a grazing lease cabin. Another 0.5 mile east, at 8 miles from McPherson, is the Painted Rock Trail Camp.

This camp, fenced to keep out range cattle, has 3 sites with tables, firepits and an outhouse toilet, but no water. The camp is named for the many Chumash rock paintings in the caves here. These fragile paintings may be observed and photographed, but strict laws protect them in every way.

(Lion Canyon Trail starts to the east at the gate to the camp and turns south down into the canyon. It's a steep, rough rocky trail.)

From Painted Rock Trail Camp, continue on Sierra Madre Ridge Road and descend easily for 1.8 miles along the north side of the ridge across the head of Lion Canyon. The large sandstone outcroppings there have been eroded into shapes that are fascinating. At the low point on this part of the ridge, you come to the large Pine Corral Potrero. Its large, scattered sandstone rocks look like whales swimming through the grass. Save some time to explore the rocks and caves here.

You climb 400 feet on the south side of Salisbury Mountain. Near a gate here, the Sweetwater Trail can be seen crossing another potrero south and below the road. After a level 0.4 mile to the east, you come to the head of the Newsome Canyon/Bull Ridge Trail.

Newsome Canyon/Bull Ridge Trail/ Perkins Road: This last 12.2 miles takes you into New Cuyama. When you leave Sierra Madre Ridge Road and turn to the north onto the signed Bull Ridge Trail (26W01), you first ride a short road down to a ranch on Salisbury Potrero. As you start down, be sure to look ahead over the large meadow sloping to the east and take note of the far ridge line on the north side. The trail you want to follow crosses that ridge at a noticeable dip almost directly northeast of you and a little to the right of the ranch buildings.

The road drops 170 feet in 0.4 mile to a low area in the huge meadow, turns right, and descends to the buildings and corrals below. But you need to keep straight ahead on a much less-traveled track, climbing slightly across the hillside to regain 60 feet in 0.5 mile to the notch on the ridge.

Passing through the notch, you leave the Sierra Madre potreros behind as suddenly as you entered them. For the next 2 miles, you descend on an old road through mixed pines and chaparral. There is a wire fence gate across the road just above a saddle, where you climb a bit before resuming the descent. The trail gets narrower where it heads down across the grass-covered mountainside, with switchbacks at the steeper places. After more steep descending on the ridge to the canyon below, you are finally down on much more level ground in the canyon.

Turn right and head down the canyon. The trail gradually improves in the next mile, becoming a road where you pass another wire stock gate. (If you open a gate to pass through, be sure to properly close it behind you to prevent cattle from straying.) Another mile of easy descent and you are at the fork in the canyon with Lion Canyon on the left. Now it's a very easy mile to the locked gate with the parking area just beyond on the right.

The Johnston Ranch is to the left as you pass the corrals to head for the town of New Cuyama, 4.2 miles ahead on paved Perkins Road. You also pass the Perez Ranch (cattleguard) on your right and then an old Richfield refinery. Pass a road to the left (it goes to a landfill) and then descend through fenced range land to Highway 166 on the west side of town. Please stay on the open roads described here—riding on private land will lead to trail closure.

(For directions on riding up Newsome Canyon to the ridge road, see the following ride description.)

Options: For those who want even more mileage, instead of turning down Bull Ridge Trail, continue on Sierra Madre Ridge Road 5.2 miles to its eastern terminus in Santa Barbara Potrero. Here it joins road 9N11. If you go left on 9N11 it takes you 15 miles through Santa Barbara Canyon to Highway 33. Or, a right on 9N11 leads through the wilderness corridor between the San Rafael and Dick Smith Wilderness areas and on into the lower Santa Ynez River. For more details on 9N11, see the following section.

66 Newsome Canyon/ Lion Canyon Loop

Distance: 17 miles.
Difficulty: Ranges from easy to very difficult and technical.
Elevation: 2,300' gain/loss.
Ride Type: Loop on dirt roads and trails.
Season: Spring, summer, fall.
Maps: Peak Mountain, New Cuyama, Hurricane Deck, Salisbury Potrero.
Water: None.

Overview: The highlight of this ride is Lion Canyon, best known for its spectacular sandstone rock formations. Water and wind have sculpted the rock into benches, caves, domes, spheres and pinnacles visible from Highway 166, 12 miles away. *Be forewarned:* The trail through the canyon is difficult—technical, steep, narrow and brushy.

Getting There: From the west end of New Cuyama, head south off of Highway 166 onto Perkins Road past the Burger Barn. Perkins Road is paved and climbs gradually straight south past fenced range land. At 2.7 miles from the highway, take a left fork. Past here the terrain levels out as it passes through the Cuyama oil fields—stay on the main road and don't let the many prospect roads confuse you.

An old Richfield refinery, located on the east side 3.1 miles from Highway 166, tells you you're going the right way. Next, cross a cattleguard and pass the Perez Ranch. As you approach Newsome Canyon, directly ahead and to the south, the road descends and passes the Johnston Ranch corrals on the right. At the corrals, a right fork heads uphill to ranch property and the left fork goes up into the canyon. Take the left fork to the east side of the canyon up to the parking area. Park at the circular turnout, 0.2 mile from the corrals, 4.2 miles from the highway.

Route: Backtrack from the parking area to find Newsome Canyon Road (26W01), then turn left (south) and ride up to the locked gate where a USFS sign reads: *Jct. 27W04 - 1 mile, Jct. 26W01 - 1 mile.*

Riding up Newsome Canyon Road to Lower Newsome Spring is a fairly easy 3-mile ride. Past the spring, Bull Ridge Trail climbs 5 miles to Sierra Madre Road. This steep trail isn't much better than a cow path just above Lower Newsome Spring, but it improves farther up and becomes almost a road for the last 3 miles. Please stay on the open roads described here—riding on private land will lead to trail closure.

From the locked gate to the Newsome Canyon/Lion Canyon fork, it's a very easy 1.0 mile. Pass the fork and continue to the left (east) up Newsome Canyon with a few short, steep climbs; it is mostly easy travel farther into the canyon.

2.0 miles past the locked gate, there is a barbed-wire stock gate. Here the trail travels through areas of loose sand. Past this gate, the road quickly becomes a singletrack (almost a cow path) and, at 3.0 miles, crosses a meadow with a fenced corral and a small group of trees on the east side. At the upper south end of the meadow, the trail breaks into a confusing maze of cow paths which crisscross Lower Newsome Spring, fouling what would otherwise be a good source of water.

The trail up Bull Ridge (your route) climbs the ridge east of the meadow. It starts just across the creek a little *downstream* from the "tree corral." This trail climbs right up the open grassy ridge and is very steep for 0.5 mile before it levels off for about 0.25 mile, with good views of the Cuyama Valley, and then climbs steeply once again. One more short level section, then the trail veers left and up, switchbacking to join a ridge coming up from the north.

At 6 miles from the locked gate, the trail enters a well-defined cut on the west side of the ridge. This tractor

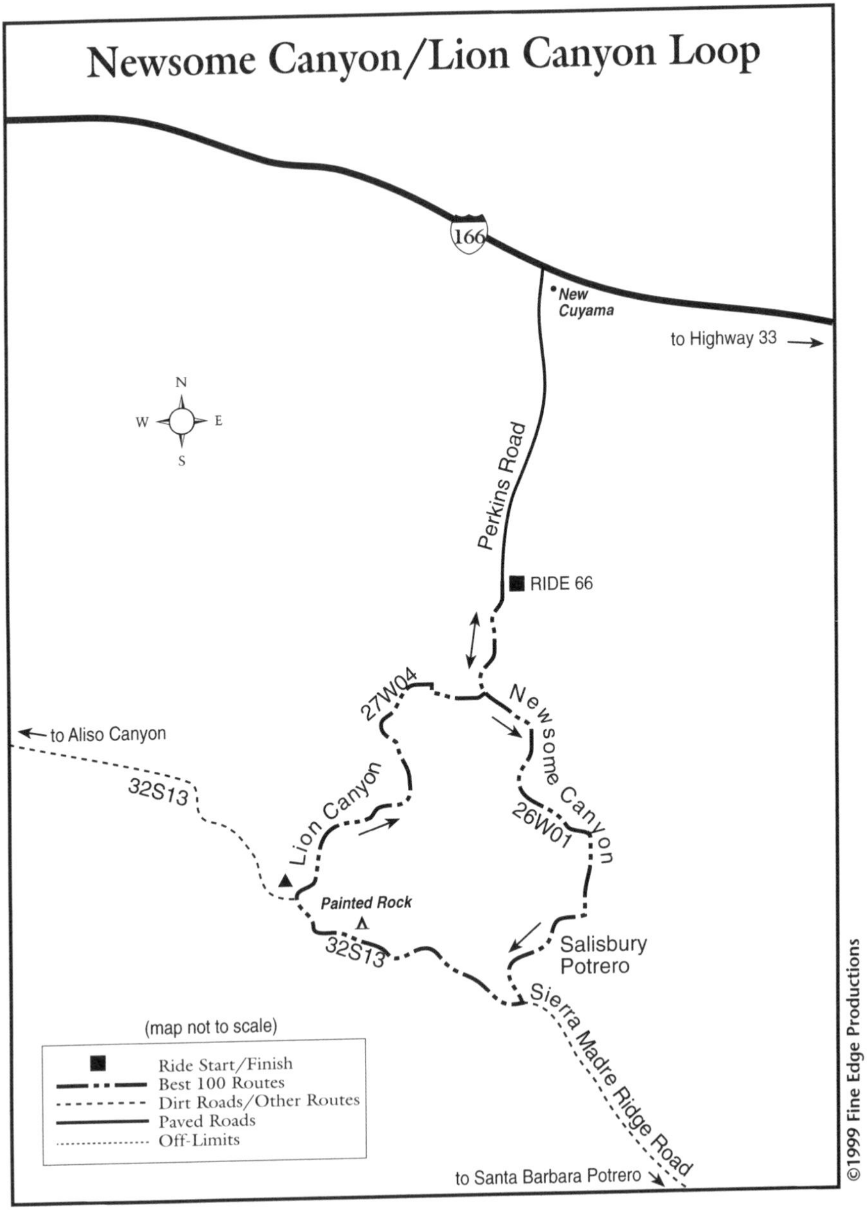

Newsome Canyon/Lion Canyon Loop

166

• New Cuyama

to Highway 33 →

Perkins Road

■ RIDE 66

27W04

Newsome Canyon

← to Aliso Canyon

32S13

Lion Canyon

26W01

▲ Painted Rock
▲

32S13

Salisbury Potrero

Sierra Madre Ridge Road

(map not to scale)

■ Ride Start/Finish
▬▪▬▪ Best 100 Routes
- - - - Dirt Roads/Other Routes
▬▬▬ Paved Roads
········· Off-Limits

to Santa Barbara Potrero ↘

©1999 Fine Edge Productions

road gradually improves. Within 0.2 mile, the trail dips across a small meadow on a ridge. You leave the grass slopes and enter chaparral and pines. Just above the meadow there is another fence gate and the trail improves even more, becoming almost a road.

For the next 2 miles, you have a steady climb into a more forested region, with a discouraging false summit. At the actual second ridgetop, you have a sudden, startling view across Salisbury Potrero, overlooking a beautiful, high, grass-covered valley a mile wide. The valley slopes down toward the east, and in the center there is a well-kept ranch. The trail crosses to the west and above the ranch buildings, and joins a road that climbs easily south and east to the Sierra Madre Ridge Road (32S13). From this point you can look south over the San Rafael Wilderness.

Go right (west) on 32S13. You will like the level travel at 4,900 feet on the south side of Salisbury Mountain (5,182 feet). It is 0.4 mile to a gate. Sweetwater Trail can be seen crossing another potrero south and below the road.

As the road descends, ahead and below you have a sudden view of the large Pine Corral Potrero. Its large scattered sandstone boulders emerge from a sea of grass and remind me of whales. This is an easy descent of 400 feet in 1.5 miles. Save some time to explore the rocks and caves here. At 4,500 feet you've reached the lowest point of the ridge road. West from Pine Corral Potrero, you have a gradual climb on the north side of the ridge, 1.8 miles to Montgomery Potrero. Along the north slope, the view into Lion Canyon keeps revealing more and more of the fascinating sandstone cliffs and rock carved by wind and water.

At Montgomery Potrero, a sign reads: *Sweetwater Trail 3.5 miles (east); Jackson Trail 1/2 mile (west); McPherson Lookout 8 miles (west)*. To the north, across from this sign, a road leads 100 yards to Painted Rock Trail Camp. This camp, fenced to keep out range cattle, has 3 sites with tables, firepits and an outhouse toilet, but no water. The camp is named for the many Chumash rock paintings in the caves here. These fragile paintings may be observed and photographed, but strict laws protect them in every way. On the south side of Montgomery Potrero, maps show 5 springs—these are not reliable water sources.

From just outside the gate to Painted Rock Camp, Lion Canyon Trail (27W04) starts right (east) over the grass-covered hill and then traverses the east side heading north. The first part is not well defined and is unsigned. About 1.5 miles down through grassland, past large sandstone "sentinels," there is a 4-inch post—these posts and an occasional trail sign are found farther down the trail.

The trail soon enters chaparral with occasional stands of pine trees. Then come the switchbacks, with a descent on the west side of the ridge into a hollow formed of wind-carved sandstone. The trail climbs, then descends to a USFS gate. Here the trail follows a sandstone ledge 8 to 10 inches wide, with a shallow cave above. The cave, quite long, has small, barely visible "steps" chipped into the rock below it. These steps, called Nojoqui in the southwest, were carved long ago by Native Americans.

The next 0.5 mile is a fairly nice ride, but then a steep, rocky section begins as the trail heads east and down toward Lion Canyon. After the brushy, rocky switchbacks start, they seem never to end, although it's not really that long. Finally you cross the creek and the hard part is over. From this point, it's a fairly easy 1.2 miles to Newsome Canyon Road, and another 1.3 miles to the parking area.

Santa Barbara Canyon and Wilderness Corridor

Santa Barbara Canyon, the northeastern gateway to the Los Padres National Forest, has much to offer the mountain bicyclist. The terrain, sandstone rock formations, and vegetation are varied and unusual. The weather can be sunny and beautiful when the coast is foggy and dreary. In the spring the wildflower displays are outstanding. This canyon was a major north-south trade route for the coastal Chumash Indians, and you can almost feel their presence as you ride through the area. Native American art and artifacts are strictly protected by the Antiquities Act and you should go out of your way to respect this law and leave no trace of your visit here. This is a lovely and remote area, and your careful and considerate use of it will allow others that same privilege.

Access to Santa Barbara Canyon is off Highways 166 and 33. Don't count on any services or water being available—come prepared.

(For more rides in this general area, see the Cuyama section in the Ventura County chapter.)

67 Santa Barbara Canyon

Distance: 34 miles.
Difficulty: Lower canyon is easy to moderate; upper canyon more difficult.
Elevation: 2,500' - 5,000'; 2,500' differential.
Ride Type: Out-and-back on dirt and paved road.
Season: Spring, summer, fall.
Maps: Fox Mountain, Salisbury Potrero.
Water: None.
Comments: This is remote country. Be prepared to be self-sufficient.

Overview: This ride is a good choice for seasoned riders who like exploring remote areas. Less-experienced riders can simply turn around when they've had enough. The truly hard-core cyclist can ride through Santa Barbara Canyon and continue through the wilderness corridor, 9N11, to the lower Santa Ynez River in a single, very long day. *That* would be some shuttle ride—more than 50 miles! This is best attempted by very fit, experienced cyclists, or as an overnight venture.

Getting There: Take Highway 166 to Highway 33. Head south on Highway 33 for 2.7 miles and turn right onto Foothill Road. If you're coming north on Highway 33, the turn is 0.8 mile north of Ballinger Canyon Road. A sign on Foothill Road reads: *Road closed ahead*. Park here.

Route: Continue on Foothill Road. At 1.2 miles a gate sign reads: *Flooded road closed*. Take either of the two dirt roads around the gate if the area is not flooded. Pavement ends at 1.5 miles. Cross the river bed (gravel) for 200 yards. Same as above with a second closed gate and the roads around the gate. You reach the intersection of

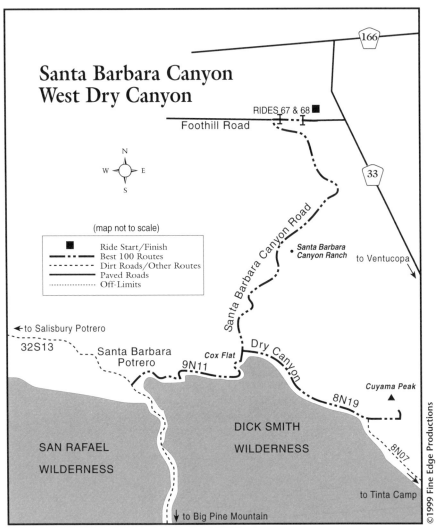

Santa Barbara Canyon
West Dry Canyon

RIDES 67 & 68 ■
Foothill Road

(map not to scale)

■ Ride Start/Finish
—··— Best 100 Routes
------- Dirt Roads/Other Routes
——— Paved Roads
·············· Off-Limits

Santa Barbara Canyon Road

• Santa Barbara
  Canyon Ranch   to Ventucopa

←to Salisbury Potrero
32S13   Santa Barbara   Cox Flat Dry Canyon
         Potrero
              9N11

Cuyama Peak ▲
           8N19

DICK SMITH
WILDERNESS

SAN RAFAEL
WILDERNESS   8N07

                          to Tinta Camp

↓ to Big Pine Mountain

© 1999 Fine Edge Productions

Santa Barbara Canyon and Foothill roads at 2.1 miles.

From the intersection, head east on the paved road. At 2.5 miles, cross a cattleguard and head east on the south side of the river. You hit another cattle crossing at 3.4 miles and another at 4.0 miles. You drop steeply into Santa Barbara Canyon itself at 4.6 miles. Cross the river bottom (flooded during storms). A USFS sign reads: *Santa Barbara Canyon to right; Hwy.*

33 - 1.5 miles to left (washed out - no through road). Head up-canyon. At 6.0 miles, you cross a double cattleguard. The fields here have numerous varieties of wildflowers in the spring season.

At 7.9 miles, there is yet another cattle crossing and sign: *No off-road vehicle travel.* At 8.3 miles, pass a hiking trail to the left (south), followed quickly by two more cattle crossings at 8.4 and 8.6 miles. Note the brick

Mining debris, Figueroa Mountain

Jamie Griffis

Y junction at Cox Flat. The road to the left is signed: *Dry Canyon Road 8N19; Tinta Canyon 6 miles; Cuyama Peak Lookout 9 miles.* The Dick Smith Wilderness Area is directly ahead. Stay to the right on 9N11.

Stay to the right at 13.9 miles. At 14.5 miles, follow a small creek up and, at 14.6 miles, reach a pullout or bivouac site. At 14.7 miles, there's a locked gate and a sign: *No motor vehicles.* This is the eastern end of Sierra Madre Ridge Road (32S13). The small gate to the left is for use by foot traffic and bicycles. It's signed: *Please close the gate.* The double-track above here is used by horses.

Route 9N11 continues due west for about 3 miles to the junction of 32S13 on the right and the continuation of 9N11 on the left. This is the turn-around point for this ride.

Extension option: From here, 9N11 south to Big Pine Mountain and, eventually, to the Santa Ynez River, is simply a corridor—the width of the roadbed itself—between the San Rafael Wilderness on the west and the Dick Smith Wilderness to the east. This area has been used extensively by backpackers and equestrians for years, and mountain bikers are the new kids on the block. Respect the wilderness rules—no bikes except on the road itself. While it is legal to ride through the corridor, taking your bike off the road onto side roads or trails is prohibited. If you should care to explore into the corri-

colored stone in the canyon on the right. Sign: *The destruction or removal of any object from the Santa Barbara Canyon and the Sierra Madre Ridge is prohibited. National Forest Service Lands are protected by the Antiquities Act.*

There's a fork in the road at 9.6 miles. Santa Barbara Canyon Ranch is to the left. Bear right and cross to the north side of the canyon. The road turns to dirt at this point. Cross a cattleguard at 9.9 miles. Note the beautifully colored sandstone cliffs at 10.1 miles. Just beyond, pass the umpteenth cattleguard with a small canyon on the right. At 12.8 miles a sign declares: *Private Land.* There is a

dor, be mindful of this and be especially courteous to any fellow travelers on the road. Not a bad idea anyway since you are miles from help or any real civilization should something untoward happen.

If you decide to continue all the way through the corridor, 9N11 (Buckhorn Road) continues to Hidden Potrero Camp where it joins 5N15 (Camuesa Road). You can take 5N15 south to Upper Oso Campground off of Paradise Road (see the Lower Santa Ynez section of this chapter) where some kind-hearted friend can pick you up.

68 West Dry Canyon

Distance: 38 miles; 12-mile out-and-back addition to previous ride.
Difficulty: Strenuous due to length.
Elevation: 2,500' - 5,875'; 3,375' gain/loss.
Ride Type: Out-and-back on doubletrack, dirt and paved roads.
Season: Spring, summer, fall.
Maps: Fox Mountain, Cuyama Peak.
Water: None.

Overview: Best done as an addition to the previous ride, this route follows the northern boundary of the Dick Smith Wilderness Area with views into the Wilderness. You also have the option of climbing Cuyama Peak.

Getting There: Follow the directions for the previous ride and begin in the same spot.

Route: Follow the directions for the previous ride to Cox Flat at 13 miles. At the Y junction there, go left onto signed Dry Canyon Road (8N19). From Cox Flat you drop down, cross the creek bed and head east, upcanyon. Here there is a double gate, usually open. The road now turns to doubletrack. The Dick Smith Wilderness is on the right (south) side of the road. At 4.5 miles from the junction, there is a bivouac site to the left. Pines start to appear and the road gets very steep and rocky. You cross a narrow saddle at 5.4 miles and pass through an old barbed wire fence, dropping steeply to the east.

You drop down into Tinta Canyon at 5.9 miles from Cox Flat. There is a metal fence which marks the start of the unmaintained section of Tinta Road (8N07). Motorcycles use this route—a very rough, narrow canyon that drops to Tinta Campground and, eventually, to Highway 33. (See Ride 99 in the Ventura County chapter.) Road 8N19 continues left uphill (north) to Cuyama Peak Lookout at 5,875 feet. This is a steep, dry road, climbing about 500 feet with little shade. If the weather is reasonable, the view from the top is worth the effort.

When you've had enough, turn around and re-trace your steps.
Caution: Going back downhill through Dry Canyon is very fast. Watch excessive speed.

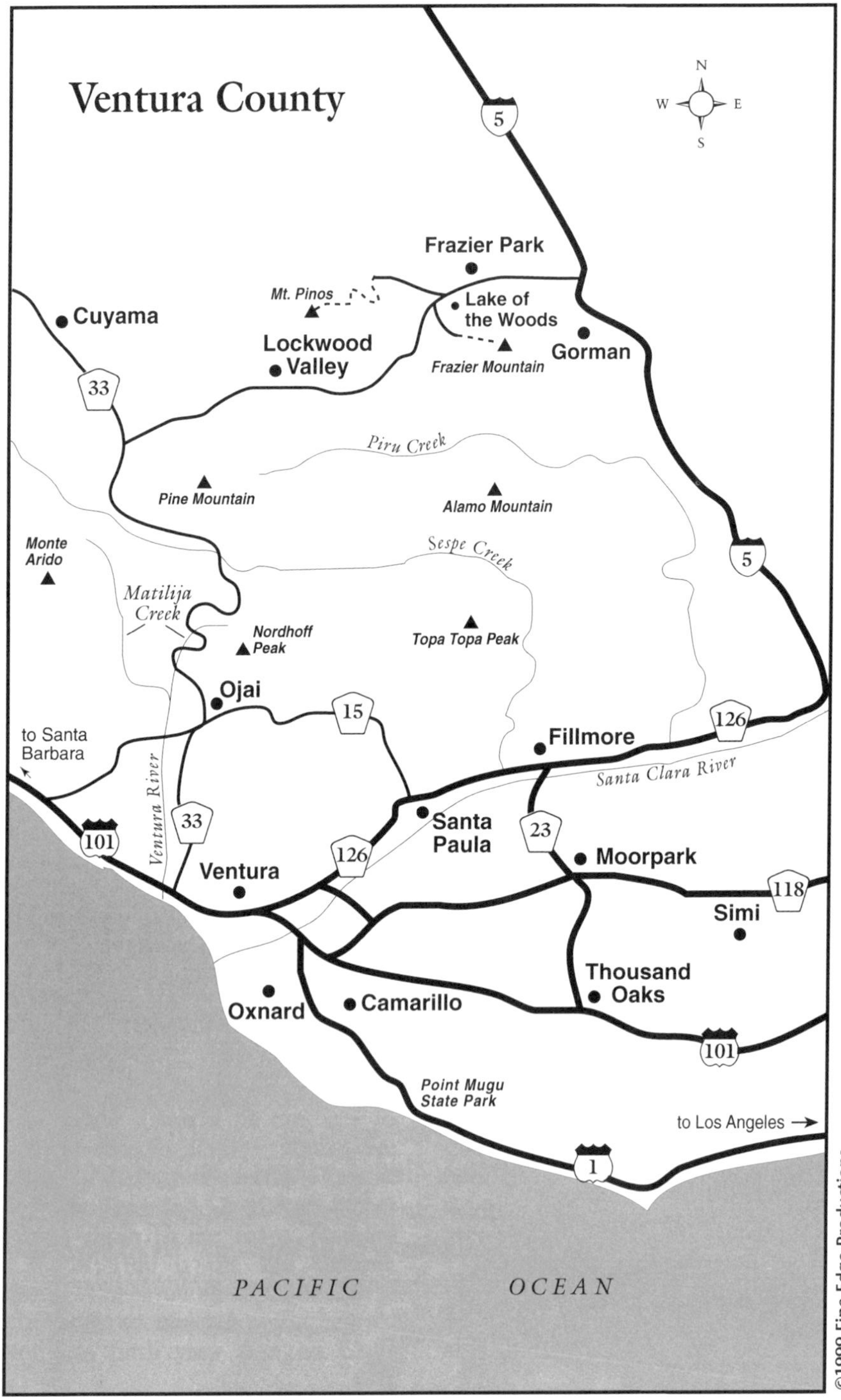

Ventura County

N
W · E
S

5

Frazier Park

Mt. Pinos
Cuyama
Lake of
the Woods
Gorman

Lockwood
Valley
Frazier Mountain

33

Piru Creek

Pine Mountain
Alamo Mountain

Monte
Arido

Sespe Creek

Matilija
Creek

Nordhoff
Peak
Topa Topa Peak

Ojai

15
126

Fillmore

to Santa
Barbara

Santa Clara River

101
33

Santa
Paula
23
Moorpark

126
118

Ventura
Simi

Thousand
Oaks

Oxnard
Camarillo
101

Point Mugu
State Park

to Los Angeles →

1

PACIFIC   OCEAN

©1999 Fine Edge Productions

CHAPTER 4

Ventura County

By Mickey McTigue, Kevin Woten, Jamie Griffis,
Mark Langton and Delaine Fragnoli

Ventura County is located on the Southern California coast adjacent to and directly west of Los Angeles County. It is a small county by California standards, only 45 miles east to west and 60 miles north to south.

Although small, Ventura offers a great diversity of terrain for the mountain biker. Starting from sea level at the beach and rising to nearly 9,000 feet at the

Great views can be found in the Ventura backcountry

summit of Mt. Pinos, you will find wide ranges in climate, elevation, trail and road conditions, and proximity to "civilization."

Almost all the population lives in the southern half on the coastal plains and river valleys, while the Los Padres National Forest takes up most of the mountainous, less-populated northern half. The many miles of trails and dirt roads in the forest, combined with a mild climate, make mountain bicycling an exciting year-round sport here.

As with the other parts of the Los Padres National Forest documented in the previous chapters, this part of the forest is also broken up by large sections of wilderness. In 1992, the Chumash and Sespe Wilderness areas were established, resulting in the loss to mountain bicycling of many roads and trails, including the incomparable Sespe and its hot springs.

Fortunately, many miles of roads and trails remain for your exploration, whether you are a novice or an experienced rider.

Point Mugu State Park

Point Mugu State Park is one of the most popular bicycling areas in the Santa Monica Mountains. It has spectacular scenery and several loop options for bicyclists. The main trail—actually an old fire road—is relatively flat and connects Newbury Park in the San Fernando Valley with the beach, where there is camping at Sycamore Canyon Campground.

The park offers five miles of ocean shoreline, two long rides in canyon bottomland, and a long ridge ride overlooking both the canyon and ocean. La Jolla Valley (currently closed to bikes) has one of the finest displays of native grasslands left in California. Bluffs near the ocean are among the few places in the world with giant coreopsis, a small tree-like shrub with bright yellow spring flowers. Silvery sycamores, thriving on deep underground water, mark the canyon floor and put on a wild display of color in the fall.

Point Mugu is inhabited by several large mammal species, including at least two mountain lions (one called Big Tail). In winter, thousands of Monarch butterflies come through during their migration south from colder climes. Because Point Mugu is located on the northwest tip of Santa Monica Bay, it provides an excellent viewing point for the California gray whale migrations in winter and spring.

Four miles northwest of Sycamore Cove, an observation platform on the west side of Pacific Coast Highway overlooks the saltwater Mugu Lagoon. There is a picnic table here, and it's a good place to watch for birds. Point Mugu Rock, a popular bouldering area for climbers, is located one mile to the southeast. From the observation platform, you may spot several rare or endangered birds, including the brown pelican, clapper rail, Belding's savanna sparrow, California least tern and marsh sandpiper. To the east of the lagoon grows the giant coreopsis. Do not disturb these birds or plants; they are protected species. *Note:* The property behind the fence belongs to the government. Unauthorized persons must stay out.

Many archeological sites from the Chumash culture have been discovered at Point Mugu State Park. Ranching began during the Spanish period when the area was known as the Guadalasca Land Grant. Most recently it was the Danielson family ranch. The Danielsons sold the land to the State to be preserved as a park. This was a critical event in the development of the Santa Monica Mountains National Recreation Area, since there were plans for developing a hotel and golf course on the Point Mugu park land. Local environmentalists joined efforts, and eventually this western cornerstone to the Santa Monicas was acquired for public use.

Sycamore Canyon in Point Mugu State Park draws big crowds. Use extra caution if you ride here, especially on summer weekends. For a more pleasant ride, we suggest cycling during the week or in winter.

Overlook Trail, Pt. Mugu State Park, with Boney Mountain in background

Mark Langton

69 Sycamore Canyon

Distance: 16.4 miles.
Difficulty: Easy, but with a stiff climb at the north end.
Elevation: Sea level to 800'.
Ride Type: Out-and-back on dirt road, some pavement.
Season: Year-round.
Map: Fine Edge Productions' Santa Monica Mountains Recreation Topo Map.
Water: Satwiwa Cultural Center, Sycamore Canyon campground.

Overview: From the beach side of Pacific Coast Highway, Big Sycamore Canyon fire road (also known as Big Sycamore Canyon Trail) begins at the north end of the Sycamore Canyon Campground. It winds along the bottom of deep, enclosed Sycamore Canyon through sycamore and oak

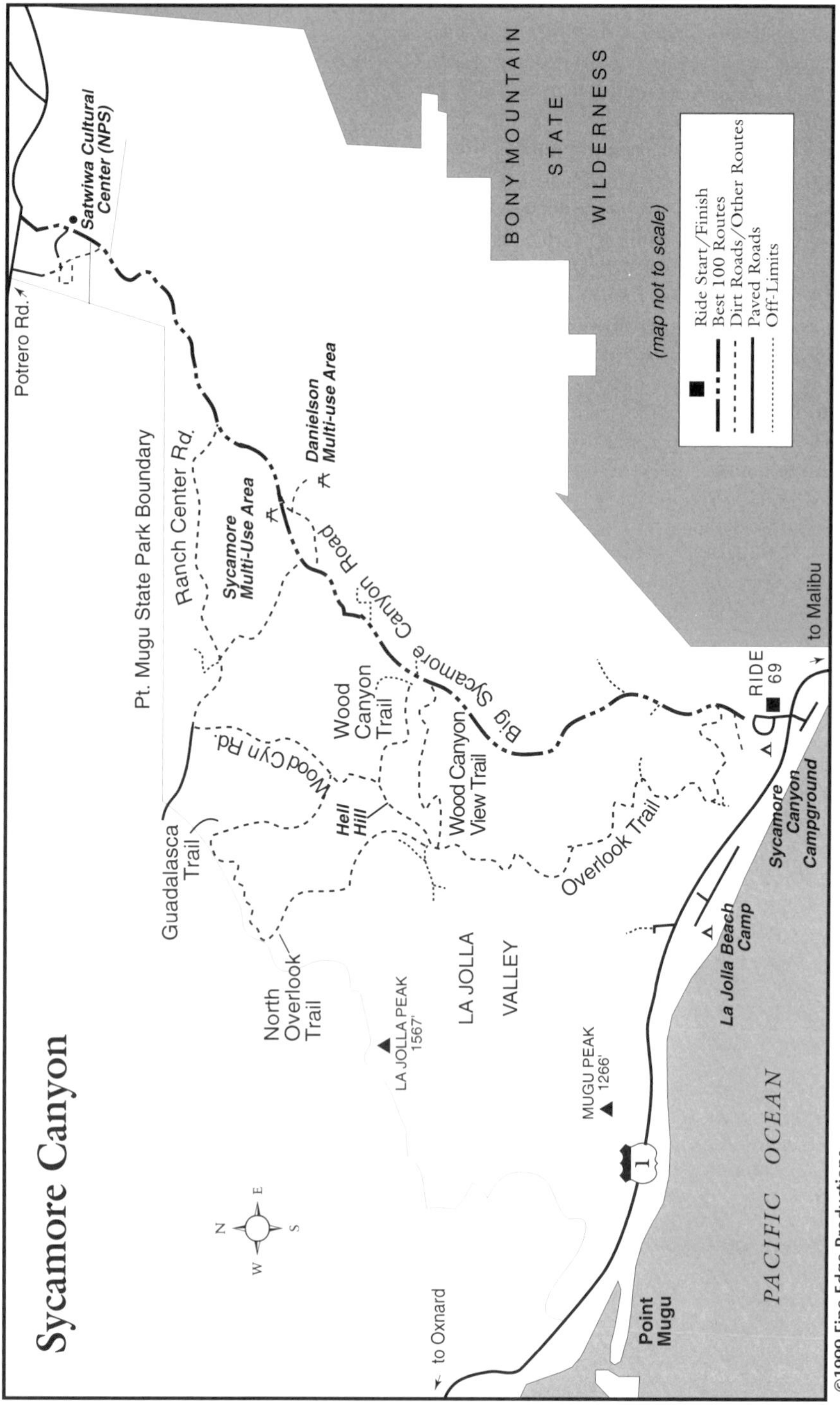

Sycamore Canyon

BONY MOUNTAIN STATE WILDERNESS

Satwiwa Cultural Center (NPS)

Potrero Rd.

Pt. Mugu State Park Boundary

Ranch Center Rd.

Sycamore Multi-Use Area

Danielson Multi-use Area

Big Sycamore Canyon Road

Wood Cyn Rd.

Guadalasca Trail

Wood Canyon Trail

Wood Canyon View Trail

Hell Hill

Overlook Trail

North Overlook Trail

LA JOLLA PEAK 1567'

LA JOLLA VALLEY

MUGU PEAK 1266'

Sycamore Canyon Campground

La Jolla Beach Camp

RIDE 69

to Malibu

Point Mugu

to Oxnard

PACIFIC OCEAN

(map not to scale)

■ Ride Start/Finish
Best 100 Routes
Dirt Roads/Other Routes
Paved Roads
Off-Limits

N
W   E
S

©1999 Fine Edge Productions

groves near a seasonal stream. The shade and frequent stream crossings make this a great hot-weather ride. It's an excellent choice for families or those just getting into the sport.

Getting There: The best access is from the beach at Sycamore Canyon Campground, 5 miles north of Leo Carrillo State Beach on Pacific Coast Highway (Highway 1). An entry fee is required for campground day use. Ride directions are from this starting point.

You can do this ride from the San Fernando Valley to the north—simply reverse the ride directions. If you're coming from Newbury Park or Ventura, take Freeway 101 and exit on Wendy Drive, turning left (south) toward the mountains. In 3.2 miles, Wendy ends at Potrero Road. Turn right. At the junction with Reino, bear left on Potrero Road, then turn left on Pinehill (at the stop sign) onto a dirt road. Follow the dirt road to the parking lot. This is the current

entrance. By mid-1999, however, a new entrance, including a cultural center, will be located off Potrero Road across from the Dos Vientos development.

To get to this new entrance from the 101 Freeway, exit Wendy Drive and go south (toward the beach) to Lynn Road. Turn right on Lynn to Reino Road, where Lynn becomes Potrero. Continue on Potrero 1.5 miles to the park entrance on the left. From this parking lot, trail mileage will increase by approximately 0.5 mile. Ride your bike around the locked fire gate to enter the park.

Route: Begin at the Big Sycamore Canyon fire road at the back of the Sycamore Canyon Campground. At 2.0 miles, you pass a picnic table under a huge overhanging oak tree. At 3.9 miles on the left is the entrance to the Wood Canyon View Trail, a 1.8-mile singletrack that climbs up to Overlook Trail. It is moderate to diffi-

Overlook Trail, Point Mugu State Park

Mark Langton

cult most of the way, a good challenge for experienced riders.

Keep right at the Wood Canyon Junction, mile 4.0. At mile 4.4 is the fire road cutoff to Ranch Center Road on the left. Keep right. At mile 4.7 is a junction with a paved road. Stay left on the pavement and watch for occasional cars. (Right leads to Danielson Multi-Use Area.) At 5.5 miles, keep right at the fork. Ranch Center Road (paved) goes left.

Just short of 6.6 miles, you pass a California Wilderness Area trailhead signed *Closed to bikes*. Begin a steep hill. Climb to the top of the hill at a water tower at mile 7.2. The road drops down to Satwiwa Nature Center at 8.2 miles and out the Newbury Park exit.

Return the way you came, or see Ride 70 and 71 for more options.

70 Sycamore Canyon/Guadalasca Trail Loop with Wood Canyon View Trail Option

Distance: 13.2 miles.
Difficulty: Moderate, with some steep climbs and descents.
Elevation: 2,700' gain/loss.
Ride Type: Loop on mostly dirt roads and singletrack.
Season: Year-round.
Map: Fine Edge Productions' Santa Monica Mountains Recreation Topo Map.
Water: Sycamore Canyon campground.

Overview: While there are several options available to both the recreational and hard-core mountain biker, this ride offers the best that Point Mugu has to offer. Riding this route in reverse would add fire road climbing and singletrack descending.

Getting There: The best access is from the beach at Sycamore Canyon Campground, 5 miles north of Leo Carrillo State Beach on Pacific Coast Highway. An entry fee is required for campground day use.

You can do this ride from the San Fernando Valley to the north. That would add 8 miles round trip. (See the previous ride for directions.)

Route: Begin at the Big Sycamore Canyon fire road at the back of the Sycamore Canyon Campground. At 2.0 miles you pass a picnic table under a huge overhanging oak tree. At 3.9 miles on the left is the entrance to the Wood Canyon View Trail, a 1.8-mile singletrack that climbs up to Overlook Trail. It is moderate to difficult most of the way, a good challenge to experienced riders. You may choose to descend this trail back down into Sycamore Canyon after climbing Guadalasca Trail. (See *Option* at the end of the ride description.)

Continue past the entrance to Wood Canyon View Trail 0.1 mile to Wood Canyon Trail. Bear left and continue to Deer Camp Junction at mile 4.8. Turn right (to the left is the infamous Hell Hill climb) and go to mile 5.2 and the intersection of Guadalasca Trail on your left.

The trail starts out fairly wide and groomed, as it used to be an old ranch road that serviced the Spanish Guadalasca Rancho. Climb through a beautiful riparian oak forest and then gain elevation into scrub oak. At 6.0 miles, a singletrack comes in from the left. Take the singletrack and begin climbing several perfectly radiused switchbacks.

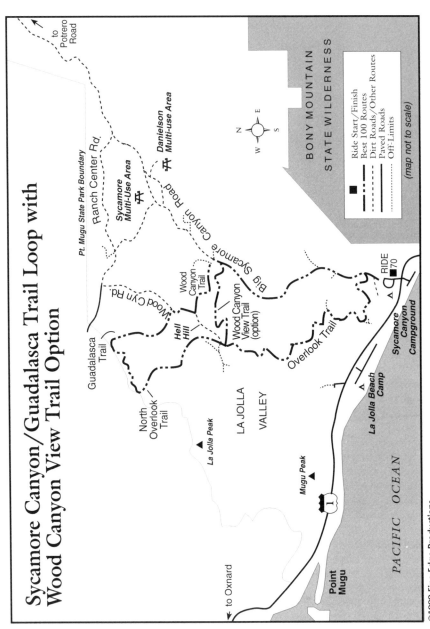

Sycamore Canyon/Guadalasca Trail Loop with
Wood Canyon View Trail Option

Wood Canyon View Trail, Pt. Mugu State Park

At mile 7.8, you come to the intersection with North Overlook fire road. Turn left up a short hill and then descend to the intersection of Hell Hill and Overlook Trail just past mile 9.

Option: Just a few yards past this intersection on Overlook Trail is the upper entrance to Wood Canyon View Trail to the left. Turn left here to descend the moderate-to-difficult singletrack back to Sycamore Canyon. Turn right at Sycamore Canyon

to return to the campground.

For the main route, continue straight on Overlook Trail for about a mile of gentle climbing and then a great descent back into Sycamore Canyon with panoramic views of Sycamore Canyon and the Pacific Ocean. At mile 12.7, you meet up with Big Sycamore Canyon fire road. Turn right and ride 0.5 mile back to the campground for a total of 13.2 miles.

Northern Santa Monica Mountains

The north end of the Santa Monica Mountains presents perhaps the most diverse and abundant riding opportunities of all the park regions in the Santa Monica Mountains National Recreation Area, including the Conejo Open Space Conservation Agency (COSCA) in Ventura County. COSCA property is maintained by the City of Thousand Oaks as an integral

part of the lifestyle of the Conejo Valley, and in the case of the Los Robles Trail, it abuts National Park Service land at Rancho Sierra Vista.

Because of the differing use policies affecting state, national and COSCA properties, please try to be aware of what land you are riding on and obey all rules. Local mountain bikers are fortunate to have access to the singletrack in COSCA, along with hikers and equestrians. Residents are proud and devoted to keeping COSCA suitable for multi-use recreation. The Conejo Open Space Trails Advisory Committee, a multi-use board made up of residents from the community, has been a remarkable model of establishing multi-use guidelines.

The Conejo Volunteer Patrol, a multi-use patrol modeled after the CORBA Mountain Bike Unit and equestrian Mounted Patrol Unit (NPS), is representative of the cooperative use of the area by hikers, equestrians and cyclists. The patrol keeps a vigilant watch on COSCA property, as does a concerned and protective constituency of individuals. Both these groups are intolerant of reckless or irresponsible behavior, so it is of utmost importance that cyclists conduct themselves in the most care-ful manner possible. Ignoring prudent riding behavior could threaten the use pattern for cyclists in the future, as well as present a physical danger to other users. *Always control your speed and be watchful of other users around every turn!*

Virtually all of COSCA property is rugged and steep, with only a few short, easy fire roads for riders of less than intermediate ability. There is a significant amount of challenging terrain in a relatively short distance, which makes the riding very strenuous yet rewarding. There are also several other areas in COSCA that can be accessed, but because they are interspersed in and around the Conejo Valley and must be connected by traveling streets and entering trailheads that are still not completely identified, we are including only the Westlake Open Space/Los Robles Canyon Open Space.

71 Los Robles Trail

Distance: 10 miles one way; 16-mile loop via Potrero Road.
Difficulty: Moderate, with some difficult, technical singletrack sections.
Elevation: 2,500' gain (approximate).
Ride Type: One-way with shuttle or loop on dirt roads and singletrack.
Season: Year-round.
Map: Fine Edge Productions' Santa Monica Mountains Recreation Topo Map.
Water: At trailhead, Satwiwa Cultural Center.

Overview: Los Robles Canyon Open Space offers several miles of interconnected singletracks and fire roads with a variety of terrain and vegetation. Although surrounded by much development, you can quickly ride into narrow canyons rich with riparian vegetation, and onto ridges with spectacular views of the Conejo and Hidden Valleys that make it seem like you are far away from the city. Yet you are never more than a few minutes from civilization. Still, the rides are challenging, and in season there are many wildflowers. *Caution:* The area is heavily used by equestrians, especially on weekends.

The main Los Robles Ridge Trail runs 10 miles west to east between Newbury Park and Westlake Village.

(Continued on Conejo Crest map, Ride 72)

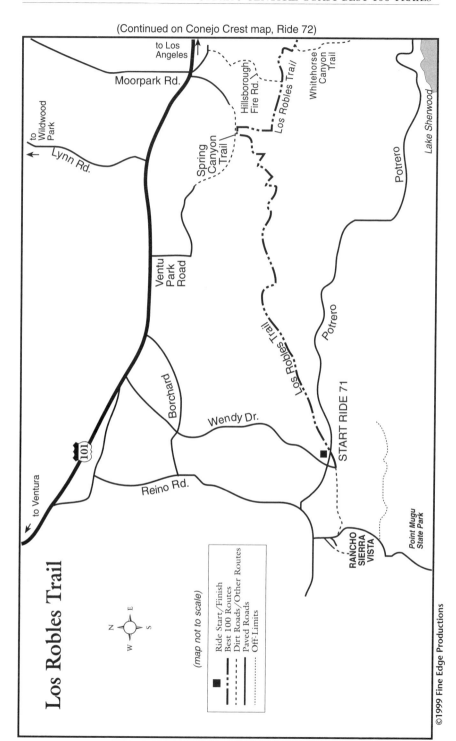

Los Robles Trail

(map not to scale)

Ride Start/Finish
Best 100 Routes
Dirt Roads/Other Routes
Paved Roads
Off-Limits

©1999 Fine Edge Productions

View of Thousand Oaks from Los Robles Trail

(Hidden Valley and Rancho Sierra Vista are to the south.) There are several connectors coming in from the north and south along the way. At the east end, the main trail forks to three different trailheads: Fairview, Triunfo Park and Lake Sherwood (see the following ride). The trail described below goes from west to east, but you can ride it in either direction. If you do it as a one-way, you need to arrange a shuttle or pick up.

Getting There: From 101, exit at Wendy and go left toward the coast. When Wendy ends at Potrero, go left 0.5 mile to gravel parking lot on left. There's water and trail information at the trailhead. Other access: Moorpark Road/Fairview Road/Triunfo Park/Lake Sherwood.

Route: Starting at the trail heading out from the gravel parking lot, you climb a short way to a private driveway. Go straight across and follow the

trail to the right. Just a few yards up the hill (0.2 mile), the trail veers left downhill to a singletrack on the right. Follow the trail as it dips and rolls, with residential property below you. At 1.3 miles, you come to the intersection with Felton Street Trail coming in from the left. This leads to Felton Street and Lynn Road.

Continue up and to the right for the Los Robles Trail. There will be a series of steep climbs and descents along a double rail horse fence. At 2.0 miles, turn left at the Y. At 2.2 miles, turn left at the fork heading uphill. Do not go straight as it leads to private property. The trail will switchback several times and come to another intersection at mile 2.6. (The left trail, called "4136" by locals—as of this printing it has no official name—leads to a great 1.8-mile descent that winds down to Lynn Road in Newbury Park, just west of Ventu Park Road.) Go right to continue on Los Robles Trail.

At almost 2.8 miles, you come to

another intersection just below private property. Do not go onto private property. Bear left at the intersection to continue. At 3.1 miles, you come to a wide dirt road which is a private driveway extension of Ventu Park Road. Do not go up or down this road. Go straight across to the singletrack trail on the other side.

Climb the short steep hill and two switchbacks, and follow the contour of the mountain for approximately 1.5 miles. The trail then begins descending a mile-long section with a series of switchbacks. Be careful of other users coming uphill. *Note:* Use extreme caution through this entire section. Control your speed and avoid skidding through the turns.

Installing trail sign, Los Robles Open Space (COSCA)

At mile 5.7, at the intersection with Spring Canyon Trail, cross a metal bar, bear right and climb to a fork. Go right at the top of the hill, following signs to Lake Sherwood and Triunfo Park (left goes to Moorpark Road). Climb the steep hill. At 6.3 miles, you pass a picnic table in an oak grove where you go left at a junction just past the sign: *Los Padres Road .5 miles, Fairview Road 4 miles, Lake Sherwood Road 4 miles.* Climb the steep hill, cross a dirt road and then go through the center of Upper Meadow (upper plateau).

You come to an intersection with a gate on the right. To the left is Hillsborough Fire Road which leads down to Moorpark Road. Climb past a metal gate at mile 7.7. The trail forks at 7.9 miles. To the right is the White Horse Canyon Trail (see the following ride). To ride the rest of the Los Robles Trail, continue straight on the main fire road to the Open Space. (For continuation of this trail, see the map for the next ride, Conejo Crest/White Horse/Triunfo Park.)

Options: There are several choices once you get to the Westlake Open Space. 1) You can turn around and go back the same way, which in itself is very different from the direction you just came. 2) Many riders take Potrero Road back to their cars at Potrero near Wendy for a loop. If you choose to do this, turn right back at the White Horse Canyon Trail. Make no turns off the main trail and you eventually come to Potrero Road and the equestrian center. Once you are on Potrero Road, turn right and ride back to your car.

Upper plateau, Los Robles Trail

Mark Langton

72 Conejo Crest/White Horse/ Triunfo Park

Distance: 6.8 miles, with shorter loops available.
Difficulty: Moderate to difficult; some advanced technical singletrack skills required.
Elevation: 1,500' gain (approximate).
Ride Type: Loop on dirt roads and singletrack.
Season: Year-round.
Map: Fine Edge Productions' Santa Monica Mountains Recreation Topo Map.
Water: None.

Overview: The technical single- and doubletrack trails in this area offer a variety of options and lots of fun. This particular loop provides great views of the Santa Monica Mountains and Westlake.

Getting There: There are several access points to the Westlake Open Space. From the east side, you can enter at Fairview off 101 at Hampshire or across the street from the equestrian center off Potrero Road in Westlake Village. From the west, you can access the upper plateau before the Los Robles Ridge Trail by taking Moorpark Road off 101, going south to Los Padres, left to Hillsborough, and right to the top of the hill. Access is on the right. However, the majority of the trail network is off Hampshire to the east.

To reach the Hampshire trails, go north on Freeway 101 to Thousand Oaks, exit Hampshire Road, go south toward Westlake to Willow Lane (the

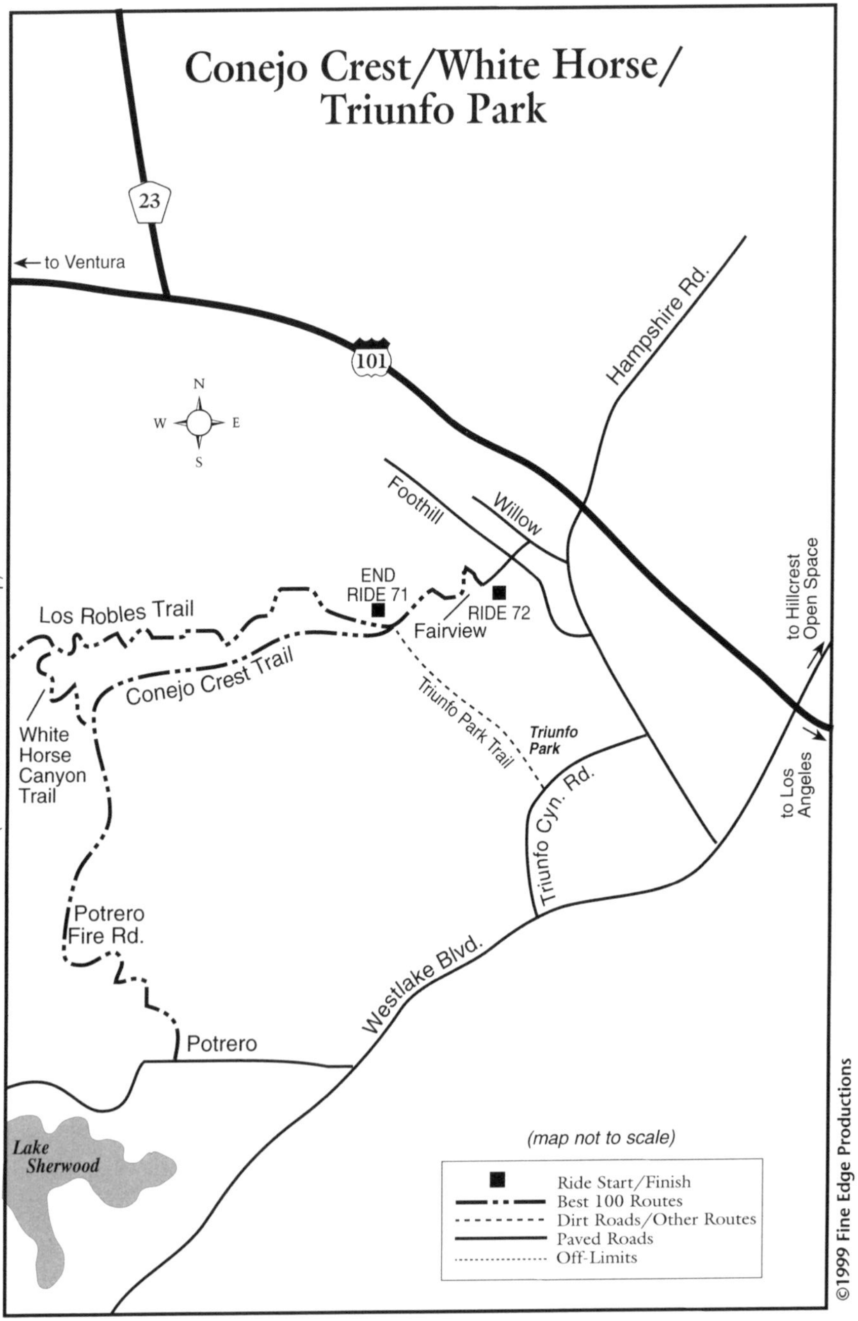

Conejo Crest/White Horse/ Triunfo Park

23

← to Ventura

101

Hampshire Rd.

Foothill

Willow

N
W E
S

Los Robles Trail

END
RIDE 71

RIDE 72

Fairview

(Continued from Los Robles map)

Conejo Crest Trail

Triunfo Park Trail

Triunfo Park

White
Horse
Canyon
Trail

Triunfo Cyn. Rd.

to Hillcrest
Open Space

to Los
Angeles

Potrero
Fire Rd.

Westlake Blvd.

Potrero

Lake
Sherwood

(map not to scale)

■   Ride Start/Finish
—··—··—   Best 100 Routes
-------   Dirt Roads/Other Routes
———   Paved Roads
············   Off-Limits

©1999 Fine Edge Productions

first street after you go under the free-way from San Fernando Valley/ Agoura or after turning right off the freeway coming from Ventura). Turn right on Willow to Fairview Road, then left on Fairview. Fairview ends at

Rocky Peak from the east, Santa Susanna Mountains

quickly and then climbing steeply to another intersection at mile 1.2. (To the right you can see a fire road descent, which is the Los Robles Canyon Trail over to the Los Robles Ridge Trail. Just behind you, back down the steep climb, is the entrance to Triunfo Park Trail. This is a very technical single-track of 0.9 mile that goes down to Triunfo Park in Westlake.) For your route, the Conejo Crest and White Horse Canyon Trail, turn left uphill at this intersection onto the narrow, rocky doubletrack.

Continue climbing until the hill tops out at a T. Here you have a beautiful view of the Santa Monicas to the west. The road winding up behind the rocky knob hill across the valley is Decker Road. To the left you can see part of Westlake Lake, and above that and to the right is Westlake Reservoir. Go right from the T-intersection to continue on Conejo Crest (left drops quickly to houses).

You will be on a ridge trail that is known as The Cobbles because of the rocky surface of the trail. At mile 1.9, you come to a descent that is very steep and loose. *Please use caution.* At the bottom of the steep descent (mile 2.0), there is a trail to the right that takes you directly into White Horse Canyon. Continue straight on this fun, rolling doubletrack to mile 2.2 and a fire road T. Going right takes you into White Horse Canyon; left goes to the beginning of the White Horse Canyon Trail.

Continue to the left downhill, and then up and over another rise. At 2.4 miles, there is a sign on the right for the White Horse Canyon Loop.

Foothill Road. Straight ahead you see a dirt road going between some houses. You can drive up this road to a locked gate, but the road is not well suited to vehicular travel, so park at the intersection.

Route: At Foothill and Fairview, set your odometer to 0.0. Continue up the fire road to a pump house on the left and a locked gate at mile 0.3. Go over the gate and turn right on the fire road. At almost 1.0 mile, you come to a three-way intersection. Straight ahead you can see the fire road as it dips down into a saddle and then reappears under a row of wire towers. (Left takes you back toward Westlake and houses; to the right is a steep climb that leads to a very technical singletrack that ends up back down at Freeway 101 and Rancho Road.)

Continue straight, descending

(The Equestrian Alternative Trail to the left is a route down to the houses below. The fire road straight ahead will take you to Potrero Road and the equestrian center.) Turn right onto the White Horse Canyon Trail for a short singletrack (lots of fun!) that takes you over the main fire road at 2.7 miles into White Horse Canyon. Turn left downhill to mile 3.4 and the main Los Robles Trail. Left takes you to the upper plateau and Hillsborough trailhead (and Los Robles Trail); right takes you back to your vehicle.

Continue right on the fire road for a fun-filled descent followed by a series of moderate switchback climbs. To your left is the Conejo Valley and Freeway 101. At 4.6 miles you arrive back at the three-way intersection and the entrance to Triunfo Park Trail. From here you can go back to where you started or descend Triunfo Park Trail.

Options: 1) If you choose to take the Triunfo Park Trail, you come to the end of the trail at a locked gate. To the left is a trail that takes you around a sand volleyball court toward a steep walk-up. Continuing uphill, it flattens out a bit and then gets very steep again. At the top of this second steep section, turn left and follow the fire road up to the first three-way intersection you came to when you began your ride (just short of mile 1.0). Turn right and continue back down to the locked gate and pump house on your left (Fairview).

2) For a less strenuous loop, instead of following the fire road up after climbing the two steep sections, go left downhill about 50 yards from the knoll you're on, and turn right at the bottom onto a narrow double-track. Just a short way down is a motorcycle trail on the left going straight down into a small valley. On the other side, you can see another fire road, the one you want to access. Drop down the motorcycle trail and follow it up the other side of the valley to a trail that merges you into the fire road. Stay on the main fire road, bearing right past the first Y in about 50 yards, then left at another Y, mile 1.6. Continue to a locked gate and pump station (mile 1.9), then turn right to go back down to Fairview.

Santa Susanna Mountains

To the northeast of the Santa Monica Mountains lies a short mountain range known as the Santa Susanna Mountains. This area is comprised of several small parcels, but is most noted for Rocky Peak Park, administered by the Santa Monica Mountains Conservancy, that rests on the border between the Simi and San Fernando valleys. In fact, both valleys can be seen sprawling below to the west and east from several view points along the Rocky Peak Trail. You will quickly see why it is called Rocky Peak, with its spectacular rock outcroppings and moonscape appearance.

Like many of the open areas in Southern California, the Santa Susannas were (and still are) home to large cattle ranches. As well, many locations still serve as sets for the television and movie industries. Large tracts of land are privately held, and you can often find yourself on private property if you're not careful. Please watch for fences and No Trespassing signs, and above all else respect private property and livestock.

Simi Valley from Rocky Peak Park

Mark Langton

73 Rocky Peak/Chumash Trail Loop

Distance: 12 miles.
Difficulty: Moderately strenuous and technical.
Elevation: 1,300' gain/loss.
Ride Type: Loop on fire road, singletrack and pavement.
Season: Year-round; summer can be very hot and smoggy.
Map: Simi Valley East.
Water: Santa Susanna County Park.

Overview: Although it requires quite a bit of pavement riding to fashion a loop, this ride combines a steep—but not too long—climb with a challenging, but fun, singletrack descent through some great rock outcroppings and with views of the San Fernando and Simi Valleys.

Getting There: From the east (405 freeway, San Fernando), take the 118 Freeway to Rocky Peak Road exit. Go left over the freeway, then right onto Santa Susanna Pass Road. Where it meets Kuehner Drive, turn left onto Katherine Street and go 0.2 mile to Santa Susanna County Park on the right.

From the west (23 Freeway, Simi), take the 118 Freeway to Kuehner Drive, turn right (south) and follow Kuehner as it curves to the east. Where it meet Santa Susanna Pass Road, turn right onto Katherine Street and go 0.2 mile to the county park. Park here.

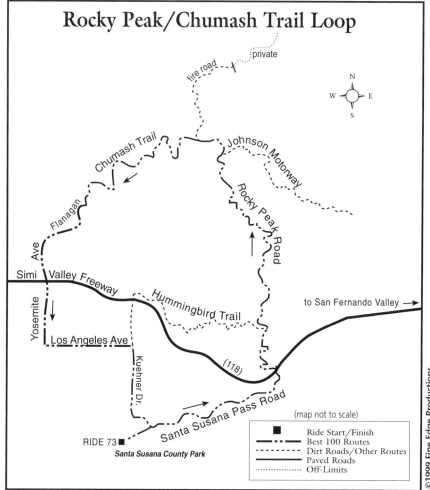

Route: From the park, backtrack to Santa Susanna Pass Road and go right. Begin a 2-mile climb to the Rocky Peak trailhead. Go left on Rocky Peak Road over the 118 Freeway to the trailhead. There is a locked gate and room for parking here. Starting at the county park, rather than at the trailhead, lets you get a nice warmup before the stiff climb up Rocky Peak.

Head around the gate and up. You climb from 1,571 feet to 2,700 feet in 2.4 miles to reach the high point of

the trail, just below Rocky Peak itself. That's steep, and it does hurt. The trail is fairly relentless, offering few breaks from climbing. After the summit, you still have several more steep climbs and descents to the end of the trail.

At 3.1 miles from the locked gate, Johnson Motorway comes in from the east (right). About 0.5 mile farther you come to the Chumash Trail on the west (left). You're going downhill and it's easy to bypass the trail. Watch for it.

Mark Langton

Heading down from Rocky Peak

Go left onto Chumash Trail. It pitches and rolls through some very loose and technical sections, but also has some sections where you can catch your breath and recover your nerves. It is almost always rocky.

The trail comes out at the end of Flanagan Drive beside a housing development. The property to the east at the bottom of the trail is parkland for several acres next to Flanagan, but there is no egress from the property as it is private to the east.

To loop back to your starting point, go down Flanagan to Yosemite, left to Los Angeles Street, left to Kuehner where it joins Santa Susanna Pass Road, and right to the county park.

Ojai Valley

For cyclists, Ojai has it all. Surrounded by mountains, Ojai Valley offers mountain views from every point. Rural roads pass through orange groves and under spreading oaks, and a bike path follows the old railroad bed, providing opportunities for the road cyclist to explore the valley at an unhurried pace. Challenging mountain highways are used by local riders for training and racing; some of these riders have gone on to Olympic medals and professional careers.

As either a destination or a starting point, Ojai Valley is a mecca for mountain biking. Everything a mountain biker needs can be found here. Food,

lodging, supplies, hospital (hopefully not needed), ranger and sheriff stations, bike shops, entertainment and—in a place noted for its tennis tournament—lots of tennis courts. Stores, motels and resort hotels, golf courses and campgrounds provide a good base for non-riding family members who can entertain themselves while others are out enjoying the trails.

Winter rains in January and February may make riding something to dream about, but the rest of the year is fine. However, some summer days can be so hot that riding only in early morning is advised. Unless you are used to extreme heat, don't ride in the noon sun. Most of the local rides are short and close to town, so a bike is transportation enough. Longer day rides are possible, especially if there is a driver who can drop you off so you can ride back over the mountain to Ojai.

To get to Ojai Valley from U.S. Highway 101 in Ventura, take State Highway 33 north. In 11.2 miles, State Highway 150 joins in from the west. Stay on 150 to the east when Highway 33 branches northwest 2 miles farther. Another mile puts you in downtown Ojai with its famed arched arcade sidewalk cover. Highway 33 passes through the valley and continues north into the Los Padres National Forest where there's more excellent mountain bicycling; you may want to try those areas while staying in the Ojai Valley.

74 Sulphur Mountain Road

Distance: 18 miles.
Difficulty: Moderate, not technical.
Elevation: 300' to 2,600'; 2,300' difference.
Ride Type: Out-and-back or loop on dirt road and pavement.
Season: Spring, summer, fall; winter can be muddy.
Maps: Matilija, Ojai, Santa Paula Peak.
Water: None.
Comments: Road open to local vehicles.

Overview: Sulphur Mountain Road is a county road, graded dirt and gravel. It is closed to motor vehicles except for property owners, the Edison Company, and Ventura County vehicles. It's open to walkers, bicycles, and horses. This ride is good all year except just after a rainstorm, when it usually is muddy. There is no drinking water available; bring plenty, it can be a hot ride. The views of the mountains to the north and Lake Casitas to the west are exceptional.

Getting There: Turn east off Highway 33, between Casitas Springs and San Antonio Creek Bridge, 6.5 miles south of Ojai and 7.4 miles north of Highway 101 in Ventura. Travel east on the paved road past the Girl Scout Camp on the left to a locked gate. Park at the turnout on Sulphur Mountain Road and Highway 33 (milepost 7.40). Do not block the locked gate. Past the gate, all the land on both sides of the road is private and posted: *No Trespassing.* You must stay on the road. The side roads are also private and posted. Only the main road is public property and open to bicyclists. This is a very popular bicycle route and you should be alert for other riders going the opposite way, and especially for hikers and equestrians.

Route: Past the gate, you climb and turn to the north. About 100 yards up the dirt road, you encounter heavy black oil on the right side of the road; a little farther up you will see the source—a natural oil spring that has been running for years, maybe centuries. Sometimes it runs out onto

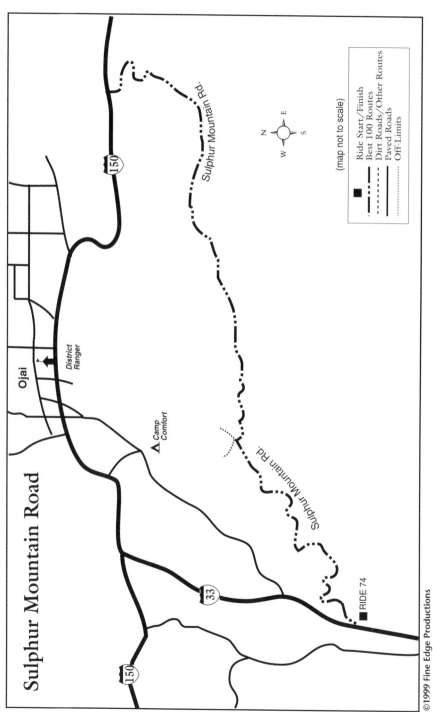

Sulphur Mountain Road

Ojai

Sulphur Mountain Rd.

Sulphur Mountain Rd.

District Ranger

△ Camp Comfort

150

33

150

■ RIDE 74

(map not to scale)

Ride Start/Finish
Best 100 Routes
Dirt Roads/Other Routes
Paved Roads
Off-Limits

N
W E
S

the road and the mess is hard to avoid.

The first mile is a steep but rideable climb through oak forest and the shade is welcome. After a short level section the climbing resumes at an easier grade; this is typical for most of this route. You climb to the east along the ridge of this mountain, first on the south side toward the ocean, and at other times on the north. There your view is of the whole Ojai Valley with the rugged mountains beyond that ring the valley.

The earth here is covered mainly with grasses, live oaks, and scattered sage. It's quite green in early spring with lots of flowers; later it becomes very dry and brown. Those who travel silently and watch carefully may see wildlife. I have seen several coyotes, some bobcats, deer, quail, hawks, snakes, and lots of small birds. Tarantulas, those large (6-inch diameter), black, hairy, scary-looking spiders, are sometimes common on the road in late afternoon in the fall. Just steer around them and you shouldn't have any trouble.

Often there are cattle on the road, including large bulls. Slow travel and patience are the best ways to get past them. Give them time and they usually get off the road. Don't run or chase them, just move slowly past. Close all gates you open.

As the road goes on and up to the top, you have views of Topa Topa Bluff, Sisar Canyon, and Santa Paula Peak. The southern view, after your

Lake Casitas from Sulphur Mountain Road

Jamie Griffis

initial climb out of Ventura River Canyon, looks across Cañada Larga to Ventura, Oxnard and the Pacific Ocean. On clear days, you can see several of the coastal islands: Anacapa, Santa Cruz, and Santa Rosa. There are occasional days of Santa Ana northeast winds when you can see all seven of the islands, including Catalina, Santa Barbara, San Nicolas and San Miguel.

You can turn around anywhere and return, or continue on to the top and beyond. *Loop Option:* After 9 miles, the road is paved and you may loop on through to Upper Ojai and Highway 150. Turn left (west) onto Highway 150. Continue on Highway 150 to 33, go left (south) back to Sulphur Mountain Road and your car.

75 Fuel Break Road

Distance: 2.3 miles from Gridley Road to Stewart Canyon/Pratt Trail Road.
Difficulty: Moderate; trail access is very rough and steep.
Elevation: 1,200' – 1,800'; 600' differential.
Ride Type: One-way on dirt road and trail.
Season: Spring and fall best; summer is very warm and winter can be muddy.
Maps: Matilija, Ojai.
Water: None.

Overview: A wide fuel break has been cut along the south side of Nordhoff Peak between Gridley Canyon and Stewart Canyon. For fire fighting and maintenance purposes, a fire road was built along this fuel break. Being so close to town, it makes a nice training ride although the road surface is often loose from being graded. There are excellent views of the Ojai Valley and no long hills to climb, but the trail down to Stewart Dam is rocky and somewhat technical.

Getting There: The best access is at the upper end of Gridley Road, reached from Highway 150.

Route: Just below the turnaround,

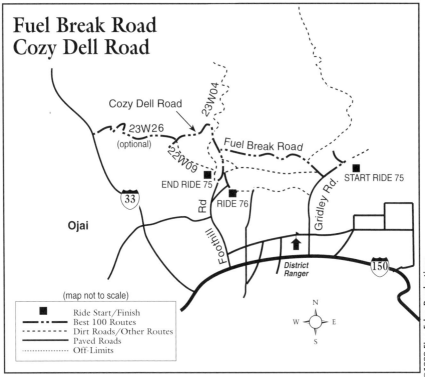

Fuel Break Road
Cozy Dell Road

ride and walk north on the signed Gridley Connector Trail (22W05). You climb steeply a short way to Gridley Road (5N11). Turn left and travel downhill 0.3 mile and take Fuel Break Road on the right uphill toward the west. Here you alternately climb and descend to the west and then drop into Stewart Canyon.

At the junction with Pratt Trail (23W09), you can turn left and travel down the canyon and come out at the Stewart Canyon Debris Dam. There is parking for trail users here.

Options: From here, you can return the way you came, or loop back to Gridley by way of Shelf Road. (Street access to the debris dam from Ojai is by traveling north on Signal almost to the end at Shelf Road; turn left at a very large water tank; within 100 yards you see the dam.)

You can also travel up Pratt Trail from Fuel Break Road by turning right and heading up the canyon on a road that takes you up on the ridge between Stewart Canyon and Cozy Dell Canyon. On that ridge, the Pratt Trail branches off and climbs on up the mountain; the road there doubles back and drops down into Cozy Dell Canyon (see the following ride).

76 Cozy Dell Road

Distance: 4 miles.
Difficulty: Moderate to difficult; steep climb.
Elevation: 1,400' - 2,080'; 680' differential.
Ride Type: Out-and-back on fire road.
Season: Spring, summer, fall; winter can be muddy.
Map: Matilija.
Water: None.

Overview: This is a nice ride in a canyon with oak trees that shade the road. Cozy Dell Canyon Road—a continuation of Fuel Break and Pratt Trail roads—drops down Cozy Dell Canyon from Pratt Trail (23W09) and heads out to a gate at the Quaker ranch in the mouth of the canyon.

Getting There: From Highway 150, turn north on Ventura to Signal. Turn off the north end of Signal Street near a large water tank and head west to the Stewart Canyon Debris Dam. Park in the space provided near the corrals.

Route: Take Pratt Trail (23W09) up

the canyon here, passing many residences. There are twists and turns to the trail before you finally get beyond the homes to the dirt road section of Pratt Trail. Continue up the canyon past Foothill Trail (22W09) and Fuel Break Road, both to your right. Continue climbing until the road crosses the ridge on the west side of Stewart Canyon.

Cozy Dell Road begins at the saddle; take it west and downhill. At the next fork go right, down into the canyon. (The left fork climbs up to the ridge and ends.) At the bottom of this side-canyon, there is a road heading into upper Cozy Dell Canyon that dead-ends at some water works.

Ignore this and continue left and down past Foothill Trail on the left. About 100 feet farther on the right is Cozy Dell Trail (23W26). Continue on Cozy Dell Road about 0.5 mile.

You reach a locked gate at the ranch—turn around here.

Loop Option: Take Cozy Dell Trail to Highway 33 where a left turn takes you back to Ojai.

Nordhoff Ridge

Rising abruptly out of Matilija Creek and climbing 12 miles to the east to Topa Topa Bluffs, Nordhoff Ridge separates Ojai Valley and Sespe River Canyon. This 50-square-mile area is characterized by steep, narrow canyons and even steeper ridges. The chaparral-covered sloping terrain contains only small streams and in summer most of these dry up. Water can usually be found at springs and where canyons are the steepest and narrowest, the water flowing over bedrock. Snow can occur in winter above 3000 feet, and rainfall can be very heavy in storms that may last several days, turning the gentle streams into raging torrents. Nordhoff Ridge receives an average rainfall of 28 inches a year, about twice that of Ojai Valley, just 5 miles away. Most of this rain occurs January through March.

The vistas from Nordhoff Ridge are spectacular. You see Ojai Valley, the Pacific Ocean and Channel Islands to the south, and to the north are repeating peaks and ridges separated by deep canyons across the Sespe Wilderness. A fire road travels the length of Nordhoff Ridge, and other roads and trails switchback up out of the lateral canyons and ridges from Ojai Valley on the south and Rose Valley to the north. The shortest way to the ridge is by Chief Peak Road (5N42.2) from Rose Valley.

Many types of rides are possible here: out-and-backs, traverses and loops. West Fork Lion Canyon, The Pines, and White Ledge trail camps are all located

Kevin Woten

Forest Service marker, biking trails

near year-round water sources. Gridley Spring trail camp was washed away by flood water, but there is a plan to relocate it nearby with volunteer labor. Campgrounds accessible by automobile are Wheeler Gorge on Highway 33, and Rose Valley, Middle Lion, and Lion camps along paved Rose Valley Road.

77 Upper Ojai to Ojai over Nordhoff Ridge

Distance: 24 miles (33 miles if you ride from downtown Ojai).
Difficulty: Difficult; occasionally technical.
Elevation: 1,600' to 5,200' to 800'; a 3,400' climb.
Ride Type: One-way on dirt roads and singletrack requires shuttle; the longer version is a loop.
Season: Spring, summer, fall.
Maps: Ojai, Lion Canyon, Topa Topa Mountains, Santa Paula Peak.
Water: Sisar Creek, White Ledge Spring, Wilsie Spring. Treat all water.

Overview: This route along the Ojai Front Range is difficult due to the elevation gain, the long distance and the descent along the Gridley Trail singletrack. Start early and plan for an all-day ride. You should not attempt this ride if you dislike narrow trails or have little or no experience on singletrack. The route links Sisar Canyon Road in Upper Ojai to Gridley Trail, which leads toward downtown Ojai. You may ride in the reverse order if you prefer or just part way and return.

Getting There: First, you have to get to Sisar Canyon Road, 9 miles east of Ojai on Highway 150. Park along 150 next to Summit School. Very strong riders might just ride out from Ojai, but be aware of the 850-foot climb. If you have two cars, leave one in Ojai, near Gridley and Highway 150, and one at Sisar Road to be picked up later; maybe someone can drop you off and take the car back to Ojai.

Route: From Highway 150 just east of Summit School, Sisar Canyon Road (4N15) heads north, climbing

3,400 feet in about 8 miles. It has an almost continuous grade and is usually in good condition, although in winter snow occurs at upper elevations and in summer it can be very hot. Start at dawn and ride up in the shade on the southwest slopes to avoid the worst heat.

As you leave Highway 150, Sisar Canyon Road passes homes on both sides of the road. Past the last house, the road turns slightly right and you need to stay on the main road by keeping to the right, avoiding left forks until you reach the Forest Service locked gate. Beyond this gate there is one more right fork, a private road to a remote ranch—keep out.

The road soon switchbacks up Sisar Canyon, and at 3 miles, you are at the junction with trail 21W08. (White Ledge Trail Camp, located about 1 mile up the trail, is a pleasant spot shaded by pungent bay trees. The spring there runs all year at considerable volume.) Past this junction, stay on Sisar Canyon Road (4N15) as it leaves the canyon and crosses a ridge out to the west of Sisar Canyon. Along

Upper Ojai to Ojai over Nordhoff Ridge
Sisar Road/Nordhoff Ridge/Red Reef Trail Loop

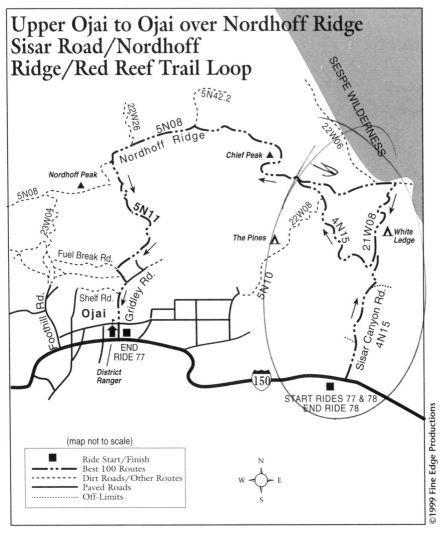

(map not to scale)

■ · · Ride Start/Finish
— · · — Best 100 Routes
- - - - - Dirt Roads/Other Routes
——— Paved Roads
· · · · · · · · · Off-Limits

©1999 Fine Edge Productions

the right side of the road at the 7-mile point, water is piped to a water trough from Wilsie Spring just above the road.

Near the top of Sisar Canyon Road, Horn Canyon Trail (22W08) crosses the road. *This steep rough trail is not recommended for bicycle use.* Just another 0.5 mile, and Sisar Canyon Road ends at the top of Nordhoff Ridge and meets Road 5N08. From this ridge, you get your first view to the north, looking out over the Sespe

Canyon, past the Piedra Blanca sandstone formation to the cliffs of Reyes, Haddock and Thorn Point peaks.

This marks the end of the 8-mile Sisar Canyon Road section of this ride. It's a good turnaround point if you just want a 16-mile out-and-back.

Turn left (west) onto Road 5N08 at its junction with Sisar Canyon Road. Continuing on Nordhoff Ridge, the next section is more moderate riding with some steep downhills and a net

Winter cycling in the Ventura backcountry

Kevin Woten

elevation loss of 1,600 feet in 7.6 miles. You quickly get a break, descending 250 feet in a mile on the north side of the ridge. At a low point on the ridge, you start a long climb around the east and north sides of Chief Peak, regaining the altitude you just lost. It's not very steep and the scenery makes up for it. On the northwest side of Chief Peak, the road travels on Nordhoff Ridge and drops and climbs very steeply for about a half-mile. Some hills can be climbed with the momentum gained coming down the previous hill. This is also the highest elevation of the trip. There are places along the ridge where you look right down to Ojai Valley.

At 13 miles, Chief Peak Road descends to the right past a cattle-guard and gate. Continue on the ridge ahead to the west, easily descending 500 feet in 1.5 miles to the junction with Howard Canyon Trail (22W26). When you look west

over Nordhoff Ridge, you can see Nordhoff Peak at the same elevation as you are. It once housed a lookout and the steel tower is still standing. Now the road begins a much steeper descent to Gridley Saddle—900 feet in almost 1.3 miles. At the saddle, you will have ridden 16 miles from Upper Ojai. Gridley Trail, the third and last leg of this ride, is to your left (south) at the saddle.

Gridley Trail (5N11) hugs the side of the canyon and winds down into the valley with many switchbacks. Most of it isn't very steep (you go from 3,600 feet to 1,600 feet in 6 miles), but it is considered technical because of the huge drop-offs over the edge. (Go slowly or—if you're not sure of your skill—get off and walk, and live to ride another day.) About halfway down, the trail widens where it used to be a road. Water is available about a half-mile down at Gridley Spring, a former camp that washed out. A plastic pipe carries water to a horse water trough; your water (treat it!) is from the stream above the trail.

After a break, continue down the west side of the canyon, passing avocado groves. Take the right (west) fork at the saddle; you are now on a road. Go down this road 0.3 mile and, at the out-bend, take the marked trail on your left steeply downhill. You nee ¹ to walk the first part of this short connector trail, and might as well walk all of it due to rocks.

Now at 22 miles, you are on paved Gridley Road and it's a smooth ride back to Highway 150 and town. Watch your speed down this steep twisty road until you get to the straight part. A right turn at Grand Avenue heads to town. A left turn on Montgomery Street takes you to Ojai Avenue.

78 Sisar Road/Nordhoff Ridge/ Red Reef Trail Loop

Distance: 17.5 miles.
Difficulty: Strenuous; trail is technical.
Elevation: 3,400' gain/loss.
Ride Type: Lollipop-shaped loop on dirt road and singletrack.
Season: Spring, summer, fall.
Maps: Ojai, Lion Canyon.
Water: Sisar Creek, White Ledge Spring, Wilsie Spring. Treat all water.

Overview: In the mid-1960s, roads were built along Nordhoff Ridge past Chief Peak and Topa Topa Bluffs out to Hines Peak and down Sisar Canyon to Upper Ojai. These roads generally followed the route of the trails they replaced. In Sisar Canyon, though, the road takes a completely different route from one mile below White Ledge Trail Camp. This leaves a 3-mile section of the original Red Reef Trail intact in Sisar Canyon— providing a singletrack return from Nordhoff Ridge. Before the roads were built, the Red Reef Trail went from Upper Ojai over the mountains and down Red Reef Canyon (thus the name) to the Sespe (now largely closed to bikes because of the wilderness areas).

Getting There: Start at Summit School on Highway 150 (see previous ride).

Route: Follow the previous ride route description, riding up Sisar Road (4N15) to Nordhoff Ridge (5N08), reached at 8.0 miles. Go right (east) on 5N08 along Nordhoff Ridge.

The road circles around the north side of the first hill with little elevation gain before crossing a saddle to climb moderately to the south side of Sisar Peak. Here, after one mile and 300 feet of climbing, you are at the top end of Horn Canyon Trail (not recommended for bikes) and just south of Sisar Peak, easily recognizable by all the repeater radio antennae on towers there.

As you continue traveling east close to the ridgetop, the cliffs of Topa Topa Bluffs provide impressive scenery ahead. Enjoy some easy riding while descending slightly for the next mile; at the second saddle on the left, make note of Lion Canyon Trail (22W06), marked by a sign. (This very difficult trail could be used to connect with the rides described in the following section; it's open but may be in poor shape.) Just 0.5 mile ahead on the right is the top of Red Reef Trail (21W08).

Head down 21W08. Between Nordhoff Ridge and White Ledge Camp, the trail is steep and rocky with many switchbacks in the brush. White Ledge is a nice camp although level ground is limited. Springs here run all year and produce an amazing amount of water. The campsites are in a grove of bay trees and the pleasant smell permeates the air.

Below the camp, the trail follows the creek, keeping to the west side for one mile. Although the trail here is a little rough, it is not very steep and could be ridden up as well as down. The trail ends at Sisar Road at 14.5 miles. Head left on Sisar Road and enjoy descending what you worked so hard to climb earlier. At 17.5 miles, you're back at your car at Highway 150.

Sespe Creek and Rose Valley

To mountain bicyclists, the Sespe was a place that had the best this sport has to offer—long and short rides as well as fishing, swimming and camping by the big pools on the river. And, of course, there are those fabled hot springs—so much boiling water it creates a hot creek. The water cools as it flows downstream, so you can find a pool with just the right temperature.

The Sespe River is a place that seems timeless; change is so gradual it's hard to see. The greatest changes came with land management practices that allowed roads to be constructed along the river. Then, with more people gaining access to gate keys, the barriers were opened to everyone in the early 1960s. A nightmare of abandoned vehicles, drugs and suspected murder ended when the floods of 1969 and 1972 washed out enough road to prevent 4WD traffic. Motor vehicles were then prohibited, but bicycles were still allowed. Trails across Sespe Canyon made it possible to ride from the Lockwood Valley area to Ojai or Fillmore.

On June 19, 1992, the Los Padres Condor Range and River Protection Act was signed into law. This bill placed 219,700 acres of forest land along the Sespe Creek into wilderness status. All man-made structures—including stoves, tables, and corrals—are to be removed except for artifacts, foot trails and registered historic buildings. Trail camps will be restored to a natural condition, and trails will be maintained at more primitive standards using only hand tools. Chain saws, some other motorized tools, and certain mechanical devices are prohibited. Sadly, this includes bicycles.

Yes, bicycles are now prohibited from the Sespe. That's the law, and we have to live with it. Six years of lobbying while this bill was before Congress had no impact, and many miles of trails are now off-limits to bicycles. (This guidebook, revised with the cooperation and assistance of the Forest Service, describes only those trails that are outside the current wilderness boundary.) A few trails and roads in the Sespe, upstream from the wilderness area, are still open to cyclists. Some of these connect to adjoining areas.

Four drive-in campgrounds are located in this area. Beaver Camp is beside the Sespe Creek off Highway 33 at milepost 28.07. Rose Valley Falls, Middle Lion, and Lion Canyon campgrounds are all accessible by car over paved Rose Valley Road (6N31). Turn off Highway 33 at milepost 28.84. Campfire restrictions may be in effect, so check ahead with the Forest Service.

Summer temperatures here are usually very hot, with low humidity, and swimming in pools along the Sespe Creek is a popular pastime. Winter storms bring heavy rain and snow, causing road closures and raising stream waters to dangerous levels.

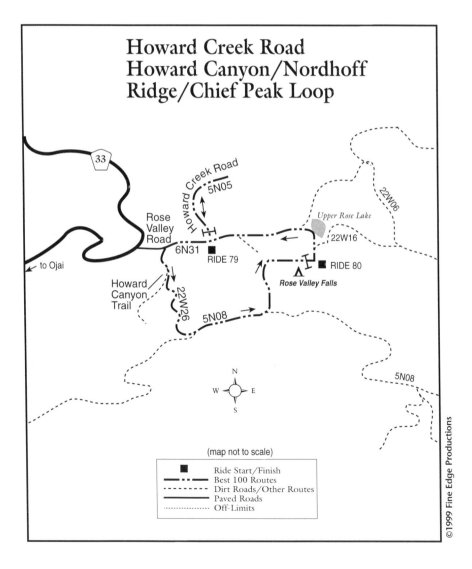

Howard Creek Road
Howard Canyon/Nordhoff
Ridge/Chief Peak Loop

(map not to scale)

■	Ride Start/Finish
▬·▬·▬	Best 100 Routes
---------	Dirt Roads/Other Routes
▬▬▬	Paved Roads
··············	Off-Limits

©1999 Fine Edge Productions

79 Howard Creek Road

Distance: 4 miles.
Difficulty: Easy; good beginner ride.
Elevation: 3,400' - 3,300' (almost level).
Ride Type: Out-and-back on dirt road.
Season: Year-round; winter and spring can be muddy.
Map: Lion Canyon.
Water: None.

Overview: Howard Creek Road (5N05) has little elevation change and is an easy down-and-back route, good for everyone, especially novice riders. Spring wildflowers are usually good here, and there is a seasonal creek. Do watch out for local dogs.

Getting There: From Ojai, take Highway 33 north and turn right onto Rose Valley Road (6N31). Take it 1.6 miles to just past the Howard Creek ford. A locked gate here restricts traffic to residents with cabins and homes at the road end. Watch out for occasional traffic and respect the rights of private property owners.

Route: Head north on 5N05. This 2-mile dirt road meanders north along Howard Creek from Rose Valley Road to Sespe Creek. The route is straightforward, with no crossing roads or trails.

80 Howard Canyon/Nordhoff Ridge/Chief Peak Loop

Distance: 11 miles.
Difficulty: Strenuous; technical.
Elevation: 1,600' gain/loss.
Ride Type: Loop on pavement, singletrack and dirt roads.
Season: Year-round; winter and spring can be muddy.
Map: Lion Canyon.
Water: None.

Overview: There is no easy way to get to Nordhoff Ridge from Rose Valley. Of the two routes (Howard Canyon Trail and Chief Peak Road) which climb to the ridge, Howard Canyon Trail is the less difficult ascent (notice we didn't say easy). If you prefer to descend on singletrack, you can push your bike up Chief Peak Road and descend Howard Canyon. Once on the ridge, you can combine these routes with some of the roads and trails described in the previous section.

Getting There: It is a 4-mile drive or ride from Highway 33 and Rose Valley Road (6N31) to Rose Valley

Falls Campground. Park next to Upper Rose Valley Lake, just below Rose Valley Campground. Do not park in campsites.

Route: Backtrack along Rose Valley Road (6N31) toward Highway 33 for 3.5 miles. About 0.5 mile east of Highway 33 on the south side of Rose Valley road, before some large pipe posts, is the new Howard Canyon trailhead (22W26). (The trail used to pass through private Rancho Grande, 0.75 mile farther east. In the late 1960s, a new road to Nordhoff lookout from Rose Valley was started but never finished. It is this road which crosses Howard Trail and is now your starting point in order to avoid ranch property.

The trail was abandoned long ago because it traveled through a shooting area that was much abused. The shooting has since been banned, and local cyclists, USFS personnel, and other volunteers have restored this important trail. Although in many places the track is narrow and brush needs cutting back, serious single-track riders can enjoy the challenge of riding this trail uphill. Downhill is even better!)

From the trailhead, start south on Howard Canyon Trail by crossing a small drainage, keeping to the east side of the trail which has been washed out. Head right and up fairly steeply to the old roadbed and follow it uphill, passing through a dense growth of Scotch broom. You climb over a low ridge, pass through a road cut and descend to the west side, where you turn off to the left on the trail.

The trail climbs with a gentle grade interspersed with very short, steep sections along the east side of the mountain and in and out of small canyons. The second canyon is larger, and sometimes in spring it has water flowing in it. Just past here on the north side of the mountain, the trail passes through a grove of oak trees—welcome shade on a hot day. Turning again onto the east side of the mountain, you can see down into Howard Canyon where there are two small lakes. The trail continues on like this until you come to a slide area shored up by steel posts with board cribbing. Above here, the trail is much steeper and more difficult for about 0.25 mile, and then you are almost at the top.

At the ridgetop, the trail continues down and to the south to intersect Nordhoff Ridge Road (5N08). (You could also turn left on the ridge, climb steeply a short way, and come out on the ridge road where it crosses over.) Nordhoff Ridge Road goes west to Gridley Saddle (see Ride 77) and east to Chief Peak Road. You head east (left) for 1.5 miles. The road stays on or very near the ridgetop, making a 500-foot ascent on its way to the top of Chief Peak Road.

Paved, but very broken, this road is extremely steep, dropping 1,600 feet in 2.5 miles. (Fit riders take over an hour to climb it.) This is your descent route to Rose Valley. Watch your speed and stay in control. [*Editor's Note:* The first time one of our authors, Mickey McTigue, rode this road was in 1959 on a Sears-Roebuck J.C. Higgins coaster-brake bike. By the time he reached the bottom, he reports that "my brakes were smoking, popping and sizzling."]

At the bottom, go around the locked gate and head left through the campground to the lake to finish your loop.

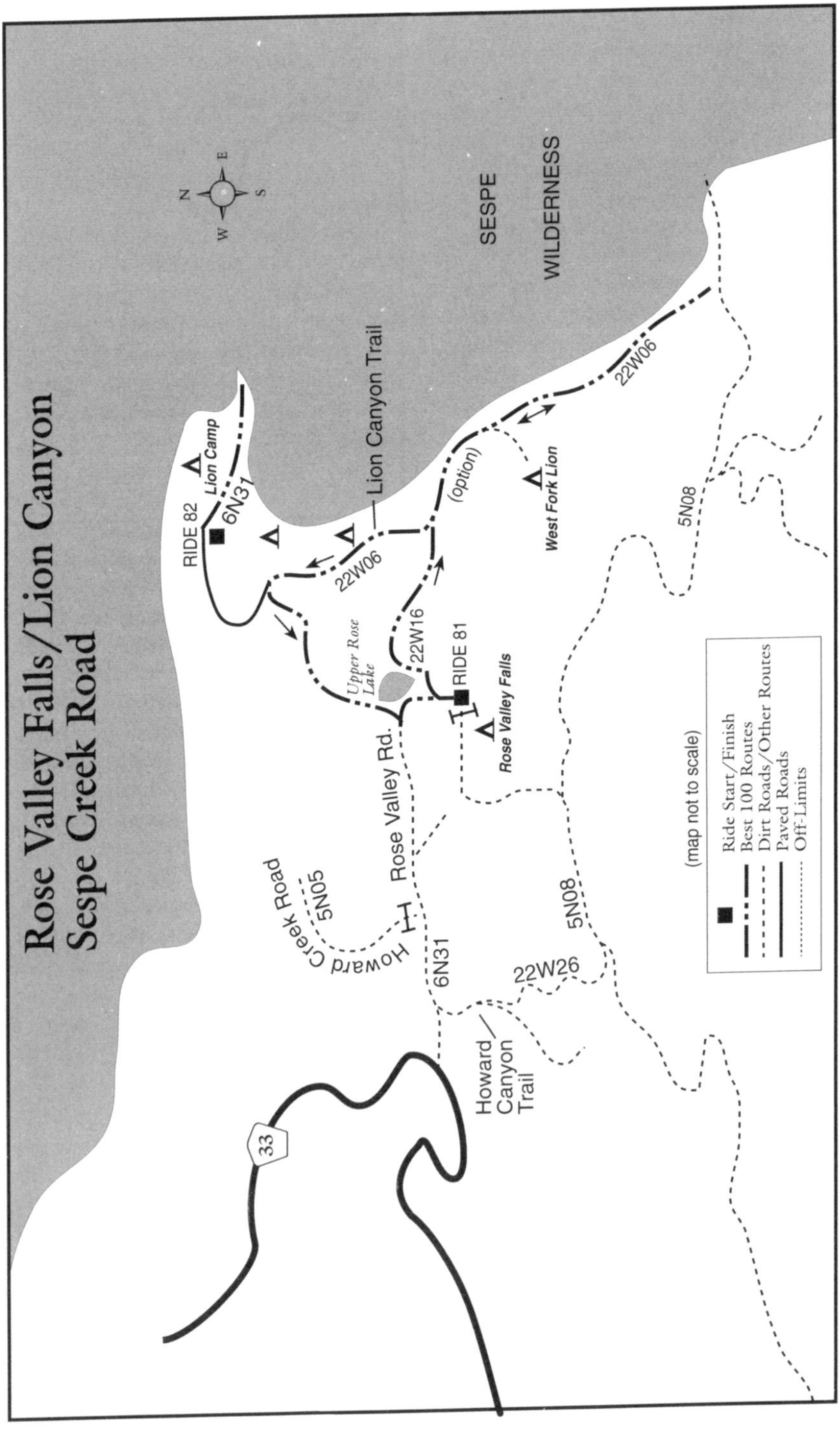

Rose Valley Falls/Lion Canyon
Sespe Creek Road

SESPE

WILDERNESS

22W06

Lion Camp

RIDE 82

6N31

Lion Canyon Trail

(option)

West Fork Lion

5N08

22W06

22W16

Upper Rose Lake

RIDE 81

Rose Valley Falls

Rose Valley Rd.

Howard Creek Road

5N05

5N08

6N31

22W26

Howard Canyon Trail

33

N
E
S
W

(map not to scale)

■ Ride Start/Finish
     Best 100 Routes
     Dirt Roads/Other Routes
     Paved Roads
     Off-Limits

©1999 Fine Edge Productions

81 Rose Valley Falls/Lion Canyon

Distance: 5.5-mile loop.
Difficulty: Moderate to difficult; trail is narrow with some exposure and steep sections.
Elevation: 3,400' - 3,600'; 200' differential.
Ride Type: Loop on trail and pavement.
Season: Year-round, but winter can be muddy.
Map: Lion Canyon.
Water: In creek east of Rose Valley Falls or in Lion Creek (treat all water).

Overview: This very pleasant loop climbs over the ridge between Rose Valley Falls Campground and Lion Canyon. The climb is steep in a few spots, with some exposure. You then loop down Lion Canyon Trail (22W06) through scenic Lion Canyon and back on paved Rose Valley Road to Rose Valley Falls Camp.

Getting There: It is a 4-mile drive or ride from Highway 33 and Rose Valley Road (6N31) to Rose Valley Falls Campground. Park next to

Upper Rose Valley Lake, just below Rose Valley Campground. Do not park in campsites.

Route: From the parking area, go around the south side of the lake below the camp. In this marshy area, the trail 22W16 can be hard to find. From the south side of the lake, the trail goes east and up a small creek that drains into the lake from the southeast. Soon you come to a steep climb across a rocky slab and into a brushy place before arriving atop a saddle.

Mickey McTigue

Upper Lion Canyon

At the saddle, you have views down into Lion Canyon. Here at the intersection of 22W16 and Lion Canyon Trail (22W06), head north (left) down-canyon to finish your loop. Use care in descending because of deep ruts and washouts. The trail disappears as you cross Lion Creek, but it picks up again on the east side of the creek.

You pass Middle Lion and Lion Canyon camps on your way to Rose Valley Road. Once at the paved road, turn left to return to Rose Valley Campground.

Option: From its intersection with 22W16, Lion Canyon Trail also climbs south toward Nordhoff Ridge. From the intersection, it is a nearly level 0.5 mile to a meadow with a 3-way intersection. The trail to West Fork Camp is on the right. A rough 0.4-mile ride will get you to the camp with 3 sites and seasonal water. (To the left is the trail to East Fork Camp which lies in the Sespe Wilderness (bicycles are not allowed). It is a 0.5-mile hike to that camp.)

Straight ahead the main trail climbs the central ridge. From here, it's a serious climb with lots of rocks and shale slides on its way to Nordhoff Ridge. The trail is open but may be in poor shape. If you make it to the ridge, you can connect with the roads and trails described in the previous section. The easiest return route is back the way you came.

82 Sespe Creek Road

Distance: 2.5 miles.
Difficulty: Moderate; rocky sections and badly eroded trail surface.
Elevation: 3,000' - 2,950'.
Ride Type: Out-and-back on rutted dirt road.
Season: Year-round.
Map: Lion Canyon.
Water: Piedra Blanca Creek, sometimes Trout Creek (treat all water).

Overview: The Sespe Wilderness boundary takes a jog around two parcels of private property that lie along the river to just below Trout Creek. The boundary crosses the old road at a gate where you start to climb away from the Sespe Creek. You may ride bicycles from Lions Camp to this gate, but no farther.

Getting There: Park along Rose Valley Road near Lion Camp just before the creek crossing.

Route: After crossing Sespe Creek at Lion Camp heading northeast, you come to the junction of Piedra Blanca Trail, Middle Sespe Trail (22W04) and Sespe Road (6N31). Head east on the road and cross Piedra Blanca Creek at 0.6 mile and Trout Creek at 1.1 mile.

A fast down-and-back takes about 30 minutes, so take your time to savor the scenery and watch out for people doing the same on foot. This is just a sample of what the next 15 miles are like. Come back with your hiking boots and get into the wilderness for a while.

Matilija

The same bill that created the Sespe Wilderness also included the 29,600-acre Matilija Wilderness. However, Upper North Fork Matilija Trail is the only route closed to bicycles because of wilderness status. Trails and roads bordering the Matilija Wilderness are open to bicycles and are described below.

This area of long, narrow, twisting canyons is bordered on the east by Highway 33 and on the west by a long ridge along the Santa Barbara County line. Before Highway 33 was extended north of Wheelers, the Matilija Upper North Fork/Cherry Creek Trail was the main access to the Upper Sespe. Fishermen, hunters and cattle ranchers traveled this way, packing in supplies and even driving cattle on this trail. John Dent and his family, long time Ventura County ranchers, traveled this way from their Ventura ranch to their Pine Mountain ranch. The Dent family home, formerly on North Ventura Avenue, was sold and moved by its new owner to the end of the paved road up Matilija Canyon. Imagine what John Dent would say if he could see where his house ended up!

Ridge-top trails and roads, very steep in some places, provide views of wilderness both near and far. Streams have water all year and some have native trout. This area receives the most rainfall in the county and streams become impassable at flood stage, so take care while riding during the rainy season. The abrupt turns of the canyons offer remote solitude and make self-reliance a must for riding here. Trail camps are located at Murietta Canyon, Cherry Canyon and Ortega Ridge.

83 Monte Arido Road/ Murietta Canyon

Distance: 25 miles; shorter out-and-backs possible.
Difficulty: Moderate to Potrero Seco; more difficult to Monte Arido; very difficult near Old Man Mountain; many steep hills, long distance.
Elevation: 5,080' to 6,000' to 3,400'.
Ride Type: One-way on dirt roads; requires shuttle.
Season: Spring, summer, fall.
Maps: Wheeler Springs, Old Man Mountain, White Ledge Peak, Matilija.
Water: None—bring plenty.
Comments: Winter storms bring heavy snow, and the adobe mud is bad during spring thaw. Riding in on frozen roads in the morning can leave you stuck by a noon thaw miles from the highway. Be self-sufficient—nearest services are in Ojai.

Overview: This ridge-top road provides exceptional views of wilderness landscapes with few human alterations. Most of those are historic ranches at the northern end of the road between Highway 33 and Potrero Seco. In this area, the road runs near the border of the Dick Smith Wilderness, and from many high points you can look out over most of the wilderness to the northwest. The southern 15 miles of the ride take you along the border of the Matilija Wilderness to the east, with great views down into remote, steep, narrow canyons. Following the ridge, the road climbs and drops many times.

Excellent day-rides can be enjoyed by parking at the upper roadhead and traveling into Potrero Seco, returning the way you came in. Three miles one way takes less than an hour, with only a net descent of 150 feet. Coming back, however, you face a 600-foot climb over the same 3.5 miles. A more strenuous effort will take you farther out to Three Sisters Rocks, 7 miles beyond the gate at Highway 33. Bring a map, compass, and binoculars to locate distant landmarks and help you find exactly where you are. Riding past the Three Sisters puts you farther into the mountains on a ridge that gets tougher as you go along. Somewhere about the 10-mile mark, you need to decide whether to go back or continue past the point of no return.

Getting There: Park on Highway 33 at Pine Mountain Summit Pass (milepost 42.7). To leave a second vehicle at the parking area at the locked gate end of Matilija Road, just before Murietta Camp, take Lake Matilija County Road west from Highway 33, 5 miles north of Ojai at milepost 16.28. Go past Lake Matilija and continue to a parking area at a locked USFS gate.

Route: Starting from Pine Mountain Summit Pass, head west on Monte Arido Road (6N03) past the locked gate. Watch out for occasional motor vehicle traffic operated under special permit from the Forest Service. Right away you have a steep descent, then climb to a saddle at 0.3 mile. (A good road branches to the south and climbs slightly for 0.2 mile to a locked gate posted: *No Trespassing.*) Continuing west from the saddle on Road 6N03, you climb a little more easily to the ridge.

Riding close to the ridge top, you can see a deep canyon to the south; past that you cross a cattleguard (0.8 mile). A spur road branches southwest here to the Dent Ranch, while the main road passes between pine trees to the west. There is easier riding and you start passing the first large grass slopes. At the top of a grade (1.6 miles), you can see down across Potrero Seco and the headwaters of the Sespe. Two ranches are located along the creek among the cottonwood trees. The descent to the ranches has two downhill runs separated by a slight climb over a saddle. As you approach the ranches, keep right, cross a cattleguard (2.2 miles), and climb toward the west across a gently sloping field.

Just before a large green tank, take a road on the right for 100 yards to Potrero Seco Trail Camp, 3 miles from the start. The camp is set in a hollow with hills on three sides, open to the east. There are three tables and fireplaces shaded by oak and pine trees, but no water. Just northeast is the abandoned site of the old Potrero Seco Guard Station.

Going farther south on Monte Arido Road (6N03), you climb moderately for a mile; then, on the right, pass the Loma Victor Road (7N05) that descends on a ridge along the Dick Smith Wilderness boundary to Mono Creek and Don Victor Valley. Past this junction, you climb a little more and make a steep descent to a saddle where there is a short side road south to a dam and pond. From this saddle, at 6.2 miles, Three Sisters Rocks can be seen ahead. A short

steep climb gets you to these surprisingly large, isolated sandstone boulders at 6.8 miles. Shade and wind

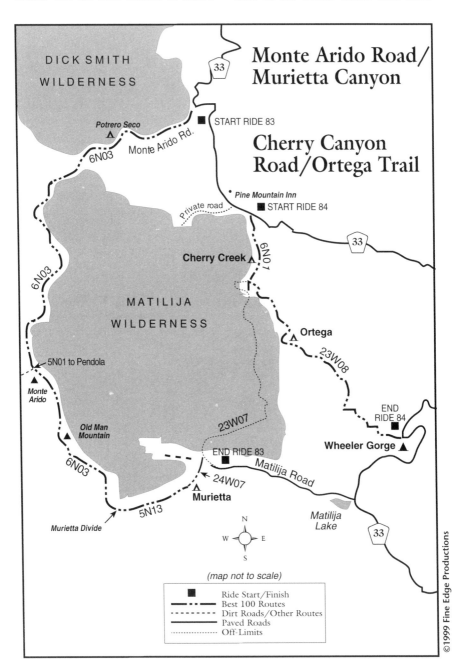

Time to rest and explore

protection is available here, making it a good rest stop.

(Hildreth Jeepway (6N17) starts past a locked gate on the north side of the rocks and can be seen along the ridge out to Hildreth Peak to the west.) From Potrero Seco, 6N03 has been gradually turning to the south and, for the rest of the way, heads generally south.

A gate at 7.0 miles is the start of a very fast section, slightly downhill on good graded road. The climb ahead is typical, with some short, steep, walk-and-push hills mixed with rideable areas—you go over a peak, down a steep hill, and repeat. Another gate (locked) at 12.2 miles is next to a dam and pond on the west side of the road. Climb again to the northwest side of Monte Arido and, at 12.45 miles, pass the Pendola Jeepway (5N01) which heads down into an open saucer-shaped canyon before descending the ridge to Pen-

dola Station at Agua Caliente Canyon. (Experienced mountain bicyclists seeking a tough, challenging ride can start at Juncal Camp—see the Santa Barbara chapter—and ride up past Murietta Divide, making the steep climb to Monte Arido and returning by the Pendola Jeepway.)

At 13.2 miles, Monte Arido, 6,003 feet, is the highest point on 6N03. (If you want, take the short walk to the summit, just west and a little above the road.) The next 1.5 miles has the steepest descent, so use your brakes carefully—you may even want to lower your seat. From another saddle on the north side of Old Man Mountain, the road climbs around on the west slopes of this double peak, giving you a good view looking down to Juncal Dam and Jameson Lake. Finally, you lose altitude rapidly, with many switchbacks across a barren landscape.

The scene changes suddenly as

you make a short climb past pine trees growing among large sandstone boulders. There is another steep descent across a boulder garden until, at 19.0 miles, a road to your right leads to a small lake, too improbable to be overlooked. One more mile, at 20 miles even, you are at Murietta Divide, pleasantly level after so much downhill. Go left (east) on 5N13 and ride another 5 miles down Murietta Canyon to your shuttle vehicle.

84 Cherry Canyon Road/ Ortega Trail

Distance: 10.5 miles.
Difficulty: Moderate to difficult; Ortega Trail is technical.
Elevation: 4,100' to 5,000' to 2,250'; 900' gain/2,750' loss.
Ride Type: One-way on dirt road and trail; requires shuttle.
Season: Year-round; summer can be hot and winter can have snow.
Map: Wheeler Spring.
Water: Infrequent; carry your own supplies.
Comments: Target shooters have been using the lower canyon on both sides of the road.

Overview: This route is best done as a shuttle since Ortega Trail is not something you want to ride up. Hard-core riders can fashion a loop by riding Highway 33 between the two trailheads—that would add about 18 miles. Less-experienced riders can ride Cherry Canyon Road up and back, omitting Ortega Trail.

The 4WD roads in this area are actually Caterpillar tractor trails left from the construction of the gas pipeline that stretches from Coalinga to the coast and follows the ridge nearby. The pipeline was built in the late 1950s, and scars created by its construction are still visible.

Getting There: Leave one vehicle at milepost 20.71 on Highway 33 at the lower Ortega trailhead just above Holiday Camp, near Wheeler Gorge. Drive a second vehicle to the upper Cherry Canyon roadhead at milepost 38.22, near Pine Mountain Inn.

Route: Cherry Canyon Road (6N01)

is a good road with a moderate grade except for a short, steep hill near the top. The road was used during construction of a gas pipeline that crosses Sespe Creek and goes up the ridge east of Cherry Creek. It is now open to OHV (Off-Highway Vehicle) traffic, so watch and listen for 4WDs and motorcycles.

This route is rideable except during snow or high water at Sespe crossing. One trail camp, although not in good repair, is located two-thirds of the way up on the right. (To reach the camp, cross the creek and climb up to the tables and fire pits.)

At the top of Ortega Saddle, Cherry Canyon Road connects with Ortega OHV Road and 23W08 to the east. The Matilija Wilderness boundary is all along the west side (on your right headed uphill) of Cherry Canyon Road. The boundary curves to the east at the saddle, cutting across Trail 23W07 where it descends into Upper North Fork Matilija Canyon—closed to bicycles. From the saddle down, you have 3 miles of rough 4WD road and 5 miles of rocky motorcycle trail. You stay on ridges almost all the way with no real stream crossings.

To ride Ortega Trail from the top of Cherry Creek Road (6N01), take Road 23W08 left (east) along the ridge and then down on the south side of Ortega Hill. It starts as a 4WD road and soon becomes a very steep downhill run. At the bottom, the trail climbs a wash and comes out on the ridge between Tule Canyon and Matilija North Fork Canyon. On this ridge, the 4WD road ends and the route continues as trail. 4WD clubs have created the present Ortega Trail Camp (no water). Old maps and a couple of stoves show where the original Ortega Camp was located— almost 3 miles farther down the trail. At its lower end, the Ortega Trail switchbacks down to Highway 33 at a 180-degree turn of the highway just above the Holiday Group Camp. This is your pickup point or where you left your shuttle vehicle. As mentioned, hard-core cyclists could loop onto Highway 33 back to the start (an additional 18 miles).

The Ortega Trail is an historic trail once used to get to the upper Sespe before the paved highway was built past Wheelers. It was an alternate, usable when high water or downed trees blocked Upper North Fork Matilija Canyon Trail. Sheep sometimes grazed in the area of the old Ortega Camp. The drainage from around the old camp crosses the trail 0.5 mile below the camp, passing under very large boulders and out of sight of anyone on the trail.

There's a local story about a sheepherder who would water his animals by lowering a bucket down to the water between the boulders. Sure enough, only about 30 feet upstream from the trail, are some very deep openings between the boulders where there is water in early summer. If you were to fall or somehow get stuck in one of these deep remote holes, you might not be found for a long time.

Another historical note: About a mile up from the lower trailhead is a carved rock next to the trail on the south (uphill) side. An outline of a church and *J. B. KING JAN 30 1908* is carved very neatly, except for the N in KING, which is done backward.

85 Murietta Road

Distance: 10 miles.
Difficulty: Easy to moderate; last mile is steep and rough.
Elevation: 1,600' - 3,400'; 1,800' gain/loss.
Ride Type: Out-and-back on dirt road.
Season: Year-round but winter and spring can be muddy.
Maps: Wheeler Springs, Old Man Mountain, White Ledge Peak, Matilija.
Water: At roadside springs. Treat all water.

Overview: This road travels 5 miles on the north side of Murietta Canyon from Matilija Creek to Murietta Divide. It is a good option for those

not up to doing all of the previous ride.

Getting There: You can get to the trailhead by taking Lake Matilija

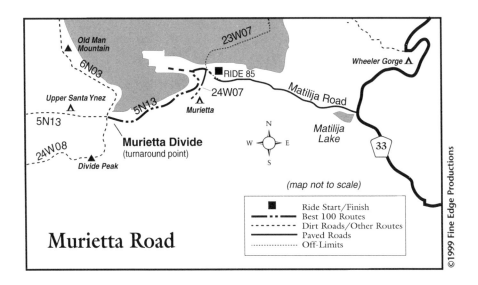

Old Man Mountain ▲

6N03

23W07

Wheeler Gorge ▲

■ RIDE 85

24W07

Matilija Road

Upper Santa Ynez ▲

5N13

Murietta ▲

N

5N13

Matilija Lake

24W08

Murietta Divide
(turnaround point)

▲ Divide Peak

W ◇ E

S

33

(map not to scale)

■ Ride Start/Finish
━━━ Best 100 Routes
- - - - - Dirt Roads/Other Routes
─── Paved Roads
.... Off-Limits

Murietta Road

©1999 Fine Edge Productions

County Road west from Highway 33 (milepost 16.28), 5 miles north of Ojai. Go past Lake Matilija and continue to a parking area at the locked Forest Service gate.

Route: Ride on the Forest Service easement past a relocated old house and cross Matilija Creek twice on the dirt road. You pass the wilderness trail to Upper North Fork Matilija (23W07) on the right. Next, on the left, Trail 24W07 is a pleasant, short 0.5 mile to Murietta Trail Camp alongside the oak-shaded creek. A volunteer trail project has connected 24W07 from Murietta Camp to the main Murietta Road, with additional improvements planned for the future.

Continue up Matilija Canyon to the west until Road 5N13 turns left at a house and gate. Here, 1.0 mile past the paved road, you leave Matilija Canyon and enter Murietta Canyon. When water flow at the crossings is low, this first mile is very easy and a worthwhile ride in itself. By looking up to the southwest, you can see the road ahead climbing around a ridge into Murietta Canyon.

As you begin riding up into Murietta Canyon, the road switches back to the east, with a splendid view of the canyons below. Turning west again into Murietta Canyon, the grade remains very rideable. Look into the canyon at the 1.8-mile point and you can see Murietta Trail Camp next to the stream in a grove of oak trees. Continue climbing on a well-graded road; then enjoy a break with a slight descent to the spot where the road crosses a small stream with abundant water at 2.8 miles.

Past this stream, the climb keeps increasing, getting noticeably steeper and rougher around 3.7 miles. A notable feature of this canyon is the large ferns growing at the many springs near the roadside. At 4.2 miles, the ferns are very dense by a spring that is piped under the road to a water trough on the south side. Incredibly, the road gets even steeper, challenging many riders' determination to ride all the way to the top of Murietta Divide (if they have made it this far). Unless you're up for an epic ride, the easiest option is to return the way you came. Riding down the very steep and rocky upper section of Murietta Canyon requires good braking control at all times.

(From Murietta Divide, at 5.0 miles, the road continues west as Juncal Canyon Road (5N13); it also connects to Monte Arido Road (6N03) to the north (see previous ride) and Divide Peak Trail (24W08) to the south. From Murietta Divide, if you continue on Road 5N13 down Juncal Canyon about 1 mile, you find Santa Ynez Trail Camp next to a year-round running stream. This trail camp with shady oak trees and water is the only camp near the divide.)

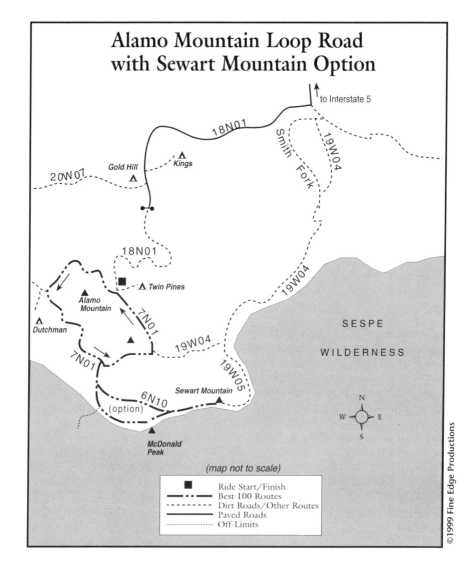

Alamo Mountain Loop Road with Sewart Mountain Option

to Interstate 5

18N01

Smith Fork

19W04

20W07

Gold Hill

Kings

18N01

Twin Pines

Alamo Mountain

Dutchman

7N01

19W04

7N01

SESPE WILDERNESS

19W04

19W05

6N10

Sewart Mountain

(option)

McDonald Peak

N W E S

(map not to scale)

■ Ride Start/Finish
— · · — Best 100 Routes
- - - - Dirt Roads/Other Routes
——— Paved Roads
· · · · · · Off-Limits

©1999 Fine Edge Productions

Alamo Mountain

Alamo Mountain is a massive peak with a somewhat rounded top. Its highest point is 7,450 feet, but the road never gets higher than 7,000 feet. At this elevation, snow occurs every year and sometimes remains for a long time. The best riding is in summer and fall. Winter can be cold. Except for the noise and speed of motorcycles at Hungry Valley State Vehicular Recreation Area, the riding here is great. From the higher elevations, you get spectacular views of seldom-seen canyons. Alamo Mountain is covered with huge trees, while Hungry Valley to the northeast is dry and desert-like.

There is much evidence of gold mining in some areas of the region. Located on the north slope of the mountain above Piru Creek, the Castaic Mine was the most extensive and successful, with two tunnels totaling over 2,200 feet in length. Mining continued here into the 1930s. Originally powered by a water wheel, the 5-stamp mill from this mine can now be seen in a historical museum in Santa Barbara. Gold panning is still a popular pastime along nearby streams.

Services and supplies are available only in Gorman on I-5. Most of the roads and trails in this area are open to motorcycles and ATVs. Car camping with limited facilities is available at Kings, Gold Hill, Twin Pines and Dutchman camps on Alamo Mountain.

Gold Hill Camp is located on a bluff above Piru Creek. The creek usually runs all year, although it's never very deep except during floods. Snow can occur here, but a lot of rain or snow is uncommon. Placer gold, washed downstream, is found along Piru Creek and in the bank under the bluff next to the camp. Panning and dredging are very popular.

Kings Camp, at the end of 8N01A, offers tables and fire pits in a grove of trees. To reach the camp, turn east from Gold Hill Road at milepost 10.25 onto paved 8N01A and continue 0.5 mile. Water is not available at this camp.

86 Alamo Mountain Loop Road with Sewart Mountain Option

Distance: 8 miles; option is 3 miles one way.
Difficulty: Easy, but the elevation is high; option is moderate.
Elevation: 6,500' to 7,000', 500' gain/loss; option 6,850' - 6,400' with several ups and downs on the ridge.
Ride Type: Loop.
Season: Summer and fall are best.
Map: Alamo Mountain.
Water: Piped spring near Twin Pines Camp and spring beside the loop road about 0.5 mile west of Twin Pines Camp, but quality is very questionable. Best to bring all you need.

Overview: You can ride your bike the 7 miles up Alamo Mountain Road on pavement, with a 2,500-foot elevation gain. Most riders, however, prefer to drive to the top and do the Alamo Mountain Loop Road. This road circles Alamo Mountain between 6,500 feet and 7,000 feet for 8 miles of cool,

Kevin Woten

Rocky crossing, dry streambed

easy riding in a mature forest of pine, oak and fir. The views from all sides of Alamo Mountain are splendid. Although you may drive a vehicle around the mountain on this road, riding a bicycle puts you more in touch with the surroundings.

Everyone who gets as far as the south point of Alamo Mountain Loop Road should consider taking the half-mile trip out to the ridge that connects McDonald Peak and Sewart Mountain. So many canyons, ridges, sandstone reefs and peaks are visible from the ridge that there's never enough time to take it all in. The views are unique, especially south into the Sespe Narrows and to the Topa Topa wall, west of the narrows. Most of the land you see is in the Sespe Wilderness. The

boundary runs along the south side of the ridge from east of McDonald Peak to Big Cedar Creek, then down that and Snowy Creek to Piru Creek.

Getting There: Alamo Mountain is accessible by motor vehicle from Interstate 5 through the Hungry Valley State Vehicular Recreational Area (motorcycle and 4WD) on a generally paved road as far as the Gold Hill-Piru Creek crossing. Take Interstate 5 to Gorman (60 miles north from Los Angeles, 40 miles south from Bakersfield, and 70 miles from Ventura). Cross to the west side of I-5 opposite Gorman and go north on Peace Valley Road 1 mile. Turn left (west) at the SVRA Hungry Valley sign onto paved Gold Hill Road (8N01). A kiosk just ahead is run by the State to collect fees for SVRA use. Maps and current information are available from the State Ranger, and information is posted on large bulletin boards. Call ahead to check weather, closures, and special events scheduled here and in the National Forest.

On Gold Hill Road, at mile 5, there is an abrupt right turn. (A dirt fork to the left is Hungry Valley Road, which leads to Snowy Creek Trail and farther on to Hard Luck Road.) Go right and continue west on paved Gold Hill Road to the 10-mile mark at Piru Creek. A gate near the creek crossing is locked during stormy winter weather, and when ice and snow are hazardous at higher elevations. Here, from the base of

Alamo Mountain, 8N01 twists and turns up the mountain's north side. Above Piru Creek, Gold Hill Road (formerly graded dirt) was paved in the fall of 1992.

As you come up the mountain, a short spur road to the east leads steeply down to Twin Pines Camp, just a little before the beginning of Alamo Mountain Loop Road. Dutchman Camp, 2.5 miles west on the loop road, is spread over a larger area with more level ground. Park at the turnout near Twin Pines Camp.

Route: The easiest way to do this loop is to ride counter-clockwise, heading west. The 2.5-mile ride out to Dutchman Camp on 7N01 meanders along the slopes, passing through groves of pines. The 200-foot elevation gain isn't difficult, since it's done a little at a time. Where the road turns south, another lesser road heads farther east. (This is the Miller Jeep Road (8N12) which connects with the many doubletracks to the campsites next to the loop. The sites are spread out in this open place among a few scattered pines of good size.)

On the 3-mile stretch from the camp out to the south point of the loop road, you travel along fairly level terrain for the first mile. For the next 2.0 miles, climb 250 feet, descend into a small canyon, climb again and end at the same elevation as the camp. Watch for rocks that fall onto the road from the steeper slopes around the small canyon.

[**Side trip:** At the south point, 6N10 to McDonald Peak and Sewart Mountain descends steeply south. It's worthwhile making the half-mile trip out to the ridge for the views down Alder Creek and out to the Sespe Narrows. Go south on Alamo Mountain Loop Road without turning to the east or west. By going this half-mile you get most of the view afforded by doing a trip to Sewart Mountain. We highly recommend it if you have time.]

Alamo Mountain Loop Road (7N01) is cut through the ridge here and turns sharply to the northeast. The view is into the upper parts of Snowy Creek Canyon which starts from the south ridge of Alamo Mountain and curves around to the northeast. After riding northeast 0.7 mile from the south point on the Loop Road, you pass Snowy Creek Trail on the right. (Snowy Creek Trail is not recommended at this time; it may be rehabilitated in the near future, however.) Continue on 1.8 miles, descending 300 feet, to complete your turn around the mountain and return to the starting point. The trees along this last section are a mixed forest of maples, oaks, and pines.

Option: To do the complete option out to Sewart Mountain, start at the southernmost point on the Loop Road and head south on Sewart Mountain Road (6N10). Be sure to control your speed since the terrain below the road is steep and rocky. At the bottom of this descent, you pass a short spur road heading down toward the former Alamo Camp, west of the saddle. Beyond this spur, the signed Sewart Mountain Road crosses over into Snowy Canyon. It passes McDonald Peak on the north and comes out of the canyon and onto the ridge east of the peak, avoiding climbs on the peak itself. (This is a good way to return to the Loop Road.)

Keep right at the Sewart Road sign and climb steeply to the ridge which here is rather rounded on top with rolling terrain. Take your time; this is one of the most scenic places in the forest and an excellent rest and lunch stop. Riding east, you drop and climb over many peaks on the ridge before joining the road that climbs back to the ridge east of McDonald Peak. There is a particularly steep place just before Sewart Mountain. (On the east side of Sewart Mountain, Big Cedar Creek Trail goes down into Snowy Creek Canyon. It is steep and rough, and currently closed to vehicle traffic.)

To return to Alamo Mountain Loop Road from Sewart Mountain, take the road where it passes north of McDonald Peak and avoid the climbs on the ridge (see above).

87 Miller Jeep Road/ Piru Creek Trail

Distance: 7 miles.
Difficulty: Very difficult; steep, rutted rough road; Piru Creek Trail is for experienced trail riders only (steep drop-off beside trail).
Elevation: 6,700' - 4,000'; 2,700' loss.
Ride Type: One-way shuttle or part of an epic loop; Piru Creek Trail can also be ridden out and back from Gold Hill Camp, 8 miles round trip.
Season: Summer and fall are best.
Maps: McDonald Peak, Lockwood Valley; or Los Padres National Forest: Mt. Pinos, Ojai and Santa Barbara Ranger Districts.
Water: None. Water in Piru Creek is questionable. Treat it!
Comments: This is a designated motorcycle route; look for safe passing places.

Overview: A steep rocky road, Miller Jeep Road (8N12) climbs a ridge from Lockwood Flat at Piru Creek to the Alamo Loop Road (7N01) on the west side of the mountain. But it is best traveled downhill, and you can do this as part of a loop trip or using a car shuttle.

Getting There: If you use only one vehicle, park at Gold Hill Camp and ride up Alamo Mountain Road and do this as a very strenuous loop. For a shuttle, your other vehicle can be parked at Dutchman Camp.

From Gold Hill Camp, ride or drive up Alamo Mountain on 8N01 and take the right (west) fork around the mountain 2.5 miles to Dutchman Camp.

Route: Miller Jeep Road (8N12) leaves the Alamo Mountain Loop Road (see previous ride) and passes just north of Dutchman Camp. Follow it west and up a hill northwest of camp where it turns and steeply descends the north side of the mountain to Piru Creek at Lockwood Flat. There you take Piru Creek Trail (20W07) east, passing Lockwood Creek Road and Sunset Camp on the way to Gold Hill Camp. (West of the jeep road, Piru Creek Trail has been completely washed out by the river.)

A 2,400-foot elevation loss in 3 miles says it all. Miller Jeep Road is an awesome downhill, very steep and rocky with boulders the first mile, followed by a steep, heavily rutted descent for the next 2.0 miles to the junction of Piru and Lockwood creeks.

Piru Creek Trail has a good blend of terrain to challenge you and some nice scenery as well. The last mile is very narrow as you ride above Piru Creek. This is one of the prettiest sections of Piru Creek. You might see

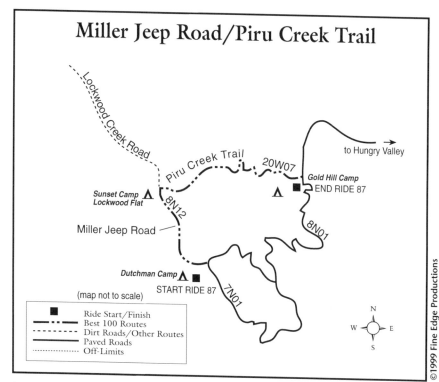

Miller Jeep Road/Piru Creek Trail

(map not to scale)

Legend:
- ■ Ride Start/Finish
- –·–·– Best 100 Routes
- – – – Dirt Roads/Other Routes
- ——— Paved Roads
- ············· Off-Limits

©1999 Fine Edge Productions

bears playing in pools below you as you ride, as well as ducks and cranes.

Option: To ride just Piru Creek Trail out and back, begin at Gold Hill Camp. Piru Creek Trail (20W07) leaves Gold Hill Camp headed uphill to the west, and can be seen crossing steep slopes northwest of camp. This first climb gets you above cliffs, upstream from the camp where Piru Creek flows through a short gorge.

Here the trail is narrow with extreme drop-offs toward the creek. If in doubt of your ability on this section, walk or go back. After passing this tough mile, the trail drops down to the creek and is much easier except for loose sand. Lockwood Flat (and Sunset Trail Camp) are at the end of this 4-mile section of trail where you connect to Lockwood Creek Road. Turn around here.

88 Hungry Valley OHV Area

Distance: Varies.
Difficulty: Trails are rated.
Elevation: Varies.
Ride Type: Use your imagination.
Season: Spring and fall are best.
Map: Available at kiosk at entry to the SVRA.
Water: None. Any stream water should be treated.

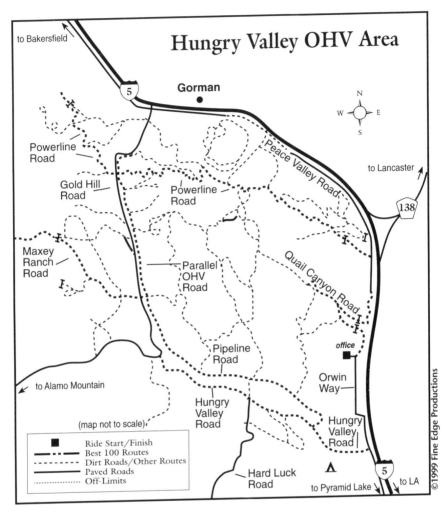

Overview: The 19,000-acre Hungry Valley State Vehicular Recreation Area (HV-SVRA) offers 2,000 acres of open riding area and over 80 miles of trails for all types of off-highway vehicles. This includes bicycles, and cyclists can find a wide variety of riding experiences here. The valley has myriad marked and unmarked trails ranging from easy to extreme with many hill climbs, ridge lines, steep descents and rolling meadow crossings. The soil is generally dirt with sandy dry streambeds.

This land wasn't set aside for bicycling, but bicycles have been declared vehicles for the purpose of keeping us out of wilderness areas. Since this is an off-highway vehicle area, why not take advantage of it? Sure, there are lots of motor vehicles zooming around, but the cyclist can still fit in. Ride during the week, in the early morning, or in winter when it's cold. At least here no one is liable to complain that you are going too fast or ruining the trails. You can't frighten the horses or hikers—we doubt you will ever see any.

For kamikaze descents, the motorcycle hill-climbing walls should be a thrill. (Trail signs rate the degree of difficulty.) Several trails continue into the Los Padres National Forest and provide longer, more remote rides, usually with more solitude than you get in the Recreation Area.

Hungry Valley has a desert-like appearance—dry with sparse vegetation. Summer days can be very hot. You should carry as much water as possible when you ride here. The 3,500-foot elevation means many days of wind, and cold winter nights with occasional snow. Spring is best, when Piru Creek and other smaller streams are full, and poppies and other wildflowers carpet the meadows.

Co-author Mickey McTigue first became aware of the area through his interest in recreational gold prospecting. Gold is found on Frazier Mountain, along Piru Creek, and in the mountains on each side of Piru Creek near Gold Hill. Old mines and diggings—as well as present-day diggers—can be found throughout these parts. Much of Mickey's knowledge was passed on to him by James Young who, in his early twenties, worked at the Castaic Mine during the Depression. Mining, hunting and ranching were the main activities then. Jim and his partner, Paul Meacham, worked the mine together. They went to town (Gorman) only one day a month for supplies.

Jim Young was always interested in the world around him, and 30 days at a time at the mine was too much isolation for him. So sometimes, after work on Saturdays, he would walk to Gorman for a night out. When the town closed for the night, he would

head back to the mine with a bottle of beer in his pocket, stories of world and local news in his head, and thoughts of renewed friendships to keep him company on the long, lonely hike. Returning to the mine at daybreak, he'd be thankful for Sunday off so he could sleep. Hiking to Gorman from the Castaic Mine is not an unpleasant walk, as Mickey once found out when, returning from a day's prospecting, a friend's car broke down not far from the mine. As they walked out in the dark, they thought about Jim Young's walks fifty years earlier. In the dark, the country probably looked much the same as it did then, but they knew that, by daylight, major changes could be seen—a paved road, power lines and many, many motorcycle trails.

The camping spots in Hungry Valley are excellent, with good toilet facilities, parking, and space between camps. Each campsite has a picnic table, barrel fire pit with a half grate to cook on, and a wooden sun overhead for shade. The campsites at Upper and Lower Scrub camps are recommended since they are a little more sheltered by a ridge and scrub oak trees.

Getting There: Take Interstate 5 to Gorman (60 miles north from Los Angeles, 40 miles south from Bakersfield, and 70 miles from Ventura). Cross to the west side of I-5 opposite Gorman and go north on Peace Valley Road 1 mile. Turn left (west) at the SVRA Hungry Valley sign onto paved Gold Hill Road (8N01). A kiosk just ahead is run by the State to collect fees for SVRA use. Maps and current information are available from the State Ranger, and information is posted on large bulletin boards. Call ahead to check weather, closures, and special events scheduled here and in the National Forest.

Frazier Mountain/Lockwood Valley

Good dirt roads and thick pine forests make for tranquil, relaxed riding on the wide ridges of this high mountain. The trees muffle and block sound, so talking with hushed voices seems right here, like in a church or library. Broken tops on the largest trees attest to the power of wind, lightning, and heavy snow, but on a bright summer day when the heat is tempered by the 7,500-foot elevation, this is a gentle backcountry. Most of the views through the trees are spectacular. The best view, of course, is at the fire lookout on the very top of the mountain at 8,013 feet—one of the few manned lookouts left in the southern forest. Visitors are welcome, but remember every day is a working day. Keep visits and distractions short.

Spring and summer thunderstorms are common with possible heavy rain and the danger of lightning on high places. In storms, keep away from tall trees and metal structures like the lookout and nearby radio towers. Heavy winter snow occurs, and strong winds cause whiteouts and severe wind chill. In the shade at this high elevation, snow and ice can last a long time. Check conditions at the ranger station on the way up or call ahead.

Mountain lions are another local hazard. This mountain is home to some big cats. There have been several sightings, and in one case, an especially large lion followed a hiker, leaving paw prints beside his tracks in the snow.

The main access road up the mountain is paved for 3 miles to over 7,000 feet. A good graded dirt road continues on to the fork at Overmeyer Flat (unsigned), a good parking place.

To the west of Frazier Mountain, the wide Lockwood Valley is surrounded by massive mountains rising over 8,000 feet in the north and east.

The valley floor at 5,000 feet can be very cold in winter and usually has some snowfall, but it doesn't last long. The nearby peaks can have snow patches lasting into May. Valley summers are pleasant with moderate temperatures. The vegetation consists of meadow grassland and sage with scattered clumps of pines.

Lockwood Valley has seen quite a few changes in recent years. Wilderness legislation creating the Chumash Wilderness Area—encompassing land on Mt. Pinos and south and west of Mt. Abel—has closed some trails to bicycles. Lockwood Creek Road has been bulldozed and a new route built above the creek. Long Dave Valley Trail is closed and Long Dave Valley Road is scheduled to be closed and re-routed sometime in 1998. Concerns about local fish, water sedimentation and damage to Lockwood Creek by OHVs led to the closures and re-routing by the Forest Service.

Lockwood Valley Road is a paved road from Highway 33 to Interstate 5 through Lockwood Valley and the communities of Lake of the Woods and Frazier Park. Supplies are available there and at Lebec and Gorman on I-5. At the southwest end of the valley, there is a Ventura County sheriff's substation and fire station (end of Chico Larson Way at mile 17.9 on Lockwood Valley Road). Kern County sheriff and fire stations are located in Frazier Park. Mt. Pinos Ranger District Headquarters is located a mile southwest of Lake of the Woods at the junction of Lockwood Valley and Frazier Mountain roads. Campfire permits, forest maps, books and pamphlets, road/trail conditions and closures, and other information—all are available here.

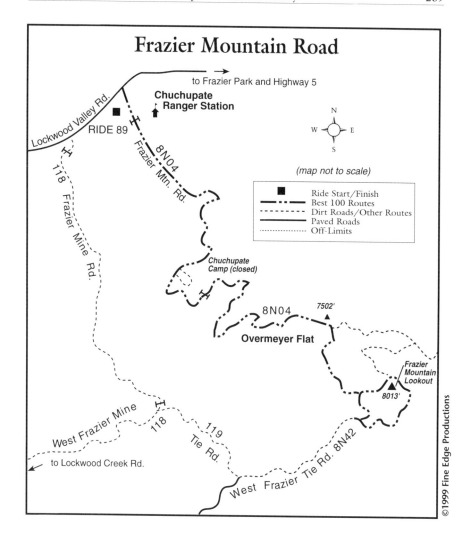

89 Frazier Mountain Road

Distance: 14.8 miles.
Difficulty: Moderate; not technical.
Elevation: 5,200' to 8,013'; 2,913' differential.
Ride Type: Out-and-back on pavement and dirt roads.
Season: Summer and fall best.
Map: Frazier Mountain.
Water: None.
Comments: Nearest services in Lake of the Woods.

Overview: This is a pretty tough hill climb—tougher than Mt. Pinos—but it provides fantastic views of the Antelope, Santa Clarita and Lockwood valleys. From here you can ride over to Frazier Mine Road to descend, or you can return the way you came for a great downhill.

Getting There: From Interstate 5, exit at Frazier Park (also signed as Mt. Pinos Recreation Area), and go west 6.5 miles to Lake of the Woods. Go left on Lockwood Valley Road 0.9 mile. Signs here direct you south (left) to Frazier Mountain Road and Chuchupate Ranger Station. Park off the road in this area. Mileages are from the ranger station.

Route: As you do this ride up the mountain, be sure to stop and survey the distant terrain. Use a map and compass to become familiar with the features of the area; they will help you find your way.

For the first mile, you climb steadily south on road 8N04 past chaparral and scattered pines. The road turns to the left a little and gets less steep at two houses—one stone, the other of logs. At 1.5 miles, the first switchback turns to the right and cuts along the mountainside which becomes much steeper. Camp buildings at 2.0 miles are on the left beyond a meadow of grasses and wildflowers where water flows out and across the road. Chuchupate Camp, at 2.5 miles, is closed due to ground squirrels infested with fleas that carry bubonic plague.

Switchback again and turn left to double back above the camp. At 3.0 miles, the pavement ends at a seasonal closure gate. The dirt road past here is rocky but good. You keep heading southeast and, at 4.3 miles, the road improves. Nearing the top, the trees are bigger and shade the road. At Overmeyer Flat, 5.8 miles, the road forks with East Frazier Road, 8N42, branching left. You can turn around here and descend Frazier Mountain Road the way you came up.

Options: 1) You can keep to the right fork on Frazier Mountain Road for a nice ride to the lookout and then loop back to Overmeyer Flat with many scenic surprises. It's 1.1 miles to the lookout junction from Overmeyer Flat.

2) Or you can take the left fork that leads 0.5 mile up to the lookout set amid an amazing array of antennas on the mountain top. You return to Overmeyer Flat by continuing past the lookout and heading south on a road that behaves itself, traveling in a half-circle to the west for 0.6 mile to West Frazier Tie Road. Turn right, travel 0.3 mile back to the fork where you turned up to the lookout.

Loop Option: For a long loop, you could head west on West Frazier Mountain Road. At 2.3 miles from the lookout, take Tie Road (119) down to the northwest to where it Ts into Frazier Mine Road. Go right and down this road to Lockwood Valley Road. A right turn takes you back to the Chuchupate Ranger Station. (See Rides 90 and 92 for more details.)

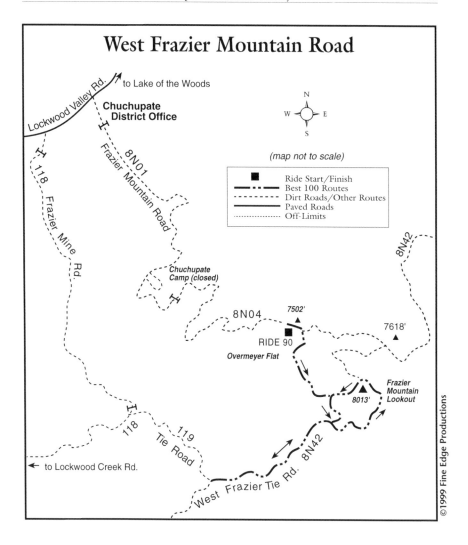

West Frazier Mountain Road

Distance: 6 miles.
Difficulty: Moderate; steep, rough road for the last half-mile.
Elevation: 7,900' - 7,000'; 900' differential.
Ride Type: Out-and-back with small loop on dirt roads.
Season: Summer and fall best.
Map: Frazier Mountain.
Water: None.
Comments: Nearest services are in Lake of the Woods.

Overview: This road can be done separately or as an addition to the previous ride. There are lots of deer up here, and some really big trees, especially on the side facing the northwest.

Include the loop around the lookout when you ride out along West Frazier Tie Road. The view there is spectacular, whereas the thick forest blocks almost all the views on the ridge road. If you start from Overmeyer Flat, go past the roads to the lookout by keeping to the right. Then on the way back, go up to the lookout on the road from the south circling counterclockwise. Ride the same counterclockwise direction when parking near the lookout. The approach to the mountain top is easier from the south.

Getting There: From Lockwood Valley Road, take Frazier Mountain Road 5.8 miles up to Overmeyer Flat (unsigned).

Route: Starting from Overmeyer Flat, ride up the right fork at the nearby sign. The road turns southwest as it climbs along the slopes through pine forest. A spring at a stone water catchment is labeled as bad water. This is a good graded road here; at 1.1 miles, you pass the main access road to the lookout. Signs at this left turn point the way, 0.5 mile up to the east. Keep riding straight ahead; 0.3 mile farther, another less-traveled road also heads east to the lookout. Take this one when you return. It climbs in a 0.6-mile half-circle up to the lookout.

You descend toward the west along the ridge. Keep in mind that you have to come back up the same way and it will take longer. The ride is through thick forest with some small open areas. At 2.9 miles from Overmeyer Flat, or 2.3 miles from the lookout, West Frazier Mine/Tie Road branches off to the north. It's nearly level on the part you see, but it soon plunges down the mountain. Riding out on that level part is easier, however, than continuing west on West Frazier Tie Road which drops steeply and is rough for the last 0.6 mile. No matter which way you go, you need to backtrack to return to the lookout.

91 East Frazier Mountain Road

Distance: 10.4 miles.
Difficulty: Moderate; not technical.
Elevation: 7,500' start; 7,800' high point; 7,350' end; 750' gain/loss.
Ride Type: Out-and-back on dirt roads.
Season: Summer and fall are best.
Map: Frazier Mountain.
Water: None.
Comments: Nearest services are in Lake of the Woods.

Overview: This is a good ride for a hot summer day. It is usually cooler at this altitude and there is plenty of shade on the road which travels along a broad ridge covered with pine forest. There are some less-traveled side roads and many clearings where you can get off the main road and enjoy the solitude. Bring a lunch, your camera, binoculars, a book, harmonica, or even a hammock. This is such a peaceful place that you should

East Frazier Mountain Road

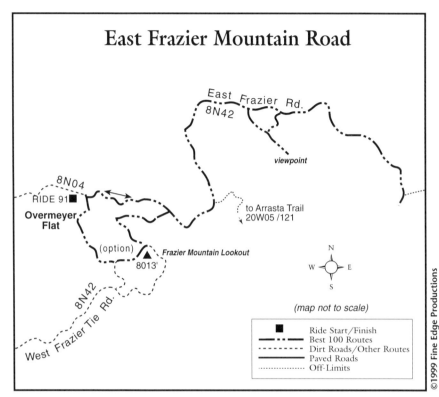

East Frazier Rd.
8N42

viewpoint

8N04
RIDE 91
Overmeyer Flat

to Arrasta Trail
20W05 /121

(option) ▲ *Frazier Mountain Lookout*
8013'

N
W ⟡ E
S

8N42

(map not to scale)

West Frazier Tie Rd.

■   Ride Start/Finish
━ ▪ ━   Best 100 Routes
- - - -   Dirt Roads/Other Routes
━━━   Paved Roads
·······   Off-Limits

©1999 Fine Edge Productions

plan time for quiet, relaxing activities to experience the mood of the mountain. Most of the ride is easy, but there are a few short steep hills where you can expend some energy.

Getting There: Park along Frazier Mountain Road at Overmeyer Flat (unsigned), 5.8 miles from Lockwood Valley Road.

Route: Ride up to the signed road fork and go left on East Frazier Road (8N42). Continue to climb moderately for 0.5 mile around the north side of the mountain. The upper end of a canyon is below to the east, and the road descends slightly toward the ridge at the head of this canyon. Near the bottom of this hill, at 0.9 mile, a rough, steep road heads up the northeast side of the mountain to the

lookout. You descend to about 1.1 miles and then climb until you reach the Arrasta Trail (20W05/OHV 121) on the right at 1.5 miles.

The road continues east on the ridge, dropping and climbing through thick forest. At 3.2 miles, a doubletrack to the right crosses the ridge for 0.45 mile to dead-end at a viewpoint. From this promontory, you can look west and see the microwave towers near the lookout. (On the way back, at 0.2 mile from the main road, another doubletrack heads east; at 3.5 miles, a doubletrack on the right seems to head back up toward the road to the viewpoint. These two may connect, but we haven't tried it.) The main road crosses to the north side of the ridge, where you can see out toward Bakersfield and down to Frazier Park. Just past that at 3.6 miles, the road divides while climbing a short hill.

Turning southeast and staying on the ridge top, you pass East Frazier Trail (19W06/OHV 120) at 5.1 miles. In this area, there are many places between the trees where you can see out across the Antelope Valley to Lancaster. The road descends more to the south and ends at a turnaround circle, 5.2 miles from Overmeyer Flat. (For an easier trip, skip the last steep rocky descents and turn around at 5.0 miles.)

Option: If you want a more strenuous ride, go up to the lookout first on Road 8N04, rather than turning onto East Frazier Road. From the lookout, take the trail to the northwest which heads down the mountain to the north, turns east, and then joins East Frazier Road 0.9 mile from its start at Frazier Mountain Road.

92 West Frazier Mine Road

Distance: 11.4 miles.
Difficulty: Very difficult; rough, rocky road with very steep sections.
Elevation: 5,400' at Lockwood Valley Road; 6,600' at high point; 5,000' at Lockwood Creek Road (8N12).
Ride Type: Loop on dirt roads and pavement.
Season: Summer and fall best.
Map: Frazier Mountain.
Water: None.
Comments: Nearest services are in Lake of the Woods.

Overview: Experienced riders can test their skill and stamina on this road through rugged terrain. It's best to start from the eastern end near the ranger station and ride to Lockwood Creek Road (8N12). You can then return by the paved highway back to your start for a total loop of 11.4 miles. It's a good cross-country ride with some tough, rocky climbs and tight steep drops. Riders, as always, should bring plenty of water, especially in summer, since much of the ride is without shade. The mine has been re-opened; take safety precautions—look but keep out.

Getting There: Park along Lockwood Valley Road 0.33 mile west of Chuchupate Ranger Station.

Route: This road is unmarked at its beginning 0.33 mile west of the Chuchupate Ranger Station. Head south from the paved road and cross the eastern side of a field. Then turn west, with some rough traveling, to rejoin the old route that used to cross the field directly through private property. Keep west and avoid some confusing side routes on the way to the old road there.

Next, you turn south and climb steeply past a seasonal closure gate. The first 1.5 mile is a steep ascent to where West Frazier Tie Road joins in from above. There is another seasonal gate here. The rest of this road is mostly downhill, with many very steep sections. The vegetation consists of mixed chaparral and pines.

From the Tie Road on, you travel west along the north side of Frazier Mountain toward Lockwood Creek. The road runs out onto a ridge and then turns back to the southeast to

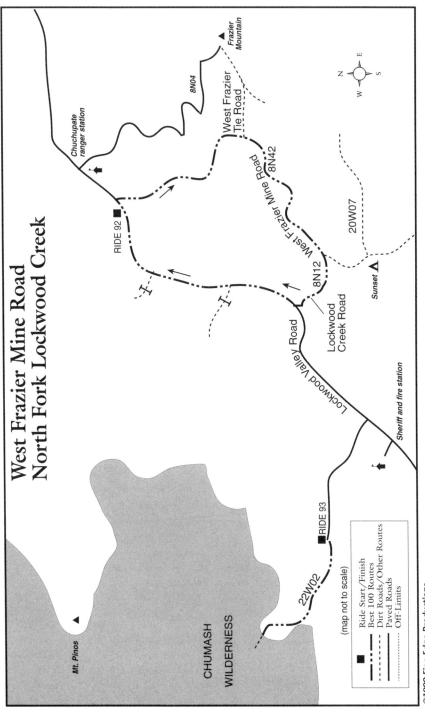

West Frazier Mine Road
North Fork Lockwood Creek

©1999 Fine Edge Productions

Lori Woten

North fork, Lockwood Creek, Frazier Mountain

descend into and cross two small canyons. In the first one, right at the switchback by the wash, is an old mine tunnel. It is partially caved in at the entrance, blocking the water that drains out, flooding the floor. *Caution:* Mines are dangerous; old mines are deadly. Look, but keep out!

The road alternates between awful and pretty good, with the last 1.5 miles pretty decent. The last 0.5 mile is down in a canyon bottom and fairly flat. Several unimproved campsites here are used often by 4WD enthusiasts. The Mine Road ends at Lockwood Creek Road (8N12). Paved Lockwood Valley Road can be reached by turning right and riding north 1.4 miles. At the highway, turn right again and ride 5 miles east to your starting point.

93 North Fork Lockwood Creek

Distance: 5 miles.
Difficulty: Easy; mildly technical.
Elevation: 5,450' – 6,000'; 550' gain/loss.
Ride Type: Out-and-back on dirt road.
Season: Summer and fall best.
Map: Lockwood Valley.
Water: Seasonal at the falls; at road end.
Comments: Nearest services are in Lake of the Woods.

Overview: This easy route rewards riders with a waterfall at its end.

Getting There: From Lockwood Valley Road (milepost 18.6), head northwest on Boy Scout Road for 3 miles to a locked gate. Park along the paved Boy Scout Road, off pavement, near Plush Ranch and the gate.

Route: A sign at the gate gives directions. Ride through the Boy Scout Camp parking area and continue straight ahead on the road at the far right side. Several stream crossings in the canyon are usually dry, but they do wash out sometimes and flash floods occur during heavy thunderstorms. This road ends just below a large waterfall. You have to walk upstream because the trail enters the Chumash Wilderness here and no bikes are allowed. Walk a short distance and look around a turn of the canyon to see the falls.

Thorn Meadows

This area of excellent summer riding is the best place for beginners due to its many miles of easy-to-ride dirt roads. Thorn Meadows gets it name from the extensive patches of wild roses that grow here. At higher elevations, many stands of large conifers, open meadow lands, and roads and trails with few steep climbs make this one of the best mountain bike areas around. Thorn Meadows is also popular with hunters due to its many meadows and abundant wildlife. The Thorn Meadows area contains the headwaters of Piru Creek—all streams here drain into Piru Creek which flows east to Pyramid Lake near Interstate 5.

Drive-in campsites at Thorn Meadows, Pine Springs and Halfmoon camps are accessible in summer and fall by auto over graded dirt road, Grade Valley Road (7N03). During winter and spring, the area is subject to snow and washouts. Due to the remoteness of this area, only vehicles in good working order with plenty of fuel, tools, and spare parts should come here; it's best to travel with two or more vehicles. The nearest supplies can be obtained at Lake of the Woods or Frazier Park, east on Lockwood Valley Road toward Interstate 5.

You can find emergency help at the Ventura County Fire Department and Sheriff's Station (805-245-3829) in Lockwood Valley at the end of Chico Larson Way (0.4 mile). Chico Larson Way is at milepost 17.9 on Lockwood Valley Road, 1.5 miles east of Grade Valley Road.

94 New Yellowjacket Loop

Distance: 15.5 miles.
Difficulty: Moderate; with some steep descents.
Elevation: 4,650' - 5,550'; 900' gain/loss.
Ride Type: Loop on dirt roads, trails and pavement.
Season: Year-round; may have snow in winter.
Map: Los Padres National Forest: Mt. Pinos, Ojai and Santa Barbara Ranger Districts.
Note: Re-routed Yellowjacket Trail and Lockwood Creek Road are not accurately depicted on this or any map.
Water: Upper Lockwood Creek at mile 3.8. Treat all water.

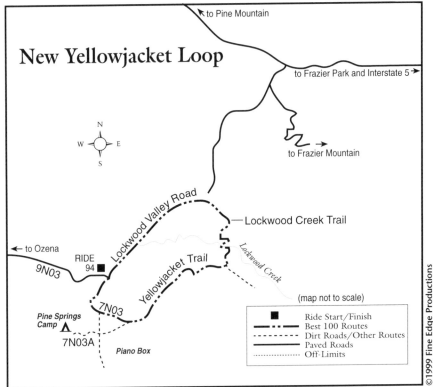

Overview: The re-routed Yellowjacket Trail captures all of the excitement and beauty of the old trail, with a challenging new downhill at its end.

Getting There: From I-5, exit at Frazier Park and go west (left) through Frazier Park to Lake of the Woods. Turn left and go southwest on Lockwood Valley Road to the gate at Grade Valley Road (7N03).

Route: From the gate at Lockwood Valley Road and Grade Valley Road, ride south up Grade Valley Road. The road is paved and in good condition. At 1.1 miles, you reach the top of the hill and the road turns to dirt. Roll along, occasionally climbing and dropping, until you reach the turn for Piano Box and Yellowjacket Trail at

2.2 miles. Go left, heading east on the dirt road.

At 3.2 miles, Piano Box Road takes off to your right. Stay left on the main road and descend to a vehicle gate and the sign for the Yellowjacket Trail at 3.6 miles. The road becomes a nice singletrack and drops about 50 feet to the bubbling headwaters of Lockwood Creek.

Cross Lockwood Creek at 3.8 miles and continue to another trail junction at 4.0 miles. Here there is another vehicle gate and a sign for Sheep Canyon on your right. Don't go this way; stay left and cross a small stream. The trail splits and climbs up a ridge about 100 feet. The trails rejoin at the top. The left-hand trail is not as steep as the right-hand trail.

As you ride on, you are high above

Jamie Griffis

Grade Valley/Lockwood Valley road crossing, New Yellowjacket Loop

Lockwood Creek gorge to your left, and you have a nice view of northern Lockwood Valley and Mt. Pinos to the northwest. The trail drops and rolls through pinyon pines and is pretty challenging in spots.

At 4.6 miles, the new trail begins. It is a doubletrack and very clean. Continue east, gradually descending to the first of four meadows. The old trail used to cross these meadows, but the new trail skirts the meadow on the right. The first meadow is small and, in winter, rain and snow melt turn it into a pond. Sometimes ducks land here to feed and you can see them swimming as you ride by.

You leave the meadow at 5.4 miles and begin to descend. Though the trail is doubletrack, it has plenty of rocks and turns, roots and drops to keep you smiling. You reach the second meadow at 5.7 miles. The new trail skirts it on the right and is a bit rocky. The second meadow is larger than the first and, like it, fills with

water in winter. Several huge pines that once stood here have toppled over into the muck, their roots saturated with water.

You leave the second meadow at 5.8 miles. The trail becomes a challenging singletrack. Continue on (east), dropping to the third meadow at 6.0 miles. This is a wide, grassy spot with pinyon trees on its north and east sides and a rock ridge on the south and west sides. The trail goes to the left here and widens to a doubletrack again. An unmarked trail joins in to the left at 6.1 miles. You stay right on the main trail and continue around the meadow to the southwest. The wide trail leaves the meadow and drops to a stream crossing at 6.5 miles.

Past the crossing, you round a large green rock formation on your left and enter the fourth and largest meadow. Deer often graze here on the moist meadow plants. Go around the meadow on the northeast side and cross another creek at 7.7 miles.

You climb a little through a narrow canyon and then descend through a shady section and cross yet another stream on the edge of yet another small meadow.

At 8.1 miles, you reach the junction with the new Lockwood Creek Road. Cross the small sandy meadow to the far left trail (Lockwood Creek Road) heading northeast. (A sign on the trail to the right says: Yellowjacket Trail, but this part now dead-ends at a barbed-wire barrier at Lockwood Creek.)

Go left and climb steeply (portage) about 250 feet up Lockwood Creek Road to the top of a ridge. Continue to ride up the ridge heading northeast to the top at 9.0 miles. You now begin a very challenging descent toward Lockwood Creek. The road is very steep in places, rutted, and has a lot of off-camber turns. At 10.0 miles, you drop into beautiful Lockwood Creek. Go left, crossing the wide, cold stream, and ride up to a parking area. (You could leave a vehicle here for a point-to-point ride.)

For the loop, ride northwest on the dirt road out to Lockwood Valley Road. Turn left here onto the pavement and ride 5 miles back to the start at the junction of Lockwood Valley and Grade Valley roads.

95 Halfmoon Camp/Mutau Creek/ Piru Creek Loop

Distance: 13.5 miles.
Difficulty: Moderate; Piru Creek Trail can be more difficult and technical.
Elevation: 4,400' - 4,800'; 750' gain/loss.
Ride Type: Loop on dirt roads and trails.
Season: Best in summer and fall.
Map: Los Padres National Forest: Mt. Pinos, Ojai and Santa Barbara Ranger Districts.
Note: The map shows Piru Creek Trail connecting to Lockwood Creek Road at Sunset Camp—it doesn't.
Water: Bring all you need; all creek water should be treated.
Comments: Halfmoon Camp is a nice camp but should be avoided on holiday weekends.

Overview: Novice riders can enjoy exploring Piru Creek Road and Grade Valley Road to Mutau Flat, while more advanced cyclists can tackle the entire loop. The pleasant road to Mutau Flat has a lot of shade and gives a nice overview of the area. Mutau Creek and Piru Creek trails provide solitude— they see little use since the Sespe Wilderness was established.

Getting There: From I-5, exit at Frazier Park and go west (left) through Frazier Park to Lake of the Woods. Turn left and go southwest on Lockwood Valley Road to the gate at Grade Valley Road (7N03). Head south up Grade Valley Road. At 2.3 and 2.8 miles, bypass Piano Box Loop Road to the east (left) and, at 2.9 miles, 7N03A to Pine Springs Camp. Continue south on 7N03. At 7 miles, cross Piru Creek (the signed Thorn Meadow Road (7N03B) is to the right). Continue on 7N03, following and crossing Piru Creek until the intersection at 12 miles. Right leads to Mutau Flat. You go left, across the creek again, on Piru Creek Road (7N13) for 0.5 mile to

Halfmoon Camp/Mutau Creek/Piru Creek Loop

Lockwood Creek ▲

7N15

Lockwood Valley Road

Lockwood Peak ▲

20W24

N
W ✦ E
S

▲

20W07

7N03

Halfmoon ▲
RIDE 95 ■

7N13

20W35

7N13

7N03

Mutau Flat

SESPE
WILDERNESS

(map not to scale)

■ Ride Start/Finish
▬ ▪ ▬ Best 100 Routes
▪ ▪ ▪ Dirt Roads/Other Routes
▬▬ Paved Roads
········· Off-Limits

©1999 Fine Edge Productions

Halfmoon Camp. Park here.

Route: Backtrack on 7N13 to the intersection and go left on 7N03 toward Mutau Flat. Mutau Road to the locked gate at Mutau Flat is an easy uphill ride with 200 feet of gain in about 2.5 miles—a good road through pine forest. At the end of the road, there is a fine view of Mutau Flat, an unusually level area of meadow (about 1 square mile) used for grazing cattle. The meadow is private property. At this point, you can also see past the flat to Sespe Canyon and Topa Topa Peak.

From Mutau Flat, take the motor-cycle trail east from the parking area above the locked gate. This trail is fairly level for 0.75 mile and then it drops down to the banks of Mutau Creek. At 3.6 miles, you reach the junction with Mutau Creek Trail (20W35) and Little Mutau Creek Trail (20W10). The Sespe Wilderness boundary is on the south side of Mutau Creek. Bicycles are no longer allowed on Little Mutau Creek Trail or Johnston Ridge Trail (20W12) to Sespe Hot Springs.

Take Mutau Creek Trail northeast (left) along Mutau Creek. This trail is used by motorcyclists and the dirt is very loose in some spots; however, the downhill isn't too difficult.

This is a pleasant canyon to explore; it comes out at Piru Creek Trail (20W07), more of a 4WD road than an actual trail. From the junction, ride up (southwest) Piru Creek Trail (20W07) to Piru Creek Road (7N13) and back to Halfmoon Camp.

Both Piru Creek Trail and Road have deteriorated from erosion and lack of maintenance. Travel is much harder on the trail than on the road. The river banks are higher and steeper, and at each stream crossing you

drop and climb the steep, rocky banks. There are many crossings.

From the Kinkaid Cabin site, where the trail becomes a road, to Halfmoon Camp, the road crosses the creek many times, and for long stretches you travel in the shallow (or dry) streambed. With almost no hills here, the only difficulty is loose sand, but much of the time there is a lot of it. Gold miners were active here in the 1930s; even now, part-time prospectors try their luck panning near Sheep Creek.

Note: Do not try to travel east on the Piru Creek Trail from the intersection with Mutau Creek Trail. The trail has been obliterated.

Mt. Pinos

Mt. Pinos, the tallest peak in the small White Mountain Coastal Range, is quickly becoming one of the premiere mountain bike areas in Southern California. Located midway

between Los Angeles, Lancaster, and Bakersfield, its pine-covered slopes, cool summer temperatures, and magnificent vistas beckon to the urban cyclist.

Piru Creek, Halfmoon Camp/Mutau Loop

Jamie Griffis

Stream crossing, Mt. Pinos area

96 Mt. Pinos/McGill Trail

Distance: 16 miles.
Difficulty: Moderately strenuous; somewhat technical.
Elevation: Begin/end 6,200'; high point 8,831'; gain/loss 2,625'.
Ride Type: Out-and-back on singletrack and dirt roads; many options possible.
Season: Spring, summer, fall.
Maps: Cuddy Valley, Sawmill Mountain.
Water: At campgrounds.
Comments: OK, so the ride is actually in Kern County, but its location in the Los Padres National Forest and its popularity with area cyclists argue for its inclusion here.

Overview: This ride has it all: great views, good climbing, wonderful spring colors (and odors!) and outrageously fun singletrack. The route described here links the mountain's best singletracks and cross-country ski trails (McGill, South Ridge and Harvest) with a touch of fire road to take you up and down Mt. Pinos.

Intermediate and advanced riders will find this a fun and challenging ride. Beginners shouldn't be put off, however. It's possible to shorten the route or to create lesser loops by starting at one of the area's three major campgrounds: McGill, Mt. Pinos and Chula Vista. Some riders like to arrange a shuttle for a downhill-only ride; still others choose to climb the paved Mt. Pinos Road (roughly a 9-mile climb) before returning on singletrack.

No matter what your skill level is, the climb to Mt. Pinos is worth the effort. The summit is surrounded by the Chumash Wilderness, created in

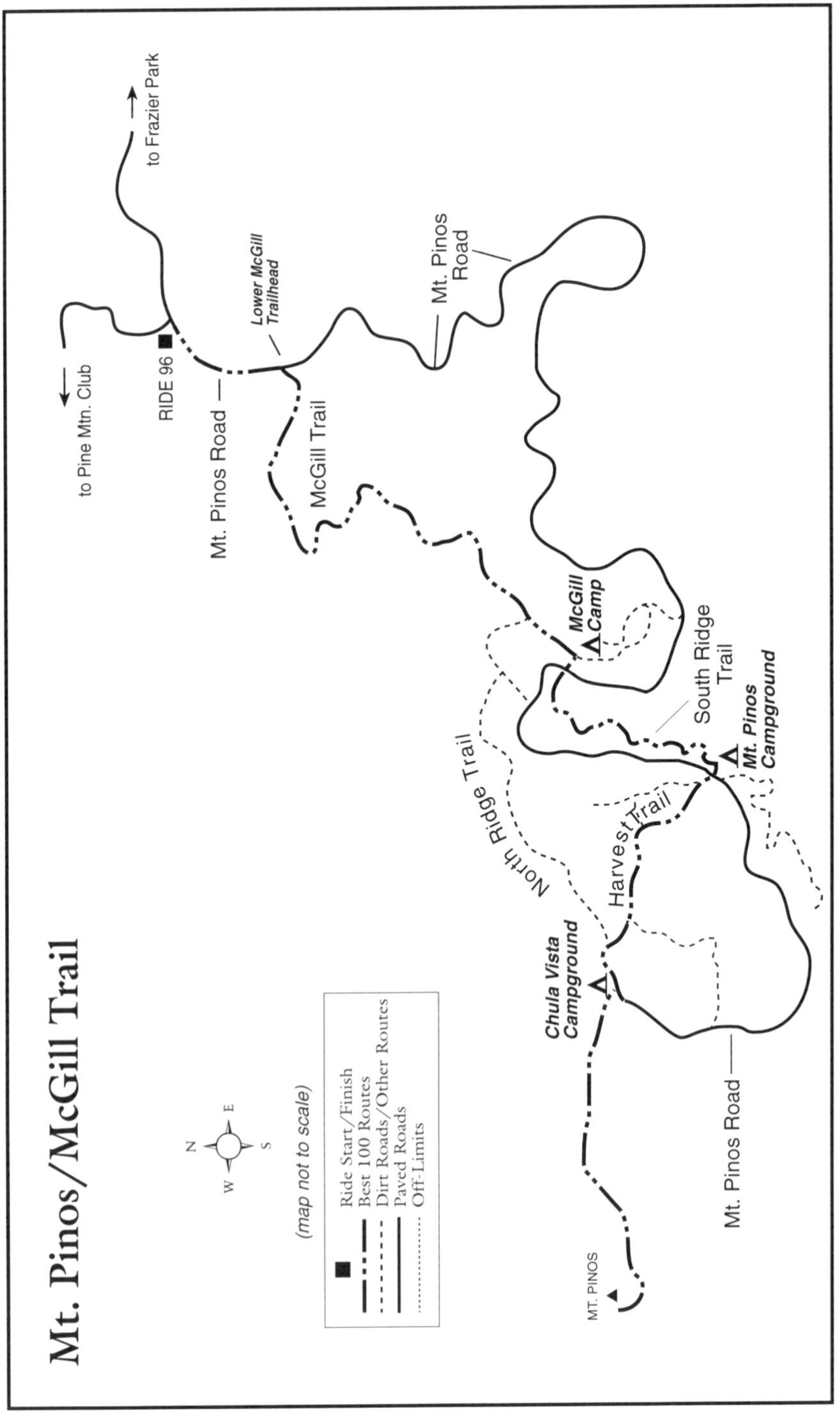

Mt. Pinos/McGill Trail

to Frazier Park

to Pine Mtn. Club

RIDE 96

Lower McGill Trailhead

Mt. Pinos Road

Mt. Pinos Road

McGill Trail

McGill Camp

North Ridge Trail

South Ridge Trail

Mt. Pinos Campground

Harvest Trail

Chula Vista Campground

Mt. Pinos Road

MT. PINOS

N
W — E
S

(map not to scale)

■　Ride Start/Finish
—··—　Best 100 Routes
---------　Dirt Roads/Other Routes
————　Paved Roads
············　Off-Limits

Jamie Griffis

View of the Sespe River from Mt. Pinos

1992. California condors have been reintroduced in the Sespe Wilderness, visible to the south, and you may catch a glimpse of these amazing birds.

Getting There: Exit I-5 at Frazier Park (also signed Mt. Pinos Recreation Area) and go left. At 6.5 miles, go straight past Lockwood Valley Road. Continue to 11.5 miles, where Mt. Pinos Road curves left. Park in the dirt lot on the right. (The lower McGill trailhead (clearly signed) is about one mile farther up Mt. Pinos Road. Route mileages are from the trailhead.)

Route: From the parking area, ride about 1.0 mile to lower McGill Trailhead, and begin by climbing McGill Trail. It's steep, but not brutally so. The trail is usually in good condition, so put it in a low gear and spin through the pines. At 1.1 miles, you reach the first of five switchbacks. After the third switchback, you begin to get fabulous views to the north and then into Lockwood Valley to the east as you traverse a more open slope. You should be able to see where you parked and be impressed with yourself for gaining so much elevation already. The grade lessens somewhat here, too, so you can take in the view without any accompanying respiratory distress.

After you swing through switchbacks three and four, the trail flattens considerably and gets downright rolly and bermy. An occasional steep rocky pitch breaks up the fun as you head onto a south slope. Most of the work is over by the 2.5-mile mark.

At 3.3 miles, you pass a bench on your right—a nice place for a break. Immediately past it is a trail junction. Go straight. Just past here is a second bench at a 4-way intersection. The two left trails drop down to McGill Campground if you need a bathroom break. (A shorter, easier loop can be fashioned by riding up the pavement to McGill Campground and down McGill Trail.) A doubletrack makes a sharp right. You want to continue straight on a relatively smooth, flat track.

You hit paved Mt. Pinos Road at 3.6 miles. Go right. Almost immediately, cross the road to where a blue cross-country ski trail sign marks the South Ridge Trail. Take this whoop-filled trail to Mt. Pinos Campground, 4.8 miles.

When you come into the campground, go right up the pavement to Mt. Pinos Road. Hang a left for 0.2 mile. Look for a big dirt turnout on the right. A dirt road starts from here, the entrance to which is covered by orange netting. Pass around the netting—there's a well-worn path.

At just over 5 miles, you come to a trail junction. A blue cross-country ski trail sign indicates Mt. Pinos Loop (easiest) to the left and Harvest Trail (more difficult) straight ahead. Take Harvest Trail and begin climbing a series of short, steep pitches. Thankfully, they're over in a little less than 1.0 mile. You emerge at Chula Vista Campground at 6.0 miles. Stay on the main trail, ignoring spurs. (Some riders choose to shuttle to this point and ride downhill from here.)

At 6.1 miles, you enter a large, paved parking lot. Head diagonally across it. Look for the large brown road sign: *Mt. Pinos, 2 miles*. Turn right and pass through an open gate to begin the climb to the summit. You pass North Ridge Trail on the right (an alternate return route).

A handful of short, steep, rocky climbs brings you to 7.0 miles. The grade lessens briefly as you approach a Y-intersection. Take the left fork. Continue on the main road past a few spurs (which lead to vista points). At 7.8 miles, stay left at another Y-intersection to begin the final push to the top. At 8.0 miles, you reach the broad, usually windy, 8,831-foot summit. No matter how warm the weather when you start your ride,

bring a windbreaker as there's often a cool breeze here.

A display announces: Iwihinmu (Mt. Pinos): A World in Balance. Two benches beckon you to sit, have a snack, and enjoy the view. Note that the trail which takes off from here leads into a wilderness area— closed to bikes. At the far end of the parking lot, a footpath leads to two port-a-potties.

To the north you can see the San Joaquin Valley and the city of Bakersfield. To the northeast, if the air is clear, you can make out the southern ramparts of the Sierra Nevada. Toward the east, Antelope Valley and the high desert stretch to the horizon. In springtime, the desert explodes with color as the California poppies bloom. The rugged Dick Smith and Sespe Wilderness areas span from west to south. These are home to the reintroduced California condor. The rare and majestic birds are sometimes spotted soaring over Mt. Pinos in search of food.

When you, too, feel in balance, head back the way you came. The fire road is fast, so watch yourself—it is open to vehicle traffic. *Option:* You have a choice here. You can opt to take the steep, loose North Ridge Trail back to McGill Campground or cross the parking lot and descend Harvest Trail. As much fun to descend as it was painful to climb, Harvest rails and rolls its way back to Mt. Pinos Road. Through Mt. Pinos Campground again, you catch South Ridge Trail, where if you're not careful, you can catch dangerous air on the whoop-de-dos. The fun factor reaches crescendo point as you swing, swoop, and berm your way down McGill Trail (don't forget those switchbacks!) back to your car. It truly doesn't get any better than this.

Mt. Pinos is laced with singletrack

Cuyama

From Highway 33 at Pine Mountain Summit, the Cuyama River and the eroded hills below and to the east look like some kind of badlands, an impressive, desolate scene. The Cuyama River is usually a wide, flat, dry wash. The hills are sparsely covered, with light brown being the prominent color. The only really green areas are irrigated alfalfa fields near the river. In recent years, several new horse ranches have sprung up near the junction of Highway 33 and Lockwood Valley Road.

The best seasons to ride here are winter and early spring when the higher elevations have snow and are cold. In summer, Cuyama is very hot and dry and you must bring plenty of water. Also, be wary of driving your motor vehicle in soft sandy soils. There are drive-in camps at Ozena and Reyes Creek, as well as at Tinta Camp, Rancho Nuevo, Dome Springs in Dry Canyon, and Nettle Springs in Apache Canyon (more rustic). Check local conditions at Ozena Forest Service Station on Highway 33 near Lockwood Valley Road.

97 East Dry Canyon

Distance: 6 miles.
Difficulty: Easy; not technical.
Elevation: 600' gain/loss.
Ride Type: Out-and-back on dirt road.
Season: Year-round, but summer can be very hot.
Map: Apache Canyon.
Water: None.
Comments: Nearest services are in Ventucopa or New Cuyama.

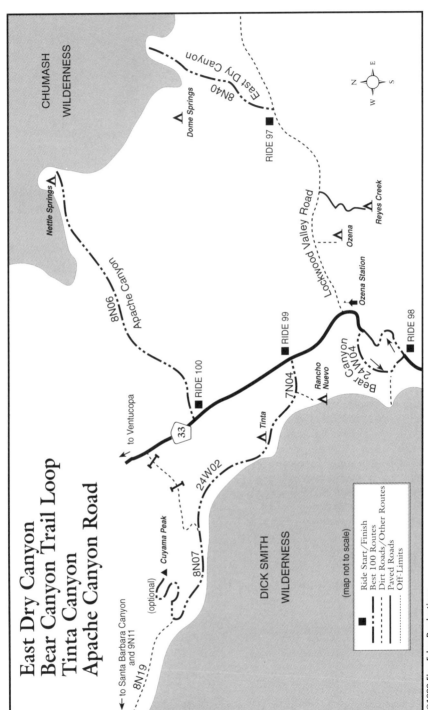

East Dry Canyon
Bear Canyon Trail Loop
Tinta Canyon
Apache Canyon Road

CHUMASH WILDERNESS

DICK SMITH WILDERNESS

Dome Springs

East Dry Canyon
8N40

RIDE 97

Reyes Creek

Ozena

Lockwood Valley Road

Ozena Station

Nettle Springs

Apache Canyon
8N06

RIDE 100

RIDE 99

7N04

Rancho Nuevo

Bear Canyon
24W04

RIDE 98

to Ventucopa

33

Tinta

24W02

Cuyama Peak
(optional)

8N07

to Santa Barbara Canyon
and 9N11

8N19

(map not to scale)

Ride Start/Finish
Best 100 Routes
Dirt Roads/Other Routes
Paved Roads
Off-Limits

© 1999 Fine Edge Productions

Overview: This is a good ride for beginners and those who are in no hurry and want to take it easy. East Dry Canyon rewards slow riders who have time to observe nature.

Getting There: Park along Lockwood Valley Road, 6.4 miles east of Highway 33.

Route: Road 8N40 takes off to the northeast from Lockwood Valley Road at milepost 6.4. Ride 3 miles up East Dry Canyon to Dome Springs Camp on this graded road, taking your time to enjoy the much-eroded landscape. Like many desert areas, Dry Canyon has some surprises—lots of trees and plant life. The soil here is

a mixture of sand and clay that turns to gumbo mud when wet.

As you head down to Dome Springs Camp, you have good views of Mt. Abel and Mt. Pinos to the northeast. The camp is located in a grove of pines; it's a drive-in camp with tables, fire pits and an outhouse. Unfortunately, it has gotten pretty shot up in recent years—not recommended.

The "Dome" is a very interesting geographic feature. It is a rounded hill of different multi-colored sand and clay layers, very similar to the formations lining Interstate 70 on the way toward Moab, Utah.

The road ends at the Chumash Wilderness boundary—no bikes allowed. Return the way you came.

98 Bear Canyon Trail Loop

Distance: 4.9 miles.
Difficulty: Very difficult in the gorge.
Elevation: 4,600' - 3,650'; 950' differential.
Ride Type: Loop on singletrack and pavement.
Season: Year-round, but summer can be extremely hot.
Map: Rancho Nuevo Creek.
Water: Seasonal water in Bear Canyon streams. Treat all water.
Comments: Nearest services are at Ozena Forest Service Station.

Overview: The upper and lower one-mile sections of Bear Canyon Trail (24W04) are rideable, but a 0.7-mile middle section passes through a narrow gorge and is very steep with several stream crossings. We recommend walking the entire gorge section.

Getting There: Park near the lower trail end of Bear Canyon Trail (signed) at milepost 47.47 on Highway 33.

Route: Ride up the highway for a somewhat steep 2.2 miles to the

upper trailhead at milepost 45.27 on a sharp bend in the road. Just off the highway at milepost 45.27, a dirt road heads steeply down to the north about 100 feet. A locked gate on the west marks the trail. Here you descend into a tributary canyon and cross a series of small linked hillside meadows. At about the 2.7-mile mark, where you are heading south, the trail switchbacks to the right and down the canyon (a lesser trail continues south). Be on the lookout for this—it's easy to miss.

You descend and cross a small stream; farther along, after that stream joins another one, you cross the combined stream. Then you cross a dry stream and go up to the Deal Canyon Trail junction at 3.3 miles. (That trail enters the Dick Smith Wilderness just west of the junction.)

The next 0.7 mile down Bear Canyon is through a beautiful, sandstone gorge with many oak and fir trees. However, the trail is very steep and slippery from leaves, so walking is recommended. The last 1.0 mile is fairly straight and level to the highway and your car.

99 Tinta Canyon

Distance: 20 miles, with shorter options possible.
Difficulty: Tinta Canyon Road is easy; Tinta Canyon Trail is moderate to difficult.
Elevation: 3,450' - 3,600' with 150' differential on Tinta Canyon Road; 3,600' - 4,800' with 1,200' differential on the trail section.
Ride Type: Out-and-back on dirt road and singletrack.
Season: Year-round, but summer can be very hot.
Maps: Rancho Nuevo Creek, Cuyama Peak.
Water: From stream in canyon. Treat all water.
Comments: Nearest services are at Ventucopa or New Cuyama.

Overview: Beginning riders can enjoy the first 3 miles of this atmospheric route through grassy meadows along Tinta Canyon Road to Tinta Camp. More experienced riders can tackle Tinta Canyon Trail as far out as they want. Tinta is a very pretty canyon with Moab-like stone cliffs.

Getting There: Park at the trailhead, milepost 50 on Highway 33, by the wilderness sign and map, or 100 yards north on Highway 33 at the Halfway Station Cafe (closed as of this writing).

Route: Most of Tinta Canyon Road (7N04) is well graded and in fine shape. It's suitable for cars, except that first you must cross the wide, flat Cuyama River. The water, when there is any, is usually shallow, but there is loose sand in the river bed. Of course, if you have 4WD, you can go farther and get stuck in the very worst places.

Nice thing about a bicycle is you can always pick it up and carry it.

This remote area doesn't usually get a lot of traffic, but because vehicles stir up clouds of dust, the best time to ride this road is during the week or when the way across the river is too rough for cars but okay for bicycles. Flash floods do occur here, and it's best to wait for the water to go down before crossing. If you are on the west side when a flood comes and have to get back, you can hike upstream on the west bank about 2 miles to the highway bridge.

From the trailhead, 1.0 mile from the highway on 7N04, a left heads south into Rancho Nuevo Canyon. (It is 0.5 mile to the camp at the end of the road.) Go straight ahead on Road 7N04, 2.0 miles, to Tinta Camp, also at the end of the road. It's not a very good camp since the turnaround is right at the campsites and the designated motorcycle trail, Tinta Canyon Trail (24W02), is situated between them. Still, it is very clean and has three picnic tables and a pit toilet.

Beginning riders can turn around here; more conditioned riders can tackle Tinta Canyon Trail. Although it has lots of easy grade, recent washouts and brush growth have made this trail much more difficult than it used to be. Right outside of Tinta Camp, the trail stays close to the stream for 0.5 mile, then switchbacks up the north side of the canyon to get above a narrow, steep gorge. The switchback section is short (0.2 mile) and not very steep, but the next part is steep; at 4.0 miles, you level out on the rim of the gorge. At 4.5 miles, the gorge is behind you and you descend to the canyon bottom.

Multi-use yield sign

From here on, the trail climbs gradually near the stream and is easier except where side gulches have cut through the trail. You have to climb in and out of these carrying your bicycle. The stream has a fair amount of water and the trail crosses it several times. Brush is a problem near the stream. One last steep hill (it's short) and you are at the upper end of the 3.8-mile singletrack where it joins a road that comes up Brubaker Canyon (8N07). (This road is blocked at a locked gate near the Brubaker Ranch below.) It climbs up over a saddle into Tinta Canyon, meets the trail, and continues up Tinta Canyon as a poor doubletrack road—but a great trail. It has a slight grade that is easy to ride, and the brush is back far enough to not be a bother.

At 8.6 miles, Upper Tinta Trail Camp, with one table and two stoves, is set among oak trees on a rise just left of the road. Nearby, there are several creek crossings and some of them have water much of the time. The last 0.5 mile is rougher due to rocks left in the road by flood waters. A gate at 10.0 miles marks the end of Road 8N07. The Cuyama Peak Lookout service road passes here from West Dry Canyon. Unless you are prepared for a long loop, ride back the way you came in.

[**Side trip:** The road up to the lookout is graded often and is in very good shape, but it's very steep. If you have the time and energy, the view is worth the effort. This is one of the few old lookouts left standing.]

Option: Strong riders may be interested in a loop option. From the end of Road (8N07), at the turnoff to the lookout, continue west on West Dry Canyon Road (8N19) down to Santa Barbara Canyon and then take Road (9N11) north to Highway 33.

These down-canyon roads are excellent riding. The return on Highway 33 is mostly level with a few rolling hills. Small stores, bars, and gas stations can be found near Ventucopa along the highway. Total distance for the loop is 41 miles, with 19 miles on pavement. (For more details about West Dry Canyon and Santa Barbara Canyon, see Rides 67 and 68 in Chapter 3, Santa Barbara.)

100 Apache Canyon Road

Distance: 18 miles.
Difficulty: Easy; not technical.
Elevation: 3,300' - 4,300'; 1,000' gain/loss.
Ride Type: Out-and-back on dirt road.
Season: Year-round, but summer can be extremely hot.
Map: Apache Canyon.
Water: None.
Comments: Nearest services are at Ventucopa or New Cuyama.

Overview: This is a great novice ride because of the gentle grade. There is not much shade and riders should bring a lot of water on warm days. There are some very nice views of Mt. Pinos and Mt. Abel as you ride up the canyon. The road is in great shape, although there are some sandy and washboard sections. Unfortunately, the camp at Nettle Springs has no water and is a bit shot up.

Getting There: Park in turnouts along Highway 33 near milepost 53.83 or at Apache Canyon Road.

Route: Apache Canyon Road (8N06) heads east from Highway 33 at the bridge at milepost 53.83. It is graded and open to motor vehicles. Off-highway vehicles travel in the

sandy wash most of the way, parallel to the road. The new Chumash Wilderness is located nearby on the south and west slopes of Mt. Pinos and Mt. Abel. The Wilderness boundary parallels the upper 2.5 miles of Apache Canyon Road on the north side and runs around the north and east sides of Nettle Springs Camp at the end of the road. San Emigdio Mesa Trail (22W21) is now in the wilderness area and bicycles are prohibited there.

Ride this graded dirt road up-canyon for 9 miles to Nettle Springs Camp. There are no trail or road intersections along the way. The camp is your turnaround point. Anything past Nettle Springs is in the Wilderness Area.

Appendices

ABOUT THE AUTHORS

Delaine Fragnoli, contributing editor to *Bicycling* magazine, is the co-author of *Mountain Biking Southern California's Best 100 Trails* and *Mountain Biking Northern California's Best 100 Trails.* She is past editor of *Mountain Biking* and *Southwest Cycling* magazines. Her freelance work has appeared in *Women's Sports & Fitness, BIKE* and *VeloNews.*

Don Douglass, one of the founders and the first president of the International Mountain Bicycling Association (IMBA), has written extensively on the need for environmentally-sound and responsible riding habits. He has been inducted into the Mountain Biking Hall of Fame.

Jamie Griffis, a professional bicycle mechanic, is the author of Terragraphics' *Touring the Los Angeles Area by Bicycle* and a co-founder of the Los Angeles Female Off Road Cycling Enthusiasts (L.A. FORCE).

Mark Langton, a former editor of *Mountain Biking* magazine, has been a long-time advocate of sound cycling principles and open trails. His writings document much of mountain biking's present and past history. He is a founding member of CORBA and has been nominated for the Mountain Biking Hall of Fame.

Mickey McTigue has been a backcountry cyclist since 1958. Active in trail building and maintenance, he leads cycling expeditions in Los Padres National Forest.

Kevin Woten pioneered many popular routes in the Saugus District of the Angeles National Forest and in the Los Padres National Forest in eastern Ventura County. He was also a co-founder of the Grapevine Mountain Bike Association and a member of IMBA's south region board of directors.

AGENCIES, MOUNTAIN BIKE CLUBS
AND VISITOR CENTERS

Alamo Bicycle Touring Company
(tours and rentals)
1108 Vista del Lago
San Luis Obispo, CA 93405
805/781-3830
800/540-BIKE (2453)

Andrew Molera State Park
c/o Pfeiffer Big Sur State Park
Big Sur, CA 93920
408/667-2315

Big Sur Chamber of Commerce
P.O. Box 87
Big Sur, CA 93920
408/667-2100

Bureau of Land Management
(BLM)
Caliente Resource Area
(for Carrizo Plain Natural Area)
4301 Rosedale Highway
Bakersfield, CA 93308
805/861-4236

Cachuma Lake Recreation Area
805/688-4658

California Coastal Conservancy
1330 Broadway, Suite 1100
Oakland, CA 94612
510/286-1015

California Department of Parks and
Recreation
Attn: Public Relations
P.O. Box 942896
Sacramento, CA 94296-0001
916/653-6995

California State Parks
916/653-6995 Touch-Tone
Information

Channel Islands National Park
805/658-5730

Concerned Central Coast Mountain
Bikers (CCCMB)
Box 16003
San Luis Obispo, CA 93406
805/528-0430
805/756-1284

Concerned Off Road Bicyclists
Association (CORBA)
818/773-3555

Conejo Open Space Conservation
Agency (COSCA)
805/449-2100

Gaviota State Park
805/968-3294

Grapevine Mountain Bike
Association
(for eastern Ventura Co.)
42762 Deerwalk Drive
Lake Elizabeth, CA 93532
805/724-9066

International Mountain Bicycling
Association
P.O. Box 7578
Boulder, CO 80306-7578
303/545-9011

Lake San Antonio
805/472-2311
800/310-2313

Lopez Lake
805/489-1122

Los Padres National Forest
6144 Calle Real
Goleta, CA 93117
805/683-6711

Los Padres National Forest
Monterey Ranger District
406 S. Mildred
King City, CA 93930
408/385-5434

Los Padres National Forest
Mt. Pinos Ranger District
HC1 Box 400
34580 Lockwood Valley Road
Frazier Park, CA 93225
805/245-3731

Los Padres National Forest
Ojai Ranger District
1190 E. Ojai Avenue
Ojai, CA 93023
805/646-4348

Los Padres National Forest
Santa Barbara Ranger District
Star Route
Santa Barbara, CA 93105
805/967-3481

Los Padres National Forest
Santa Lucia Ranger District
1616 N. Carlotti Drive
Santa Maria, CA 93454
805/925-9538

Montaña de Oro State Park
805/528-0513

Monterey County Parks
(for Lake San Antonio)
888/588-CAMP (2267)

Monterey County Visitors and
Convention Bureau
380 Alvarado Street
Monterey, CA 93942
408/649-1770

Morro Bay State Park
805/772-2560

The Nature Conservancy
Carrizo Plain Natural Area
P.O. Box 3098
California Valley, CA 93453

Rancho Sierra Vista/Satwiwa
805/375-1930

Road Conditions
800/427-7623

San Luis Obispo County Visitors &
Conference Bureau
1037 Mill Street
San Luis Obispo, CA 93401
805/541-8000
800/634-1414

Santa Barbara Conference and
Visitors Bureau
510 State Street, Suite A
Santa Barbara, CA 93101
805/966-9222
800/927-4688

Santa Barbara Mountain Bike Trail
Volunteers
225 Valdez Avenue
Goleta, CA 93117
805/683-0371

Santa Monica Mountains National
Recreation Area
(Point Mugu State Park)
818/597-9192

Ventura Visitors and Convention
Bureau
89-C South California Street
Ventura, CA 93001
805/648-2075
800/333-2989

RECOMMENDED READING

GENERAL CYCLING

Friel, Joe. *Cyclist's Training Bible.* Velo Press, 1996.

Nealy, William. *Mountain Bike! A Manual of Beginning to Advanced Technique.* Birmingham: Menasha Ridge Press, 1992.

Nealy, William. *The Mountain Bike Way of Knowledge.* Birmingham: Menasha Ridge Press, 1989.

Skillbeck, Paul. *Singletrack Mind.* Velo Press, 1996.

Smith, Jill. *The Mountain Bikers' Cookbook.* Velo Press, 1997.

Stuart, Robin, and Cathy Jensen. *Mountain Biking for Women.* Waverly, New York: Acorn Publishing, 1994.

Zinn, Leonard. *Zinn and the Art of Mountain Bike Maintenance.* Velo Press, 1996.

Backcountry Travel and First Aid

Graydon, Don, ed. *Mountaineering, The Freedom of the Hills.* 5th ed. The Mountaineers, 1992.

Lentz, M., S. Macdonald, and J. Carline. *Mountaineering First Aid.* The Mountaineers, 1990.

LITERARY

Kerouac, Jack. *Big Sur.* New York: Penguin Books, 1962.

Miller, Henry. *Big Sur and the Oranges of Hieronymus Bosch.* New York: New Directions, 1957.

REFERENCES

Dodd, K. *Guide to Obtaining USGS Information.* U.S. Geological Survey Circular 900, 1986.

Little, Elbert L. *Audubon Society Field Guide of North American Trees.* New York: Alfred A. Knopf, 1980.

Stellenberg, Richard. *Audubon Society Field Guide of American Wildflowers— Western.* New York: Alfred A. Knopf, 1979.

Stratton, George. *The Recreation Guide to California National Forests.* Montana: Falcon Press, 1991.

REGIONAL GUIDES

Berlund, Carol. *Mountain Biking the Central Coast, Volume One.* San Luis Obispo, California: EZ Nature Books, 1990. (Note: the trail information in this book is very dated.)

Dawkins, Gwen, and Dirk Franklin, *Fat Tire Fun: The Mountain Biking Trail Guide for San Luis Obispo County.* 2nd ed.1998. (A good resource for those who live in SLO.)

Rice, Andrew. *Adventure Guide to Northern California.* New York: Macmillan, 1996.

SLO Adventures. *Mountain Biking Eastern San Luis Obispo County, 1997.* (Topo map; a good resource for those who live in SLO.)

SLO Adventures. *Mountain Biking San Luis Obispo & Coastal Areas, 1997.* (Topo map; a good resource for those who live in SLO.)

ROUTE INDEX

Outdoor Publications from MountainBikingPress.com

RECREATION TOPO MAPS

(with Mountain Biking, Hiking and Ski Touring Trails,
6-color, double-sided, includes trail profiles & route descriptions)

Eastern High Sierra-Mammoth, June, Mono, 2nd Ed., ISBN 0-938665-21-9 $9.95

Santa Monica Mountains, ISBN 0-938665-23-5 $9.95

San Bernardino Mountains, ISBN 0-938665-32-4 $9.95

San Gabriel Mountains—West, ISBN 0-938665-13-8 $8.95

North Lake Tahoe Basin, 2nd Ed., ISBN 0-938665-34-0 $8.95

South Lake Tahoe Basin, 3rd Ed., ISBN 0-938665-35-9 $8.95

Laminated copies – $10 additional

MOUNTAIN BIKING GUIDEBOOKS

Mountain Biking California's Central Coast Best 100 Trails,
by Fragnoli   ISBN 0-938665-59-6
(classic routes, 90 detailed maps, 272 pages) $18.95

Mountain Biking Southern California's Best 100 Trails,
     2nd Ed., Fragnoli & Douglass, Eds.,
     ISBN 0-938665-53-7
(classic routes, 80 detailed maps, 352 pages) $16.95

*Mountain Biking Northern California's Best 100
Trails* by Fragnoli & Stuart,
ISBN 0-938665-31-6
(classic routes, 80 detailed maps, 300 pages) $16.95

Mountain Biking the Eastern Sierra's Best 100 Trails,
     by Hemingway-Douglass, Davis,
and Douglass, ISBN 0-938665-42-1 $18.95

*Mountain Biking Santa Monica Mountains'
Best Trails,* by Hasenauer & Langton,
ISBN 0-938665-55-3 $14.95

Mountain Biking North America's Best 100 Ski Resorts
by Fragnoli, ISBN 0-938665-46-4 $16.95

Mountain Biking the San Gabriel Mountains' Best Trails
with Angeles National Forest and Mt. Pinos
by Troy & Woten, ISBN 0-938665-43-X $14.95

Mountain Biking South Lake Tahoe's Best Trails
by Bonser & Miskimins, ISBN 0-938665-52-9 $14.95

Mountain Biking North Lake Tahoe's Best Trails
by Bonser & Miskimins, ISBN 0-938665-40-5 $14.95

Lake Tahoe's Top 20 Bike Rides on Pavement & Dirt
by Miskimins, ISBN 0-938665-36-7 $6.95

Guide 10, San Bernardino Mountains
by Shipley, ISBN 0-938665-16-2 $10.95

Guide 11, Orange County and Cleveland N.F.,
2nd Ed. by Rasmussen, ISBN 0-938665-37-5 $11.95

Guide 13, Reno/Carson Area
by Miskimins, ISBN 0-938665-22-7 $10.95

OTHER GUIDEBOOKS

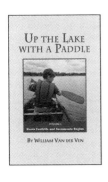

Up the Lake With a Paddle, Canoe & Kayak Guide, Vol. 1,
Sierra Foothills, Sacramento Region,
by Van der Ven, ISBN 0-938665-54-5 $18.95

Favorite Pedal Tours of Northern California,
by Bloom, ISBN 0-938665-12-X $12.95

To order any of these items,
see your local dealer or order
direct from Fine Edge
Productions. Please include
$2.50 for shipping with check
or money order. California
residents add 7.25% tax.

MountainBikingPress.com

AN IMPRINT OF
FINE EDGE PRODUCTIONS

140 North Valley View Rd.
Swall Meadow, CA 93514
Fax (760) 387-2286

Prices are subject to change.
© 1999 Fine Edge Productions

Visit our website:
MountainBikingPress.com

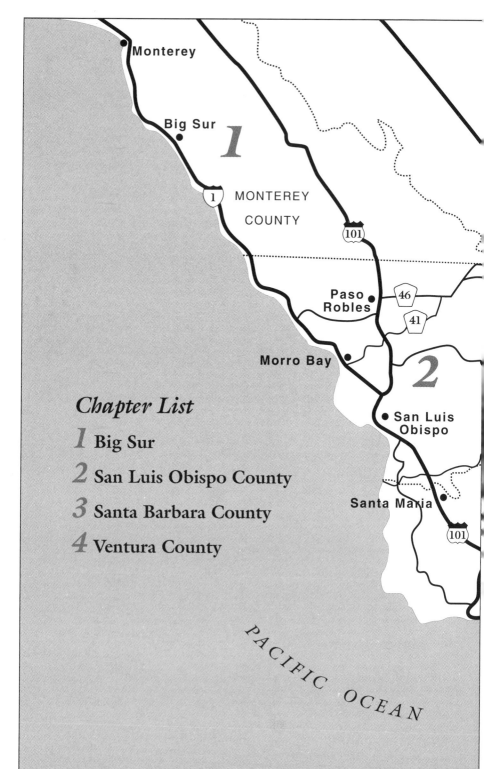

Monterey

Big Sur

1

① 1 MONTEREY
COUNTY

⑩ 101

Paso
Robles ● ⑯ 46

⑪ 41

Morro Bay

2

● San Luis
Obispo

Chapter List

Santa Maria ●

⑩ 101

P A C I F I C

O C E A N

Affirmation Books is an important part of the ministry of the House of Affirmation, International Therapeutic Center for Clergy and Religious, founded by Sr. Anna Polcino, M.D., F.A.P.A., and Fr. Thomas A. Kane, Ph.D., D.P.S. Income from the sale of Affirmation books and tapes is used to provide care for priests and religious suffering from emotional unrest.

The House of Affirmation provides a threefold program of service, education, and research. Among its services are five residential therapeutic communities and three counseling centers in the United States and one residential center in England. All centers provide nonresidential counseling. The House sponsors a leadership conference each year during the first week of February and a month-long Institute of Applied Psychotheology during July. More than forty clinical staff members conduct workshops and symposiums throughout the year.

For further information, write or call the administrative offices in Boston, Massachusetts.

The House of Affirmation
22 The Fenway
Boston, Massachusetts 02215
617/266-8792